T0197304

THE UGLIEST MAN
I KNOW
AND WHAT HE DID TO
ME AND MY FAMILY

THE UGLIEST MAN
I KNOW
AND WHAT HE DID TO
ME AND MY FAMILY

EMILY OLSON

THE UGLIEST MAN I KNOW AND WHAT
HE DID TO ME AND MY FAMILY

iUniverse books may be ordered through booksellers or by contacting:

iUniverse
1663 Liberty Drive
Bloomington, IN 47403
www.iuniverse.com
1-800-Authors (1-800-288-4677)

ISBN: 978-1-5320-5982-7 (sc)
ISBN: 978-1-5320-5983-4 (e)

Print information available on the last page.

iUniverse rev. date: 04/26/2019

DEDICATION

THIS WORK IS DEDICATED to those who helped me the most especially Dr. Tim Olson who inspired me throughout the entire process from beginning to end and convinced me that I had the skills to structure my thoughts in such a manner as to create an actual book that would make sense and help others to face their own similar problems and exercise their own demons and set themselves free from their own mental prisons. Dr. Tim Olson also assisted me in the writing of this book.

I would also like to pay homage to my deceased son Alexander who is with me twenty four hours a day seven days a week he constantly inspires me and has always been my support system in life as well as death. I love you Alex. Tim loves you too and we will all be together soon. My son was an only child he fought for this country and did one tour to Afghanistan and Iraq I was very proud of him. He was a chemical op specialist and sharp shooter. He was my boy and had my big hands.

Last but not least, I cannot forget my best friend and mentor Katie. Katie is like a sister to me. You see, when Alex died, Katie was a lifesaver she literally saved my life I was literally considering ending my life from not being able to cope with my son's death who was an only child. Katie spent hours and hours with me and enveloped me in the warmth of her soul until I accepted the truth of universal love; "I want to live".

Would like to mention all the German Shepherds that I have had in my family that are now deceased starting with: Julius #1, Julius#2, Maggie Mae #3, Spartan Warrior #4, are all deceased and have all brought me great pleasure and have all their ashes and footprints. My shelf in the Livingroom is full of ashes with my son and my dogs but Ya know what, I've had a full life and have no complaints and would not have changed a thing. I just wanted to share a little piece of me with you, thanks for reading.

Love Always;
Emily Olson

FOREWORD

THERE ARE A LOT of people in this world who harbor deep dark secrets that have a deep effect on their mental well being and for one reason or another, they keep these secrets bottled up and locked up deep inside the darkest places of their mind.

Occasionally, these memories are triggered by certain events and brought to the surface to cause serious emotional pain to the carrier and can cause such things as nervous break downs and even lead to Suicide. When this occurs its time to seek professional help.

I visited a psychiatrist and explained in detail my situation and she referred me to a therapist. The sessions were very helpful and helped me to move forward as opposed to living in the past. She was moved at the complexity of my story especially when I told her that I was raped by my grandfather when I was 6 years old and beaten by my father all my life until I was 18 years of age and then again when I was pregnant with my son at age 24 years old and to top it all off, I found out that my father accepted monetary payment from his father to keep my molestation quiet and my mother was privy to this information as well. This broke my heart but my mind was free and I felt that I could finally move forward.

Hopefully, this book will inspire those readers who might be harboring a dangerous secret to evaluate their motivation for doing so and to possibly rethink the possible outcomes for not sharing their information. I'm sure the reader can appreciate the dynamics of my story when what would have happened if what I would have remained silent. Even if I would have lived my home life and relationship with my husband would have been extremely sad and limited. Please beware.

BY: EMILY OLSON

THE PURPOSE OF THIS book is to help others who might have experienced the same problems that I have by being born to a set of parents who are both mentally dysfunctional. The marriage between my mother and my father produced seven children, three girls and four boys each of which suffer from their own unique mental problem, some more profound than others and all unique unto the individual. Six of their children, including me were born in California and one was born in Colorado. The Colorado Baby was the most memorable birth for my mother. This was a C section type birth that kept my mother in the hospital for 72 hours due to complications.

Some of the siblings harbor personalities that are destructive to themselves, while others have personalities that are destructive to both themselves and others. None of my brothers and sisters do very well in society. They were never taught and had no real desire to learn interpersonal communication skills my oldest brother might be an exception to this because he enjoys public speaking but he uses this for his own personal monetary gains. I do feel however, that there is some sort of inter-personal communication system that has been established and used between family members but it is still difficult to communicate with them on a professional level and none of the family members seem to have a clear understanding of each other's problems and this makes it rather difficult to establish any support system within the confines of the family itself. There are certain family members who seem to love one another at times, and then there are others who seem to hate and despise each and every one of their siblings and their spouses. In-fighting has become the norm as the family matures and select members try to steal from other family members. Deception and false accusation is used to acquire personal property from other family members. I was personally involved in such an accusation from my own mother. I will cover this in great detail later in the book. Myself and my siblings are all in their forty's and fifty's and only myself, a sister and a brother remain married after two attempts. Other family marriages have ended in failure. I am the only sibling of seven who has earned a college degree. Out of the nine members of our immediate family including my mother and my father, there are only three members of our immediate family, including myself who are homeowners. Four of my siblings still live in Colorado while others have moved on to find happiness elsewhere. My sister Lilly moved to Kansas. I moved to Illinois, my brother Jimmy moved to Florida and my brother Charlie who was thrown out of the house by my father at gunpoint at a very early age, moved to California. I have not seen him since. My mother has created close ties with my sister Marsha and together they manage to milk the rest of the family members and sometimes use under handed means to gain their support. However, this lifeline or whatever one chooses to call it,; will soon be closed to them as they become more and more aggressive and stealing from other family members has become very easy for them and other family members become wise to their deceptions. This book does focus a great deal on my dad because he was very brutal and extremely mean to the entire family including my mother but my mother, was extremely mentally ill as well, for example: I was sexually abused by my grandfather and this is covered in great detail in the book, but the point I'd like to make here is that I was only six years old when this happened and my mother blamed me for it and to this day I am in my late fifty's and she still blames me for it. Now I ask the reader does this sound like a sane individual?

Writing this book has been a rude awaking for me as I have learned a lot of unwelcomed information about my family. It's difficult and it makes me mad to continue, but most of all, I'm filled with a deep burning sorrow and wonder why out of all the billions and billions of people on this planet of ours could I have possibly ended up with these two individuals? Well as the old adage goes, you can't pick your neighbors and you can't pick your parents, especially when you are a child. You get what you get in this world, and it's up to us to make our own luck or our own way so to speak. Hopefully writing this book will serve as a tool and a means to help me heal my heart and my soul so that I can feel complete again and feel better about myself on all levels including the mind, the body and the soul. You see, I feel like I am broken in every sense of the word. Just remember if you feel this way or if you know someone who is going through this or is being traumatized like I'm about to discuss or needs help in any way, this book is a great resource to find the help you or they might need to get in touch with someone who cares and can offer assistance right away. Just do me a favor, don't wait like I did, always tell someone any adult if you're a kid, or any social worker, or call the police department, or get some help right away. Because the longer you wait the longer the problem festers. Remember, it's like a cut; it will never get better if you just keep putting band aids on it. Remember, it's your life and no one has the right to take it from you or control it for their own gains or pleasure. You only have one life and only one chance to live it the way you want to live it. In addition to taking care of our own well- being, lets maintain an awareness of the world around us and try to discourage abuse of any kind whether it be directed against other people who are totally defenseless or any living creature. I'm not suggesting that you should place yourself in harms way, but use discretion and by all and any means whatsoever, seek assistance.

THE FORMIDABLE YEARS

THESE ARE THE FIRST memories I have of life. And it begins with the recollection of me pounding my head on the floor trying to get my mother's attention. I was probably somewhere around eighteen months old. During later years she explained that she never knew what I wanted she just waited until I quit then placed a band aid over the damaged area on my forehead and walked away.

Another memory I have while dressed in black patent leather shoes and a blue dress and looking down over a steep cliff at the end of our cul-de-sac. At the bottom of the cliff was an unfinished swimming pool that contained no water. There was nothing between me and the swimming pool other than several hundred feet of sheer rock wall. I was mesmerized by the beauty of the pool but also heard someone call my name from somewhere in the distant background. The sound got louder and became more intelligible, "Emily I have candy", I recognized the voice; it was my mother calling out to me.

Thinking back on this episode as an adult, I remember that my mother was frantic as she called to me. I also remembered that the rock and dirt was crumbling beneath my tiny feet as it fell hundreds of feet down below before landing at the bottom of the cliff. The soil was very dry and the falling rock created a lot of clouds of dust that got in my eyes that blinded me and I couldn't see very well. My mother knew that she had just one chance to save my life because she noticed that my stance was beginning to falter. So she reached into her pockets and calmly said; "Emily come to Mama, come get the candy come now, come on honey, come to Mama". Just then I turned to look at my mother and I always believed her because she never told me a lie. So with that I wanted the candy so bad that I ran to mommy and she started to scream and cry out loud saying; "Thank you Lord, oh my God, Dear God, Thank you, I could of lost her just then!" She then immediately went over to Suzie's house next door and got candy lots of it and gave it to me and she cried all day long. Another incident which comes to mind, not because of its dynamic relevance to the story of my life, but because of its surprising personal awakening of the strength of my power of recollection. My husband always tells me that he cannot remember any incident that happened to him before his ninth birthday and to him, I am an enigma. At any rate, as my memory shows me; me and my oldest brother were outside playing on the see saw. Mom was outside too, hanging clothes on the clothes line with clothes pins, she was pregnant with my brother Charlie, this would be her third child. Anyways, my brother wanted to see how high the see saw would go up into the sky if he pushed it real hard. Now keep in mind, with the see saw; I was at the other half of the see saw standing there observing what he was doing. I wasn't really paying any attention to the movement of my end of the see saw; because I was too busy watching him. Guess what, right after the first plunge, the see saw went right into the underneath of my lower jaw and Lodged itself into my juggler vein. I was bleeding profusely! My brother ran over to my mother and shouted; "Mom, come quickly its Emily, she is bleeding the see saw is stuck in her throat, she needs help!" My Mom came running with a towel, took the see saw out of my throat, ran over to Suzie's house next door, and they took me to the emergency room. I had lost a lot of blood, but the surgeons were very good, they were real good because I went home the same day with my mom. They gave me some blood, and did their best to cosmetically repair the damage and as a result, today I am left with a small indentation under my chin and a small scar. This is only noticeable when I lift my head up. Also, once in a while I will get seizures in my throat.

I learned through experience, that Dads appetite and 57 Chevy came before the welfare of the family.

This particular incident happened when I was two and half years old. My brother Robert was 4 years old or so and Charlie was 8 months old sitting on mom's lap, in the garage watching dad work on his 57 Chevy. I even have a photo to capture the moment with my mother explaining to me that she had a black eye covered up with makeup in the picture. When I look at the picture today, it just mesmerizes me. You could see my mother's phony smile and see how sad all of us kids were. It was some hard times. Anyway, it was around lunchtime, my dad instructed my mother to go to the store and pick up a half gallon of milk, 1 loaf of bread, 1 small jar of mayonnaise, 1 package of bologna, 1 package of cheese, 1 six pack of beer. My Mom replied; "Sure, can I take the kids"? My Dad replied an emphatic, no you certainly cannot, now go. My mom trembling with fear of what this monster might do to their youngest child whispered in Robert's ear, "please try to protect your brother and don't let your father hit him too hard, she said, "I will try mommy Robert said"" I was too frightened to speak; I grabbed mommy's hand and led her to the car. At the store we were very careful to buy only what we were instructed to buy for fear of reprisal. We came home and Mom asked dad if she could fix the kids a sandwich because they haven't eaten all day. Dad said; "certainly not. Wait until after I have had my lunch, now fix me a sandwich and bring me a beer and sit and watch me work on the car". It seemed to me that Dad loved to exercise power over the family and more often than not, he wanted to keep everyone together where he could watch them and he used food as a controlling item. As an adult, I realize that people like my dad, are usually abused at work and are limited in advanced potential, but that was not the case with my dad, in fact, my dad excelled at his position as a machine technician. He invented modifications that would improve the output of the machine that he was assigned to by at least 100%. The new modifications on the machine and its increased productivity gave my dad a place in the Guinness book of World records. With his newly modified machine, he was able to break three world records for the most envelops produced in an eight hours' time frame. I don't know whether or not my dad was compensated fairly for his creativity. If not, this could be a factor in his abusive behavior, but probably not because his father was just as abusive.

If the job was not the contributing factor that led to the abuse of our family something else had to be wrong. I suspect that my father was suffering from severe mental illness. However, I am not qualified to make this diagnosis.

At any rate, the incident in the garage with the lunch continued for over 3 hours before we were allowed to eat. Charlie could barely swallow his milk because his little jaws were still swollen from the beating that dad had given him. This in itself and not going any further with the book should have been the beginning of a long prison sentence for my dad and possibly my mom. You see Charlie was only eight months old and nothing in this world that he did at this early age could possibly justify such horrid abuse from anyone and condoned by my mother.

Mom still didn't have enough milk for Charlie so she had to go next door to Suzie's house to borrow more. At this point, mom still could not produce milk probably because of lack of nourishment.

Note: The above incident provides the reader with a small taste of how brutal and how ugly my father really is. But only the surface has been scratched. Read on to gain the full appreciation of how mean and ruthless one man can be toward his own family. There is no reason for these senseless acts of brutality, but it does provide the reader with a look inside the mind of an individual who suffers from paranoid schizophrenia as told from the perspective of a victim.

So far I've talked about decisions and actions made by my mother and father that had a traumatic and financial effect on the entire family, but one decision in particular was one that was more personal to me and it caused me more pain and sorrow than all of

the horrible beatings that I suffered from the hands of my father combined.

This incident happened when I was about three maybe four years old. One day at the beginning of summer my mother decided to enter me and my brothers in a contest to model clothes for extra money to buy clothes for us kids to help out her and dad, besides like mom always said; "You can't win, if you don't play". So with that, she entered us in the contest. It was a small contest for people who thought they had beautiful children and thought they had a chance to win. The process included a session of picture taking and filling out forms that informed us that we would be notified if we won the contest.

Several weeks went by, and then we heard a knock on the door. It was Rhonda Barnet and it seems we had won the contest. Rhonda introduced herself to my mother and to me and my brothers and asked if she could come in? Rhonda Barnet if you don't know already was a famous American gossip columnist and actress, and businesswoman. I really do not know how she became involved in this contest, but here she was at our front door, covering the story and explaining the facts, so I guess it must have been a pretty big contest mom put us in. Of course, back in those days, California was really just starting out and putting things out there so anything could happen. My mom was so thrilled she said; "Yes, come in". Next mom offered her a cup of coffee, and I think Rhonda accepted. Then they began to start a conversation about the contest and what we won and the details. Rhonda explained that my brothers would be modeling clothes for a catalog I cannot recall which one or the details. Then Emily would be modeling for a catalog too, but with her we took some additional shots of her and would like to offer you and your husband a chance to let Emily do drama classes, commercials, and dance. What we are offering here is a chance for your daughter to get into Hollywood. Get her in early, teach her everything now, then maybe, just maybe she might have a chance to be the next childhood star or who knows. My mother had this look on her face I will never forget. She looked at Rhonda then she looked down at me. She was frightened for some reason, very scared for me. I guess it was too much for her to take in all at once. My mom began to think she was in over her head this time. She bit her lip and said nothing." But Katy, Rhonda said; I'm telling you she's perfect. Her facial structure, her petite body style, she's beautiful Kate. We would love to have her. Just look at her, she's a treasure. Please talk to your husband tonight, here's my card, please call me ASAP. Here's the contract please look it over carefully. Enclosed you will find the part where it says how much the parents get. Well yes, as parents of this child you will get the most until she turns 18 years old. This way, your family will be well compensated for her work, Also she will be attending school on a full scholarship for the acting and drama and dancing etc.… So please get back to me here's a couple more cards in case you lose one. Thank you so much for your time. That night mom and dad discussed the contract and all the information regarding the Rhonda Barnet offers. They argued back and forth until bedtime with no resolution. The next day my dad went to work and my mom said nothing to me or my brothers. I kept asking her, "Mommy, can I go model the clothes and go to Hollywood, maybe it will be good not only for me, but for the whole family. I can make lots of money to help out so we can have more food, and clothes and stuff mommy". My mother just looked down at me with no response, with tears in her eyes and said, "Emily go and play, those Hollywood people are no good for you. I don't want you to get involved in the drinking and smoking and drugs. It's a bad atmosphere. Besides who will look after you? No, I won't let my precious little girl get hurt that way". I responded as I screamed and cried, "mom no, no, this would be the best mom, they won't hurt me, mom, please, mom no!" The days rolled on and not a word was mentioned of this because it upset me so bad mom had her mind set on the answer of No, so, I slowly was starting to forget, I guess. Then one day a couple of weeks later we got this knock on the door I became very nervous because from down deep inside I knew who it was. Mom answered the door to the smiling face of Rhonda Barnet. "Good Afternoon Mrs. Pandora have you made a decision". My mom in an abrupt and unfriendly manner responded; "Yes I have, my daughter will not be modeling any clothes, or going to Hollywood for any type of classes, and my boys are not modeling any clothes and here's your paper work back". Rhonda responded," why Katy you went to all that trouble to enter the contest for your children to see if they were beautiful and indeed they are especially Emily, and now such a change of heart? My mom responded; "That's all I have to say". Then slammed the door shut in Rhonda's face. I cried I think for about two weeks over this and have still to this day to get over that incident. Because think of it for a moment, how different my life would have been. I can only imagine.

<u>Note</u>: I'm sure that most people at one time or another have dreamed about living a different life but the important thing to remember is that most of us have the power to live the life we want now. We can choose to be happy, we can choose to be sad, we can choose to make others happy or we can choose to make others sad. If we respect ourselves we are on the right track, If we also respect others we are well on our way and if we help those who cannot help themselves we will truly achieve success.

DAD TRIED TO DELIVER TIM WITH HIS WORK BOOTS ON

My mother was in her 9th month of pregnancy in giving birth to my brother Tim. I can't remember what day it was but mom was in the kitchen preparing dinner. Dad had just gotten home from work and an argument started over some trivial matter which was probably related to the dinner meal which I also cannot remember. I do remember however; that dad began to raise his voice and started to shove mom. I will never forget that hideous voice that sounded more like a deep loud groan from the depths of hell that left chills and raised the hairs on my neck. Dad shoved mom to the floor and started to kick her as hard as he could in her stomach. He still had his work clothes on which smelled of sweat and were heavily soiled from a hard day's work at his job. His work clothes included his steel toed black leather work boots. My mom started screaming and yelling as loud as she could begging him to stop, "You're going to kill my baby, Robert stop, stop". This seemed to add fuel to the fire. Dad began to sweat profusely and his eyes seemed to go blank as they widened with an evil stare and I don't know if I am imagining this or not but he seemed to be enjoying this. He seemed to be undergoing some sort of transformation. His breathing was deep and labored his head and arms were floundering to the left and right his whole body was moving to the left and right as he seemed to be trying to gain more energy to be directed and focused to those big heavy black heavy steel toed work boots. He could not stop even if he wanted to. He was a machine of destruction. Within seconds the entire kitchen floor was covered in blood but I knew I had to get help. Soon my mother stopped screaming and moved only when she was kicked by my dad and each time she was kicked it became more and more hideous because with every kick blood would spray profusely from her vagina and cover half the kitchen and this would excite my dad even more. I pulled on my brother Robert's arm as to ask him for help but, he was frozen with fear. The telephone was on the other side of the kitchen. So I had to slip and slide in my bare feet through the blood to reach the telephone to call 911. I could barely reach the telephone but there was a stepstool available and I had to be very careful because there was blood all over my little feet and I did not want to fall because I knew that my mom's life and that of her unborn child were dependent on me. So I picked up the telephone very carefully and dialed 911. Within several minutes the police department, ambulance, and firetruck all arrived to try to save my mother's life and to find out what happened. My mother was unconscious upon their arrival. I heard a very loud knock on the door and the police announced themselves and rushed in through the unlocked door along with several large firemen. They immediately tended to my mom while questioning in a demanding manner, "what's going on here"? At first we were all too shocked to answer, but I finally said that my dad was kicking my mom with his work boots on and she was screaming and now she is asleep and then I pointed toward my mom and then toward my dad. All of my siblings and my dad were covered in blood. The EMT's were able to revive my mom immediately and tried to find out what happened to her. The police took statements from us kids and my mother. Dad was cuffed and forcibly carted off to jail. The lady next door Suzie took care of us until family members could arrive to help out. Mom gave birth to Tim immediately upon arrival at the hospital. The surgeon that delivered moms baby said the beating she took was probably too much for her and her unborn child and that she could see repercussions from this incident later on. I guess the surgeon was right because three months later when my mom and I were changing Tim on the bed we noticed his head was a too small for the rest of his body. My mom said; "Emily, do you think Tim's head is not growing?" I said; "Yes mommy it looks like his head is much too small for his body, why?" My mom immediately called the family Physician. She then was directed to call Children's Hospital in Los Angeles. This would be my brother's home for the next four to five years or so. You see when my dad kicked my mom in the stomach as many times as he did, he traumatized not only my mother but he traumatized my brother too. What he did was injure my brother's head so it needed extensive surgery in order to fix it so it could grow normally. He also caused Tim to be completely cross-eyed. This would require again multiple surgeries to fix. So every weekend my mother and father would stay at Children's hospital with Tim. During this process my mom wanted to keep her breast milk fresh for Tim. She asked me to feed off her so that her breast milk would continue to produce fresh milk for Tim when he came home from the hospital to feed, keep in mind I was five years old at the time and can remember this like it was yesterday. When I first saw Tim, he looked like he had been in a major car accident with all the band aids and tubes it was so sad to think that this tragedy could have been prevented. Anyways, this ordeal went on for over five years then finally Tim got better and seemed to be normal except for the huge scar that he still carries on his head today that goes from one end of his ear to the other. This reminds me of the horrible incident each and every time I see him today. In our inner family circle we always favored Tim I guess because of all the surgeries and all he had to endure.

Note: At this juncture in my mom's life, I really have to question her motivation for staying married to this monster of a man. The only contribution that he has made thus far to their marriage are using her and their children as release mechanisms for any ill feelings that he may be harboring about anything at all.

For my dad, this marriage was perfect, he was a very sadistic individual and with every new child born to this family was a new opportunity for my dad to satisfy his sadistic needs. My mom should not have let this happen to her children and if I were to judge her in a court of law, in my eyes, she would be found guilty of child abuse.

DAD'S DAYS OFF WERE FOR HIS ENJOYMENT ONLY

SATURDAY'S AND SUNDAY'S WERE the worst days of the week as far as I was concerned. This meant that dad was home to make sure that his lists of demands were getting done. We had to work around the house and yard night and day. We had an RCA victor color television so he would pick the T.V. shows both early in the morning and in the evening. There was no afternoon viewing of T.V. Then usually one of the kids would get into some kind of trouble so, he would beat them in the garage in the afternoon around two p.m. He would pick up his can of beer and his hose and continue watering his Dichondra which he used as a substitute for California grass. He made us pick all the weeds out of it every weekend until it looked perfect everywhere. The quiet and calm was just an illusion, dad was a walking time bomb and it didn't take too much at all to set him off even laughter that was too loud was enough to earn me or my siblings a trip to the garage. Every Sunday mom would make a big dinner and put it in the oven either a pot roast with the fixings or meat loaf with the fixings or something that would feed the entire family and fill everyone up with no trouble at all. The boys were always hungry, so it really didn't matter what she made they ate just about anything and everything. It seemed like they were always hungry. After dinner sometimes my mom and I would make banana splits for everyone with our banana boats. The banana boats were made of glass so I had to be very careful when I handled them. After we made the banana splits we would call everyone back into the kitchen to eat them quickly so I could clean up the kitchen for mom and get ready for T.V. time. Dad had to inspect the kitchen to make sure everything was done to his satisfaction for example: the cupboards had to be waxed, the floors had to be cleaned and waxed, all the dishes cleaned and put away, all the sinks cleaned and waxed and the table cleaned and waxed. Then I could go and watch T.V. with my siblings. He would come in and say; "Great job Emily go in and find your spot". I know it sounds ridiculous but I felt really great after being complimented. Sunday was the big night for T.V. viewing but we each had an assigned spot on the floor to sit and you had to sit in that spot if you wanted to watch T.V. Our Sunday night shows were as follows: Twenty Thousand Leagues under the Sea, Bonanza, and Walt Disney's Wonderful World. Each show was an hour long and all was in color because we had an RCA Victor T.V. it really put out a nice picture. Then dad would lay in front of the T.V. in his underwear take one of the boys either Robert or Tim who was also dressed in their underwear then dad would put his arm around him and watch T.V for the entire T.V. time. Neither mom nor I approved of this and thought that dad should at least put some pajama bottoms on but no he just would not have it. He said; "It's my house and I'll do as I please". Mom also thought the boys should put some pajamas on, and once in a great while they did, but most of the time they did not and I thought that was not right. Sometimes you could see him pulling the kid closer to him to cuddle with him and I would just shake my head in disgust it really made my mom mad too. My dad did this sort of thing all the time with all the kids but not me, I knew better I had already been molested which I cover in detail further in the book, at any rate, I refused to be touched or tortured anymore by anyone and he knew not to bother me. He asked a few times but I set him straight right away. My mother was right there to back me up on that one too.

DADDY IS NO ANGEL

Bend over grab your ankles and stare at the wall. As a young child I'll never forget those words, what they meant and how they frightened me and still haunt me to this day. As I look back, I remember all the frightening times in the garage of our Beautiful Northern California Home on Palm and I can still vividly recall all the beatings, and torture the kids and I and my mother had to endure. It was horrible. When you heard those words it meant you were going to get a severe beating within an inch of your life literally. Let me explain. First, after you got into some kind of remedial type of trouble and dad found out about it, he would reach for the strap or piece of wood or whatever he had hanging up in the garage to beat your butt with. After exposing your bare rear end in front of the rest of the siblings dad, would force you to reach down grab your ankles, look at the wall, and wait for the swat. This waiting period was another little bit of torture which he seemed to enjoy with great pleasure. It was terrifying especially as a child. He would keep this up until he thought you have had enough. Sometimes it was so hard to watch, because he would beat you until your butt was bloody. If your butt was gone, he would hit your back and arms etc. Dad was as tyrant. Then after dad was tired he would send you to bed hungry. I can still remember, as I was lying in bed screaming and crying, I was asking myself, "Is this a nightmare, I can't wait until it's over"? Then I cried myself to sleep amid the moans and groans from the cries and whimpers of my siblings. This was my world and the world of my brothers and sister. It served to form our views and perspectives of the world around us. Our personalities were developed with the lessons learned from this hideous man and his distorted examples of leadership. At first, our mom protected us as much as she could from his abusive treatments. But later, it seemed that mom fell in line with his leadership style. One reason for this is because she was afraid of getting beat up herself which happened quite frequently when my dad got angry. Eventually, my mom seemed to develop some of my dad's sadistic tendencies. For example when Charlie my brother got into any kind of trouble, my mom was eager to inform my dad so that he could administer punishment. For some reason or other, my mom and dad used Charlie as a focal point for all their hatred and problems, and as a result, my brother Charlie received most of the beatings because he got in trouble most of the time. I really feel that mom and dad helped to convince Charlie that he was worthless.

Note: It seems to me that what mom might be trying to do here is an attempt to cover her own butt somewhat by sacrificing one of her children. By convincing dad that Charlie needs constant correction, maybe dad will focus most of his attention on him.

THERE'S ALWAYS A STORM BEFORE THE CALM

It was early evening just after supper time, and all of us kids were outside in front of the house playing with the neighbor kids our usual games. I just happened to come into the house because I had to go to the bathroom real quick before returning to my girlfriend Susan. We were playing hop scotch and our barbie dolls. All the barbie dolls belonged to Susan, because I only owned one that I hardly ever played with because I knew I would never get another. You see, my mother had to save up $7.50 to buy this particular barbie doll at the TG&Y store located near the Alpha Beta market. Me and my mother had to walk several blocks down the street while she was pregnant with one of my siblings and it was hot and all we had on our feet were skimpy rubber thongs. It must have been well over 85 degrees outside and the walk was long and hard on us both. But we made it. When mom and I arrived we immediately went inside the store and walked around and I found the doll in her case. Then mom and I purchased a couple of very large soft drinks in cold cups to go along with my barbie doll and off we went for the hike home. I was so happy inside my heart was pounding with joy that mom got me my first barbie. I decided to keep her in mint condition forever. We had no money for doll furniture or accessories, so I made my furniture out of colored toilet paper, for example, (a couch, or a pillow, or a bed, etc.) I still own the same barbie and on her buttock its labeled **Mattel 1953** and she is beautiful and she is in mint condition! I thought I would share this with the reader so you know how precious and little we had growing up and how I carefully kept my things very private because I knew I would not receive another. Getting back to the story, next we decided to get our roller skates and go skating around the neighborhood until night time then when my dad whistles that means I had to come in for the evening which was around 8 p.m. in the evening. Upon entering the house earlier on when I had to go to the bathroom, I heard a rumbling and loud noises and banging around in my mom's bedroom. The door was open as I walked by and saw my father throwing my mother against the wall and socking her in the face multiple times in the face and stomach and back and then threw her up against the dresser then he saw me and quickly slammed the bedroom door and continued his beating up of my mother. This continued for about 10 minutes. There was screaming and yelling and he just would not stop throwing her into the wall and socking her all over her body! I was desperate and scared. I started to pace up and down the hallway I began to sweat and did not know what to do. I was 8 years old at the time and was very scared for my mother I thought for sure he would kill her. Then suddenly I heard him say; "Now look what you made me do to my hand you son of bitch". I thought to my self he must have injured himself because he hit her so many times. Then all of a sudden the door flew open putting a hole in the wall behind it. He then went into the kitchen to wash off his hand and put a bandage on it and put a fresh pack of Pall Mall Reds cigarettes in his pocket and lit one up got into his 57 Chevy and spun out his wheels of course after he was out of his own drive way, he did not want that on his drive way only in the street and left abruptly! I waited for a couple of minutes before coming out of my hiding place and then I went to go check on my mom. As I walked into the room I found her on the floor next to the wall with her left arm over her face protecting her face. I asked her; "Mom can you get up are you ok, is there anything broken"? Mom replies;" I am not sure right now, just go and start the bath water make it hot and make sure to get two or three clean towels for me with two wash cloths and the dove soap" I responded; "Yes mom right away". Mom continued to lay there until the bath water was completely ready and then I helped her to get up off the floor. Mom slowly arose from her position on the floor with my help as she struggled with all her might holding onto my shoulders and my hands. She pulled on me with everything she had in her she got onto her knees. Then slowly with her elbows on the floor she crawled to the bed to use as an elevator to help her to stand to the up ward position. Then she sort of just caught her breath for a moment, then pulled back all her hair. Her hair was a mess from being pulled out by the roots! There was blood all over her face and arms and her clothes were ripped and torn. I was crying and could not hold back my fear for her. I was really scared as I watched in horror the pain my mother was going through and could only imagine how she was feeling inside right at this moment. I was shaking with fear. I grabbed her bloody hand and helped her into the bathroom to help her remove all her clothing, what I saw next took my breath away. As I peeled back her clothing I saw the intense damage he had caused and I began to cry more and more as I examined my own mothers body. First, she removed her shirt, and I saw her arms, which were covered with large purple and black bruises scratches, and blood. Then her back was full of fist marks and large bumps which were purple and black pumps all over everywhere and I mean everywhere all the way down to her kidneys. Next her stomach had large purple bruises that were black and blue and her breasts were each had one black blue mark and blood spots with scratches on each. Her neck had been chocked with hand prints on them and her face was back and blue with a black eye and a bloody lip and cheek bone. Both of her legs were black and blue with bruises. Then after I saw all of the damage I slowly helped her into the tub of water and she slowly sank into the bath tub to relax. All was quiet. Then she ask me to grab the dove soap and a wash cloth to wash her back slowly and very gently and I did while I was crying quietly. I have never seen such a horrific beating in my life, but yes I have seen him beat the kids pretty bad and yes he has beat me too pretty good with different objects but this somehow was different, this was horrific, this was madness and my mind captured it like film on a camera. He almost killed her this time the water was full of blood and I was definitely scared for my mother. She knew deep down she needed to do something but still refused to press charges because she claimed she could not escape his wrath, why I will never know. She soaked in the warm bath water for over an hour for an hour until she felt she could get well enough to go to bed. In the mean time I went outside to watch the kids and maybe start the supper for everyone. Dad did not come back home until late that evening, it was maybe after midnight. Then he had to get ready for work which was at 4 a.m. and he left by 5 a.m. each morning thank God. The monster was gone for the entire day to give her and the family a rest. As I reflect back at the situation, I realize that my mother made a lot of mistakes. The biggest mistake was not pressing charging in a timely manner. My mother refused to do this because of her distorted thinking process. My mother felt that pressing charges or even running away, was useless. She was convinced that the courts would not help her because of past experiences with the same issue. But then again, she has never pressed charges. She did not want to jeopardize chances of losing her share of the house and furniture. She was also convinced that her and her kids would end up living in some sort of a less than desirable half way house or safe house is what they referred to them back in those days. Her decision not to press charges left her vulnerable and open to future beatings from this monster which did in fact occur throughout her entire life.

<u>Note</u>: The decisions that my mother made not only affected her welfare but the welfare of me and all of my siblings as well. We were all in danger by living with my monster of a father and we all did receive severe beatings some of which that left us in severe shock and close to death. In this regard, my mother was thoughtless and selfish.

IN SPITE OF MY DAD, WE WANTED TO BE A NORMAL FAMILY

THERE WERE RARE OCCASIONS on weekends when dad was home we would enjoy home cooked meals and family games in the backyard, as well as evening T.V. viewing. But if anything at all happened that upset dad during these happy times it would all explode into a terrible nightmare. My mother soon tired of these many episodes and gathered up the kids and left dad. Sometimes we went to Mom's Mom and Dad, or once we stayed in the mountains up at Big Bear. Then one time we left dad for a whole year and went to Columbus, Nebraska and after mom and dad got back together and made up, things went well for a while and then got progressively worse. For example, we started to go back to church on a regular basis; my oldest brother Robert stopped performing activities as an altar boy. He seemed to lose interest in going to church altogether and stayed home with dad watching cartoons on Sunday mornings in their underwear in front of the T.V. And they would still be that way when we would all arrive home around 10:00 am in the morning, unbelievable. I found this very weird. Another dark memory, that I have is associated with weekends at home with dad. My mom would go to the dairy after church with us kids and buy bacon, eggs, orange juice, 1 gallon of fresh milk, 1 loaf bread, 1 pound butter,

1 dozen fresh sweet rolls for the family. It was just down the street from where we lived in Northern California so it was real convenient for us. After we arrived home mom started to cook breakfast for the family and us kids would play outside until it was ready. Boy did it smell good. Then dad would come in to the kitchen to check on the groceries as breakfast was being served. Dad acted differently on each occasion on one occasion in particular, dad checked the grocery list and found cinnamon rolls. Upon seeing this dad produced a hideous laugh as he attempted to make fun of mom and her obvious love for sweets. In my mind, his attempt at humor failed as he yelled out loud, "see kids, your mom will probably die with a cinnamon roll or cookie on her grave". None of the kids laughed at his comment, in fact, I felt that there was something wrong with dads mind because he kept rambling and rambling about the same thing. My mom finally cut him short when she said to him; "Robert you always have your share of the cinnamon rolls and you seem to like them as much as if not more than the rest of the family." Upon hearing this he yelled out a couple of cuss words and scampered off in a huff. It's surprising that mom was able to walk away from this episode with nothing more than verbal abuse. My mom loved sweets and purchased them every weekend for her and to share with the rest of the family and she experienced the same argument from my father. On many occasions my father was a bit more physical. For example, on one occasion she was humiliated in front of the family as my father smashed the cinnamon bun to her face and mouth while discarding the rest to the floor and yelling at the top of his lungs; "You stupid Mother Fucking Bitch". Needless to say, after hearing this and witnessing his treatment of my mother we were all petrified and frozen with fear, because these episodes are usually a prelude of something fiercer to follow. But we did not know because he was so un-predictable. What really confused me the most was that his anger and outbursts was not triggered by alcohol in fact, most of the time he had a mean hateful look on his face that seemed like a time bomb ready to explode. When he drank beer in excess he did become a bit more aggressive but beer was not the trigger and he never drank hard liquor. At times a cigarette

was enough to calm him down, and his anger was usually associated with beer and not so much hard liquor.

<u>Note:</u> There's no doubt in my mind that my dad was a very dangerous man and needed to be institutionalized in a place where he could receive help and counseling. Its terribly wrong to try to raise a family based on fear and intimidation because its takes a toll by distorting the development of the social aspects of the affected individuals and restrains their abilities to interact with others.

WHY WAS MY DAD SO MEAN

FROM WHAT I KNOW about my dad, and his family, his young childhood environment is more than likely the main contributor to the development of his personality. I was told early in life that my dad's father was heavily involved with organized crime and he was a very ruthless and mean individual who used force and brutality to get his way. In fact, he used his force as a means of interacting and communicating with his family. As a result, all family members including his wife were afraid of him. He went so far as to beat his own wife who was crippled and restricted to a wheel chair. Now as far as my father is concerned, my grandfather made him sleep outside in a cold fireplace after he had beaten him with a whip over his back until it was bloody and was denied food and water where he stayed all night. This continued for several years. During this time, my dad had a deep burning desire to get an education. He studied intensely and made sure that his grades were up to par. His ultimate goal was to go to college. When his dad was away, he secretly asked for help from his mother to complete his homework because he was weak in certain areas and wanted to get high grades in all subjects and his mother had a very high IQ and could teach him well. In addition to academic development, my dad was heavily involved in body building. He belonged to a local gym and spent many hours lifting weights and performing various other exercises. One day, my dad came home from school with his books in his arms his dad was at home and in a bad mood and grabbed my dad's book's and threw them on the floor. My dad demanded that he pick the books up. His dad refused. My dad asked him again; "You pick up the books or, I'm going to have to hurt you". My grandfather was totally shocked. He had never heard anything like this before from my father, but he still refused to pick up the books. My dad took a deep breath and stretched his massive arm, opened his hand grabbed my grandfather tightly around the neck and shoved him with brute force against the wall. My grandfather's face turned beet red he gasped for air and the sweat poured down his face. My dad said; "If you ever throw my books to the floor again, or hit me, my mother, or anyone else in this family again, I will beat the living shit out of you until you are dead do you understand that"? Grandfather could not talk so he just nodded his head yes. Dad asked him again; "Now will you pick up my books". Grandma with her frail arthritis ridden hands managed to clap her hands with tears in her eyes and smiled at my father.

Note: By challenging and defeating my grandfather, my father did a good deed and made my grandmother proud, but unfortunately my father's mental attributes and psyche was imprinted, probably at birth and nurtured throughout his life from his father and resulted in a carbon copy of his own father. How sad for me, my mother and my siblings.

THE CALM BEFORE THE STORM

ONE OF MY MOST favorite memories was when Grandma and I and my mom went to San Francisco to see my auntie Lana every month for her home-made pasta. But the trip itself was a fun filled and exhilarating experience. Grandma was driving a Chevy 4 door impala and she always left the house late, which means she had to go a little faster in order to get there on time as she promised Lana she would arrive by 11:00 a.m. sharp. So, grandma got behind the wheel and went about 70 M.P.H. in order to make it there on time and when we got to San Francisco, as you know, the roads are like a roller coaster. At any rate, Grandma was flying down those roads in order to make it on time and I was in the back seat but the seat belt was too big for me so I bobbed up and down almost slamming to the ceiling and back to the seat again. I enjoyed it, and could not contain my laughter and excitement; I was six and a half. My mom was in the front seat holding on for her dear life. She told Grandma; Mom If you don't slow down, you'll kill us all". Grandma responded; "Katy I've been driving these roads long before you were even born, and know them like the back of my hand, I would never do anything to harm you or my granddaughter just look at Emily, she's having the time of her life back there". Mom responded; "Yeah I know, but she is just a child and doesn't know how dangerous these roads can be Mom". Soon we arrived at the apartment. It was situated on the ocean side of a very steep hill so grandma was determined to use the parking brake. Upon exiting the car, there was auntie Lana outside to greet us. She seemed excited waving her hands talking Italian, and welcoming us to her home. My auntie Lana is pure Italian and this was made obvious to anyone who did not know. She wore a scarf made of silk to cover all her long gray hair wrapped around her head to keep her hair from getting into the food. She then wore a long dress below her knees with an apron to cover her clothing. Then, nylons and her shoes were leather boot type shoes that lace up above her ankles with a small heel. Also she had a small white towel to wipe her hands attached to her side at all times for whatever reason. Since I was only about six and a half years old I cannot recall too much about the apartment, but I do remember a few of the things that captured my interests. Before entering the apartment, we were all required to remove our shoes. Then it was straight to the kitchen for her famous pasta fazool lunch. I was in complete aw at the sight of the huge old table. First, the table itself was very, very old and unique it even had a strange but wonderful smell to it. The table was adorned with special handmade laced Italian style pattern floral tablecloth. Each table setting had china, Chrystal glasses, and real silver with cloth napkins for each individual to use. Auntie Lana then placed a candle in the middle of the table so we could say the prayer before eating. We were all Catholic and it was standard practice to bless the food and thank the Lord God before eating, as I still do today. She gave me a booster for my chair because I was still too small to reach the table. It was finally time to eat. So Lana and my mom started getting the food put into bowls with big spoons so people could serve themselves. I could hardly contain my excitement. The next experience was more over whelming and created sensory pleasure that could not have been equaled by the world's best Italian restaurant. My olfactory nerves were stimulated beyond repression. The first served was the fresh piping hot hand made pasta noodles. Next she served the home-made rich red and thick pasta sauce. Next came her famous meat balls oh boy, those were unbelievable. Then of course you cannot forget the fresh home-made bread, and fresh parmesan cheese. Then last but not least, one bottle of ruby red wine for my mother, grandma, and Lana of course and for me in a small porcelain pitcher was milk. Now we were ready to eat (*manga in Italian*). I was like a loose cannon and I did not need to be persuaded. At the end of the day when we went home there was always plenty of left overs for us to take with us to provide for those who could not attend. This was an added bonus.

<u>Note</u>: **Nothing triggers my memory and all of the elements associated with it like the taste of good authentic freshly prepared Italian food cooked by Italian immigrants from Sicily. These people were kind, gentle and sometimes hard to understand, but not at all like my dad.**

BLINDED BY TRUST

WRITING THIS SECTION OF the book will probably be the hardest thing I'll ever have to do but I feel that in order for me to heal it must be done. When I was six years old I thought the world was a beautiful place and I loved spending time with my father's family and I had a sense of purpose when I was given the very special job of caring for my invalid, wheelchair confined grandmother during the summer of 1966 and 1967. She suffered from severe Rheumatoid Arthritis and could not care for herself. She was a very sweet lady, but my grandfather proved to be a nightmare. He started looking at me in a rather distinct and unique way. He started buying me gifts and buying me candy and ice cream. He wanted to spend time with me because my mom was too busy with her other kids and started to neglect me more and more each day. My clothes were raged and old. My hair was unkempt. My grandfather always wanted to try to dress me and insisted on helping me brush my hair. But, I really did not need the help. I didn't know that he was a predator who preyed on small children. He was trying to use me to satisfy his own perverted needs. I felt very weird around him. At times, he just scared me to death, at night; I would lay awake, with my eyes open wondering if he was going to come for me and then one night he did. My worst nightmares came true. He crept up on me, tapped me on the shoulder and said, "Let's go". He told me to be real quiet and to never say anything to anybody or anyone. This man was very, dangerous and I knew if I ever said anything, he would come and kill me with whatever object he could get his hands on. I looked over at grandma and noticed that she seemed to be awake. I took my little stuffed animal and went with grandpa. My grandfather made me lay down beside him in a back to back position. I could feel him move and twist while moaning and groaning all night long and I asked him; "what are you doing?" then he replied, "Just go to sleep". These nightly episodes continued all summer long and became more intense. I was asked to change positions and sometimes we slept facing each other and sometimes he would place his penis between my legs to masturbate. He had a rag with him to clean himself off with. This made me sick, but I was trapped and I knew there was no one around to help. My grandmother was not blind to what was going on but she was crippled and helpless but, she could talk and on one night in a barely audible whisper she called to me as my grandfather started to carry me from the room, "Emily don't go, please don't go, I need you". I stayed to help her. Thank God for grandma. My grandfather, in my mind and from what I observed, was an extremely perverted and cruel individual. On several occasions I witnessed him carting my crippled grandma off in the middle of the night into the same bedroom that he took me. He kept her there for several hours before returning her to her own bed. She was speechless after these episodes and seemed to be crying. I'll never know what he did to her in the privacy of his bedroom but, it was by no means normal sex, her crippled body would not allow it. All I could say, being familiar with his abuse was, "oh my God grandma". One day my grandfather asked me if I would like to go for a ride in his big dump truck. I thought about it and said, sure. But I knew deep down if I had given any other answer, he would probably think that I was going to tell grandma about what he was doing, and so I went along with him reluctantly. Although, as I reflect back, I think my grandmother suspected that something was going on because of the way I was acting out when I was around grandpa.

As I recall, the truck rides were horrible. The truck itself was an oversized dump truck used for hauling heavy loads of dirt and rock. At my young age, the cab seemed to be at least ten feet off the ground and it was very noisy and extremely loud. My grandpa was constantly shifting gears or manipulating some other control which I knew nothing about. The inside of the cab was hot and dusty and the sweat just beaded off and rolled over my tiny body. It was almost unbearable, but there were moments that excited me for example, when he either dumped a load or took on a load, the entire truck would shake and rumble and felt like a small earthquake. The excitement however, was not enough to interest me for future rides. Since it was illegal to have a child in such a large work vehicle, I remember being covered with a tarp whenever there were people around. This was a very scary experience for me. The tarp was filthy dirty with a strong musty rotten smell. It was unbearable and I cried and whimpered as low as I could, afraid of what he would do to me if I were discovered by someone. These rides were anywhere from eight to ten hours long depending on the job. Going to the bathroom was a nightmare. Most of the time I had to hold it but sometimes he brought a can and a roll of toilet paper. At the end of the day he would lift me out of the truck and insist that I sit and watch him grease the truck wheels and perform any required maintenance. I was desperate to go inside to check on grandma and get cleaned up. I know now that this whole truck ride scenario was just nothing more than a ploy to keep me away from grandma so that I would not tell her about his perverted advances toward me. Grandma was becoming weaker so I decided that I could not go on any more truck rides and surprisingly enough, grandpa agreed. But I suspect that he got into some kind of trouble by taking me with him on his work trips. The rest of the summer I stayed with my grandmother to help her with her treatments. My grandfather did manage however, to molest me at home in the garage or the bathroom or whenever he had the opportunity. He became more brazen in his approach and didn't seem to care who found out. Summer finally ended and I went home. I wasn't really happy to go home because I knew what waited for me; a pregnant mother, a mean violent father and a very unhappy family atmosphere. There was no one there that I could tell my problems to and certainly no one who had the time to listen. I felt like a prisoner locked within my own terrified mind. I returned to school, but could not concentrate, as hard as I tried and no one would help me or lend assistance so I flunked the second grade. I had to repeat the second grade. After the school year ended, I was asked to return to grandmas to care for her in her ever deteriorating condition. My mom was reluctant, she said that she needed help at home, but I suspect that she knew something was not right. My mom was finally persuaded because it was thought at the time that my grandmother had limited time to live and desperately needed my help.

Note: Fear of my grandfather and father robbed me of my childhood and as a result, I matured faster than most kids of my age but, my decision to keep the molestation issue a secret was definitely the wrong thing to do. I was reluctant to tell my parents because I realized that both of my parents were mentally unpredictable, especially my father and he could have easily blamed and punished me, Ironically however, later on when my mother found out, she in fact did blame me for the molestation and still does to this day.

At any rate, reflecting back, I should have told someone at my school about the molestation, as well as, expressing my fear of my father.

THE SECOND TIME AROUND

My mother and father finally decided that I would return to help care for my grandmother for one more summer. Shortly after arriving, I realized that my grandfather was a lot meaner and more aggressive both with me and my grandmother. It was obvious that he was tired of taking care of grandma. He was more physically abusive to her. So I would jump in and tell him, "Here let me help you out with her, I will take her to the bathroom, I will be okay." He just looked at me and said; "Thank you I am really tired, from working all day and grandpa needs a break." I just smiled and took grandma as fast as I could to the bathroom without saying a word. I knew he had been abusing her because of all of the bruises all over her arms and legs and just everywhere. She looked very sad and unhappy, but very thankful that I had finally arrived to help her in her final days on this earth. After I took her to the toilet I then took her to the sink so she could wash her hands and face and whatever else she wanted to do. This made her very happy. I gave her lots of time to do the things she wanted to do and not rush or hurry her like grandpa did all the time. I would go with her on her shopping trips and help her in and out of the car and put her into her wheel chair then help with the shopping. The only tough part was getting the wheel chair down the back stairs of the house. Grandpa never took the time or was too cheap to build a wheel chair ramp. All he ever cared about was her keeping the books to the penny, and cleaning the house which he made me and my mom do for free. My mom wasn't really afraid of grandpa, but she was afraid of my dad. My dad ordered her to take care of his mother and besides that, my mother truly loved my grandmother.

TRAUMATIZED

ONE OF THE MOST unbearable memories that I have about my young childhood occurred during this second summer to assist my grandma. I remember it was right after supper and grandpa said he was going to give grandma her weekly bath. Because next week she gets her hair done and we will go to Disneyland and Knott's Berry Farm this weekend. I was so excited. So, as soon as we finished the dishes, I helped get the bathwater ready. This experience was so powerfully engrained in my mind, that I can still remember the color and scent of the towels. I can vividly see each and every detail of the bathroom and it gives birth and brings forth a river of emotions that will be with me for the rest of my life. I continued to help grandma by placing the bathmat in the tub and informed her that I would be right outside if she needed further assistance. She nodded her head yes, and grandpa said; "with a half-smile, thank you sweet heart." Grandpa closed the door but not all the way. I decided to take this opportunity to watch grandpa give grandma a bath. I did this in case I would need to assume grandpa's responsibilities and take care of grandmas bathing needs sometime in the future. But what I saw was surely nowhere near what I expected. I saw him undress her, and then he tried to pin her hair up with bobby pins and put a bonnet on her head so as to not get her hair wet. Grandma told him, "Luke, you're hurting me, those Bobbie pins are sharp and are scratching my head and making my head bleed". Grandpa got furious he said you know what; "all you ever do is complain, and bitch. Here I am trying my damnedest to try to help you out, and what do I get, nothing but your fucking bitching, complaining, and your bullshit. Well bitch, I've have fucking had it with you! Then he proceeded to sock her in the face with his fist multiple times. I had to cover my mouth shut because I lost my breath. I was in shock. Then he proceeded to pick up grandmas small fragile little broken body and throw her into the bath tub, but first he lifted her way high over his head then he slammed her as hard as he could into the bathtub. I started to cry uncontrollably and tiptoed very quietly into the kitchen and hid under the kitchen table crying quietly with my stuffed animal. Then all of a sudden grandpa screamed out; "Emily come quickly, I need help its grandma." Before I went into the bathroom I wiped all my tears away and acted like nothing was wrong and dried my face the best that I could so he could tell nothing was wrong. When I got to the bathroom I saw grandma in the bathtub with blood splatter all over. I started screaming; "Grandpa what happened." Grandpa explained that grandma fell into the bathtub and for me to go call 911 now."

Note: I was terrified of grandpa and in my young mind I knew that he would kill me if I Told the police what I saw and what he did to grandma through the crack in the door, but I could of used creativity, for example, I could have said that I heard a lot of noise and banging, then screaming and yelling coming from the bathroom.

GRANDMA FINDS PEACE

DURING GRANDMAS STAY IN the hospital, my mom and dad visited her and gave me feedback on her progress. They would tell me that she was getting better and that she would be home soon. I found this hard to believe, in consideration of the beating that she received. I asked my parents if grandpa would need my help after she returned home. They said yes. My grandfather discussed this issue with my dad and it was agreed that my help was desperately needed. Two weeks later, during the early summer, I returned to my grandmother's house. I was in total shock. My grandmother looked horrible, her bruises were green and yellow and consumed her entire body, her face was so distorted and she was barely recognizable it was covered with grotesque colored bruises and swollen. Her arms were green and yellow, her hips black and blue especially around the 12 inch long stiches. The remainders of her legs were covered with green and yellow bruising all the way down toward her crippled feet. Her feet were pointed with her toes pointed and drawn inward. Her knees were drawn toward her chest in the form of a fetal position. Her arms were drawn together with her elbows touching. Her hands were drawn to her chin with her fingers half clenched and clutching each other. Her head was bent sideways against her half closed fingers. She was clothed in a house dress that snapped down the front and was fitted over her arms. She wore pink booties over her rolled up nylons which did not extend beyond her knees. Her makeup was slight with a small amount of lipstick and a bit of face powder. I told grandma that I was here to help her and I will be staying the entire summer. So our whole family was there to welcome her home and put her suit cases away and un-pack for her. My oldest brother Robert was watching the kids while I assisted mom to help grandma get ready for the barbecue and set the tables outside under the covered patio which had two benches for the barbecue. Also in the backyard, in a slightly dirty area situated next to a shed, which housed grease guns and miscellaneous tools he kept his trucks parked. It was sort of a unique set-up, but it was a quiet and extremely somber setting with an uncomfortable sense of foreboding. I remember the shed very well it was one of grandpa's favorite places to molest me.

Anyway, dad and his father were off and busy fixing the grill up for the barbecue, while mom and me and grandma fixed or rather made the potato salad, grandma already had the coleslaw, and the fresh Italian bread for the hotdogs and hamburgers. Then on a separate dish mom cut up a head of lettuce, tomatoes, onions, and pickles which were the fixings for the hamburgers, I put the ketchup and mustard in the center of the tables for everyone to grab. Then I set out the glasses for the kids. The kids sat at a separate table from the adults. I do remember one very important thing. I had to get two table clothes. Dad made it a point because the boys were very sloppy and very hungry and they reach a lot, so he wanted them over at another table where he could feed them good and then he could enjoy his meal with his mom and dad and my mom in peace. Also, grandpa would bring out a special bottle of his finest red wine for mom and dad and him and grandma to enjoy with their dinner. Everything went fine through the lunch and after words my mother and I began the cleanup process. After the cleanup was complete, everyone said their goodbyes and went home. I stayed behind to care for my grandmother. The rest of the evening was rather uneventful; we watched a little TV, The Lawrence Welk Show; had some chocolate ice cream and went to bed. I slept with grandma so that I could help her with her bodily functions. There was a bedpan on a table in the corner of the room and when grandma whispered; "Emily I need to go to the bathroom". I would get the bed pan and help grandma relieve herself. Sometimes this was physically demanding, but I loved my grandma and I knew that if I didn't help her she would have to rely on grandpa. This continued for about three weeks and during this time grandma became progressively weaker and she continued to lose weight and her appetite diminished. The pain from the two broken hips and the arthritis took its toll and was too much for her little body to bear. Grandpa didn't seem to care for grandma at all and he kept molesting me and I was so fearful of him that I no longer had the courage to fight. One Sunday morning, as I recall, my family including my mother, father brothers and sister were visiting. Sometime during their visit my brother Robert caught my grandfather in the act of molesting me. He didn't say anything at the time, but I would certainly hear about it later. I stayed with grandma this night and she passed away with my arms tightly held around her. In the morning, I tried desperately to wake grandma and got no response so I had no choice but to go wake grandpa. Grandpa came to check on grandma and said that she had passed away. Reflecting back, I remember that grandma was very weak just before her death just before she went to bed the night before she had another confrontation with grandpa about the way that he was molesting me and this argument took its toll on her will to live.

Note: Even though my grandmother suffered from a severe case of arthritis, I truly believe that her death was hastened by my grandfather. His severe mental and physical abuse certainly took its toll and robbed her of her will to live. My grandmother was only 53 years old when she finally died in my arms.

MY MOM AND DAD FINALLY PULLED THEIR HEADS OUT OF THEIR ASSES

AFTER BEING NOTIFIED OF my grandma's death, my mom and dad immediately came to take me home, but they had also been informed by Robert Jr. about the molestations. Dad beat mom and Robert Jr. upon finding out about the molestation. This beating is something I will never understand. Why he chose to beat my mother and my brother made absolutely no sense. But then again, my father was totally irrational and I firmly believe that he is more mentally ill than previously diagnosed and he's a danger to himself, his family, and society. At any rate, my grandfather was unaware of my father's visit. Early in the morning, my mom and dad knocked on the door, I opened the door, my dad said; "get your things were leaving". My dad left in a huff to talk to his dad. I don't know exactly what was said, but there was a heated argument going on in the kitchen area and I'm sure that money was at the center of the discussion. If I were to guess, grandpa paid his way out of a serious situation and was allowed to go free while I was left with the psychological damage and future trauma that was sure to occur and have a negative effect on the rest of my life. My grandfather was free to continue molesting other children in the family which he did. After agreements were made and finalized, we left grandpa's house and we never returned while I was a child. I was not even allowed to attend Grandma's funeral because my parents felt that I had already suffered enough trauma. When in fact, I knew deep down, that the whole family knew of this tragedy and my parents were not only humiliated by this man but did not want to be in the same state as this man. This tragedy not only affected our family but it affected all the people around us, and to everyone we knew, it seemed like a plague. My mom felt humiliated by everyone and she had to move out in order to live out the rest of her life. My dad felt the same way. All the family members on both sides found out, and the news traveled like wild fire. The whole family was ashamed and my parents blamed me for the incident! I was only six. Threatened by a monster, and then blamed for not speaking up, but they were unaware that my grandfather threatened to kill me if I opened my mouth and in addition to this, my own father was paid off by his dad to forget the entire incident.(I'm just assuming this because every time my father needed money, he would call his dad and he would get money wired to him, i.e; (the farm needed a water line which was $10,000). To this day, I will never understand why my parents cared so little for me by selling my soul to this monster and then trying to justify it by blaming me for the problem. I hope all of them rot in hell, especially my father and mother. I suffer each and every night with my ghosts. For example; I have to make sure the closet door is closed or I cannot sleep, for fear of monsters. I know, it sounds silly, but when I was a little girl these monsters really did exist in my mind and did come out to haunt me, so today I just close the closet door and they are gone. My life hasn't been simple it gets kind of complicated at times, but I just deal with it. Since the incident my parents have treated me as a tainted child, for example, when I needed tonsil and adenoid surgery, my parents waited too long because they feared that I would disclose information about the molestation and when they did decide to take me to the Doctor, it was too late because I had lost most of the hearing in my right ear and have hearing problems for the rest of my life. Luckily, I have an understanding husband who recognizes that I do have serious problems and he is working with me in trying everything he can to help me live with the pain. My Husband also recognizes that I have very sick parents and he doesn't want anything to do with them. Without a good support system, it would be extremely hard to make it on my own.

<u>Note:</u> Money is the blood of life for my family, especially my mom and dad, they would do anything in the world for its attainment even if it means turning on each other. Their greed has embarrassed me on several occasions; for example, my mother used to brag to my husband about all the rich and wealthy boyfriends that she had the opportunity to marry before she met my dad. This is all that she could remember about them and my father accused my husband of being jealous over his new trailer and pick-up truck. During A Christmas party, my oldest brother took out his wallet and flashed several crisp new $100 dollar bills at me and my husband.

HEAVEN HELP US WE REALLY TRIED

LIFE WENT ON AS usual and things seemed to calm down. Dad broke his second world record at work for making the most envelopes in eight hours. He then flew to New York where they offered him a job and a house and a V.P. position, but dad turned it down saying he just could not raise his family in such an atmosphere, "Too many people and too much pollution, bad atmosphere for my family". So he came back to California and went back to Unique envelope to break his third world record and get into the Guinness Book of World records for making the most envelopes in an eight hour period. Plus he received a beautiful trophy and some monetary reward for this accomplishment complete with pictures in the paper too. My brothers and I returned to school and everything seemed to calm down. Even mom seemed sort of happy. But soon arguments between my mom and dad began to happen more frequently. I can remember this all started around dads thirty fourth birthday. I remember waking up that morning watching dad comb his hair getting dressed and he looked the same as he ever did but his demeanor was different. He started to get upset for no reason at all and became very short tempered and upset for no reason at all and he was more violent and aggressive than ever. He yelled much louder, he hit much harder, and beat mom more often and more severely. When he corrected the kids he would literally pick them up, including me, and slam us against the wall with all the force he could muster. He was relentless. He would not stop until he was exhausted. The kids would be left bloody and bruised and screaming. My mother decided that she had finally had enough and decided to leave. This she kept a secret from dad. Otherwise, this probably would have been her death sentence.

<u>Note:</u> No woman or child should ever have to endure this type of physical or mental abuse. My mother's refusal to press charges in earlier episodes were based entirely on her obsessive greed and love for money. It was based on the hope that she would outlive this monster and she would be left with all of the assets. This was a dangerous dream with no basis in reality and it placed her life as well as, the lives of her children in extreme jeopardy.

OFF TO NEBRASKA

LITTLE DID WE KNOW, that mom had been planning and preparing to leave for some time now. She even managed to set aside a small amount of money to travel. She wanted to head east because she was really tired of living in an over populated city and she felt that living in a small town would provide her and her children with the best chances of remaining hidden from our dad. So our target was Omaha Nebraska. After arriving, mom changed her mind as she decided to go to Columbus Nebraska. First thing mom needed was a job. So, she walked over to the restaurant and asked for a job. She immediately got a job and explained to her manager that she needed a place to rent for her and the children. Lucky for us he had a house to rent with rent that my mother could afford. She also explained that she needed a car. Again this angel from nowhere had a car and he offered it to mom at a price that he knew she could afford and gave her the keys so her and the kids could go home. I'll never forget the look of surprise and gratitude on my mom's face and I thought she was going to break down and cry. The manger could see her happiness and hugged her and smiled he looked at us kids and I could suddenly feel his warmth as a tear fell from his eyes. During the following weeks as we settled in, mom applied for food stamps and was approved and all of us kids got enrolled in catholic schools because that's all they had down there at the time in Columbus Nebraska. I'll never forget how mean the Nuns in the church were to me and how they would correct me with the ruler. Boy, they were too strict! They would slap the back of my hands until they were bright red for something I did that was probably really remedial or small and pulled my hair in church for chewing gum while the Priest was preaching, then make me spit it out. As soon as my mom found out about this, she went down there and told them to never hit me again, she explained that I've already had too much violence with my father and the last thing Emily needs is more violence in her life. Mom's salary was low so we didn't have many treats and our food was supplemented with what was given to her at the restaurant. We didn't have many clothes except for the catholic school uniforms which had to be ironed once a week. So mom got an iron at a garage sale so we ironed our clothes on towels on the floor. The high cost of utilities forced us to stay warm by huddling together by the stove. We had no T.V. set so for entertainment we had to find other alternatives. One of them involved my story telling abilities. We would all gather around in a group and make ourselves as comfortable and warm as possible and we would use candles for lighting and I would invent some sort of a story usually a scary tale from the darkest and deepest recesses of my mind. Sometimes the stories were so realistic that I even scared myself. The stories were consistent with our surroundings for example; the house seemed to creek and moan in support of various lines. For example; when I described; "Loud footsteps, the wind would make an eerie sound as it blew through the house and the lights would flash as the wind blew stronger". At times, the candles would flicker and the flames would completely die out when certain words were spoken. I looked at the faces of my siblings and they were white as ghosts and needless to say they were drenched in sweat. On one occasion my oldest brother begged me to stop because I was scaring him and the children. It seems however that he was the only one that wanted me to stop the story. All the rest of the other kids wanted me to finish. An argument ensued and Robert Jr. won because he was the eldest brother but I let him know of his insecurities and my passion for good story telling. He had nothing further to say. I put all the kids to bed that night reassuring them that in the future when Robert Jr. was not around I would continue to tell my stories and finish them. They were very happy to hear that. With that, they all hugged me and smiled and went to sleep.

<u>Note:</u> It's amazing to realize that no matter what religion you are or what you believe in, there is actually evil and good in this world and they manifest themselves as pure and unwavering feelings that are hard to explain but are as real as life itself. With this divine balance, we could not exist, we would destroy each other and all human life would cease to exist. So please realize how special you are and cherish your worth and the worth of others and help to maintain order in the universe because after all that is what our job is.

NIGHTMARES ARE REAL, DAD FOUND US

IT SEEMS THAT DAD had contacted a private investigator to find us. So after a year of struggling and almost starving, we got an unwanted surprise. Dad found us and decided to take the boys Robert Jr. and Charlie from the catholic school that afternoon telling the nuns that he was just taking the boys out for ice-cream and would bring them back in one hour. But he never returned. Marsha and I walked home from school without my brothers and I found that very unusual but thought that maybe they were already at home. When I got into the house no one was home. I immediately called my mother at work and told her that the boys Robert Jr. and Charlie were missing. She immediately called the school and found out that my dad had been there earlier to pick up Robert Jr. and Charlie and never returned them to the school. My mom was panicked and scared and very upset at the nuns for doing that because his name was not on the place cards of people to pick up the children. The nuns were in a great deal of trouble, but so was my mother. She now knew what she had to do. Mom felt that she had no choice but to take us kids and return to California as soon as possible. This decision makes no sense to me because shortly after returning, mom got pregnant again and gave birth to a little girl named Lilly after my dad's mother. This would be her sixth child now and my responsibilities for taking care of my siblings were greater than ever now. She said I was her; "Right hand man, and without me she would not be able to do the work". I questioned my mother's sanity especially her decision about sleeping with a man whom she hated and despised. As a young child I could not understand this and as an adult this is beyond my comprehension.

Note: **This episode proved to me, especially in my young mind, that my mother was truly mentally ill and was being taken advantage of by father, My mother should of called the police and filled a report, but instead, she followed my dad back to California and got pregnant again. This birth resulted in a 10lb baby. This was her second 10lb baby. The beatings started again several months after this child was born.**

FORCES BEYOND OUR CONTROL CONVINCED MY DAD THAT WE NEEDED TO LEAVE CALIFORNIA

AFTER EXPERIENCING SEVERAL LARGE earthquakes in the seventies, my father decided that it was time to round up the family and move out of California. My dad purchased a GMC utility vehicle. It had three bench seats and rear space for storage. But even before we thought about loading the truck, dad looked at the truck and decided that he didn't like the tires or the rims so he researched several catalogs and found new tires and rims that he thought would look good on the truck. So he called the retailer and ordered a set of tires and rims for the truck. From what I recall dad said that the tires were being shipped from another country and would arrive in Sacramento at the docks in a few days. Dad arranged to drive four hundred miles to pick up the tires and rims which he took to the retailer to have them mounted on to the truck. Dad claimed he was saving a few dollars for this effort. Then he drove another four hundred miles to make the trip back home. At the time I was only eight years old and I felt that dad was wasting a whole lot of money time and effort and to this day I cannot figure out why anyone in their right mind would drive eight hundred miles and spend a great deal of money to trade a perfectly brand new set of tires for another set of brand new tires. Initially we purchased food, a porta-potty, and a two person pup tent. This was just the beginning. Other provisions included portable stoves, lanterns, and flashlights, case of batteries, first aid provisions, blankets, and cases of water, ice chests, and clothes for the family. What seemed to be a very large space in the GMC was now very cramped with hardly any room for the passengers. But it was especially uncomfortable for my older brother Robert who was only 10 years old and who was starting to experience growing pains and there was really no room for him to move the seat back to stretch his legs. Mom kept BENGAY cream to rub his legs down with at night to help relieve the excruciating pain and would also administer Anacin. Robert cried all night every night during the whole entire trip. Mom would try to soothe him but nothing really seemed to help. Robert Jr. really did suffer in that back seat, and I really felt sorry for him and I cried in silence for him hoping this trip would be over soon. Unfortunately, this trip would be lasting at least a year if not longer. It was a very painful and horrible experience. I guess at times it was a little interesting to experience new surroundings, with different people and new landscapes. But my father was so mean and hateful that he usually ruined each and every experience for us kids so my memories of these states and their surroundings were not very pleasant. Dad designed this entire trip including the routing and the scheduling for his own satisfaction with no regard for anyone else. This entire trip was constructed for his own enjoyment. The kids and my mom were with him simply because he felt that he was obligated to do so as a parent, husband and father which were probably the result of his strong Italian heritage. Otherwise; he could care less if the family was happy or not. This trip belonged to him. Sometimes we would just simply drive through a state and keep right on going and not stop until dad got tired. Then when he was real tired he would stop at the nearest KOA campground and unpack at whatever hour it happened to be usually it was an inconvenient or very late hour and the kids were tired and hungry, ready for bed, but we still had to help unload the truck and set up camp before we were allowed to sleep. I do remember however one of our first major stops was in Las Vegas Nevada. My father allowed my mother to try her hand at the slot machines. She got lucky after a few attempts and won fifty dollars in nickels. She wanted to keep going but dad insisted that it was time to leave. She was very disappointed but left anyway. This moment of fun lasted for about an hour while we all waited in the truck for her to return. We were off again on his trip. Soon it was time for us to eat. Our dinner meals usually consisted of whatever we could purchase at the camp stores such as hot dogs stale bread and day old donuts and the food that we had in the coolers was usually soaked by melted ice or too old to eat. This would help to fill up our stomachs but it really wasn't very much in terms of nourishment and needless to say, there were a lot of illness and stomach problems during the trip. This would really upset dad. As the illness grew more frequent dad made an attempt to purchase fresher foods at local super markets and tried to keep them cold with crushed or dry ice. This was not easy to do but with a little effort it helped to relieve the strain from eating outdated foods from KOA campgrounds. Sometimes, however, dad would instruct mom to purchase whole ready-made meals to be consumed after she bought them. Dad also tried to make the meals a bit more nourishing by adding fruits and vegetables when-ever they were available. This helped as well. I don't really feel that dad was that concerned with the welfare of the kids he just didn't like his trip being disrupted by constant interruptions from the illnesses. The trip was still in its infancy and we were learning as we traveled further. We headed East toward needles California and continued East on I-40 through New Mexico, Texas and then stopped for gas in Wichita Kansas. After a brief bathroom break, we continued east.

Note: Dad was fighting a loosing battle with himself. He had a dual personality. His evil side didn't really want the kids and his wife with him on this trip while his religious fanatical side was telling him to care for your family if you want to be accepted into heaven.

FACE TO FACE WITH A TORNADO

So FAR IT WAS a nice but a boring trip, especially for the kids and dad seemed especially bored too so he decided to turn on the radio for a little down home country music or news. He got more than he wished for. The radio was blaring severe Tornado warnings for the Wichita area on I-40. Dad looked in the rear view mirror and sure enough there it was and it was closing fast right behind us. Suddenly the quiet turned into screams and yells and 70 (mph) quickly turned into the maximum of 122 (mph) and dad was yelling and screaming too "Katy get under the seat with the baby,kids get under the seats". I managed to look around and could see that cars and trucks were being sucked into the funnel. A strong feeling of sadness came over me while some of the other kids in the car thought that this was funny, but they were only Laughing because they were very scared and this was how they let out their emotions of extreme fear. This was the first time that I saw fear in my dad's eyes especially when the Tornado lifted the rear end of the truck off the ground. I am not sure how long it lasted but it felt like eternity. When the tornado stopped all of a sudden, dad just pulled the truck over to the side of the road and everything was real quiet, you could hear a pin drop. He got out of the truck and turned around to see the devastation. It was horrible. There were cars and trucks, and dead animals, and dead people in their cars, and lots of garbage everywhere. My dad just got back in the truck and started to cry saying; "Thank-you lord for protecting my family today". I have never seen my father cry too much, but I guess this was one of those times. He sat there in silence for a while to just stare at all the devastation behind us. He wiped his tears away, turned on the engine and drove away. From here dad picked up I-70 and decided to go to Colorado to visit his NANU (great grandfather), and NANA (great-grandmother) and to visit the place and house where he was born. This was in Southern Colorado. We stayed there about one week then dad decided it was time to go. We had a lot of traveling to do and, "lots of road to cover "he said; so with that we packed up the family and headed towards Utah. When we arrived in Utah and the first thing my mom wanted to see was the Mormon Tabernacle church located in Salt Lake City Utah. We spent a couple hours there dad took pictures; we marveled at the pipes on the organs it was beautiful. After leaving Utah, my dad felt tired and wanted to rest. So we decided to look for a KOA campground in Idaho. He decided to stop at a KOA campground in Twin Falls. It was summertime there but it still seemed cold at night with the evening breeze, I can still feel how cold the ground was, it went right through my sleeping bag. The morning dew was very heavy too and there was always lots of moisture on our tent. We would all get up and started to pack up the truck and make the coffee for mom and dad. I was instructed to go to the KOA store to get eggs and bread and one stick of butter and maybe sausage if they had it for our breakfast to cook on pans outside. Water was available just up the path a few hundred yards away. So after breakfast, I cleaned the dishes, and helped mom put them away and we continued our journey. The environment inside the truck seemed quiet for a while it always was until around midday when my oldest brother Robert started getting his growing pains. Then Mom would give me the BENGAY ointment and Anacin with a jug of water to help my brother in the back seat. Then his crying and moaning and groaning would start. He would just stretch his head back over the seat with his mouth wide open in pain. He seemed to be in an unconscious like state. My dad said; "Hey what's all the commotion back there?" I said, "Nothing dad it's just Robert he's having his growing pains again, he'll be okay". With that dad pulled out a cigarette cracked open his window, and listened to the news for the weather. Robert's Jr. situation could have been eliminated altogether if my dad was a bit more thoughtful before the trip started. In my opinion, he could have purchased luggage racks for the top of the vehicle which would have freed up more space in the back section of the carry all. This would have allowed us to extend all of the seats toward the back. This additional space would have provided more leg room for all of the passengers. This would have made for more of a relaxing trip. But again, this was dad's trip and as long as dad was comfortable that's all that dad cared about.

Note: Again dad's obligation to his family were satisfied by including them on his trip whether or not they were comfortable was their problem. They had the entire back area of the vehicle to arrange in any way they wanted to get comfortable.

CUSTER'S NEXT STAND

DAD CONTINUED ON HIGHWAY I-90 out of Missoula that morning, and decided to stop for coffee and donuts and gas at the nearest gas station which happened to be in Butte Montana. Dad got out of the truck to fill up both tanks, he had two tanks one was a reserve tank so you could just switch over tanks and keep on going and didn't have to stop for a long way before you needed gas. Dad filled up both sides and went in to pay for the gas and get coffee for him and mom and donuts for us kids with drinks. What happened was a totally different story. The men inside the gas station started giving my dad a hard time. Dad had slightly long hair that curled up in the back. He also had a long handle bar type mustache. There were several men inside who started calling him; "Custer, and referring to him as the man who looked like Custer or was at Custer's Last Stand". This infuriated my father. My dad immediately said; "You The one that made the remark I'll take you on by myself outside alone, the rest of you let me go and get my gun so I can make this thing even". As soon as the men heard this they all scrambled in different directions. My dad was serious and not in the mood to play their childish games. Dad grabbed the man that made the statement, by the throat and told him something that really scared the shit out of him because his eyes got really big and he started shaking.

My guess is that he will think twice before opening up his mouth again to a stranger off the road because you never know what you're going to run into. My dad jumped back in the truck put his gun back under the seat, loaded of course, and we were off again headed towards Billings Montana. Montana was beautiful, but it was mostly just grasslands and small homesteads until you arrived at the local towns. Dad says in the wintertime it really does get bitter cold here with snow drifts that can be as tall as ten feet high when the wind blows. I just sat in my seat and tried to imagine that. How lonely that would be out here all alone with lots of wildlife. We saw a lot of buffalo, deer, and antelope grazing on the hills. They looked so peaceful and beautiful. The buffalo even crossed the road in front of the truck and stopped traffic one day it was awesome to see them so close and to appreciate just how majestic of an animal they really were and how big. Dad seemed to be in a foul mood as he watched us in the rear view mirror quietly with his eyes. He kept warning us to be quiet especially Charlie in the back seat. It was a hard trip with not much to keep the boys amused but themselves and maybe a few made-up games they might have thought up for the road to keep themselves amused, but dad wasn't in the mood to hear the laughing and snickering that went on back there. But think of it, all they really had for laughing, joking and playing was each other. They were kids after all and that's what kids do. Us girls well, we sat right behind dad and had to be very quiet, Marsha slept most of the time, I was mostly quiet taking notes in my head of everything that went on and what a monster my dad really was. He could be so very heartless if and when he chooses to be. At any moment, things could change, and I knew in my mind depending on how many times he had to tell the boys to be quiet or how many times he had to raise his voice, I would count them in my head and knew it was time. I knew the next stop would be the KOA campground **Bismarck North Dakota** where he would let out his Dr. Jekyll and Mr. Hyde phenomena. He would wait for just the right moment then all of a sudden, he would start in with his fit of rage, he would usually start with Charlie and work his way around the family. Our spot on the KOA campground usually was a secluded one so no one could hear what was going on. Dad figured out that people could not be involved in his personal family affairs. Charlie was assigned the duty of dumping the shit pot every morning, He liked to twirl it around in circles to show us kids he would not spill even one drop. He was right, he did it, he twirled the bucket very fast, I mean real fast without losing a single drop. I was really impressed so were the rest of the kids. But dad happened to come up from behind the bushes when we were all having fun and he said;" Goddammit, I told you Charlie not to fool around like that". I told dad;" Dad we wanted to see if he could perform that trick without spilling a drop, and he did, it was great!" Dad explained;" I said no fooling around just dump the shit bucket, get it cleaned out and back in the pickup, but you can't do that can you Charlie". Dad started in on Charlie and all us kids defended him but it didn't work. I hated my father he was so unforgiving the way he beat Charlie and the boys and us girls for not listening to him my mother was in a daze and she too hated him I think the most. We packed up our stuff and headed towards Rapid City South Dakota which we drove through to Scottsbluff Nebraska. My sister Marsha would usually sleep through these states and wake up saying dad; "what state are we in now?" He would say;" Nebraska honey, just go back to sleep". Marsha usually put her head back on a small pillow and went back to sleep, she was very quiet for the whole trip; it was a blessing because my dad had no problems with us. That night dad ended up in Des Moines Iowa. This is where his Uncle Sam lived so he thought he would drop by to pay him a visit with the kids since it's been maybe ten years or so since he has seen him he said. I guess the last time he seen him was when I was a baby and him and my mom went to Kansas City Kansas to see him and Auntie Emma on the train. Since then Uncle Sam divorced Auntie Emma and remarried a much younger woman, and left Emma with nothing. You see, Uncle Sam is a very wealthy man he has his own tomato factory and plantation, and many workers that work for him. He also has the gout. He is a very self- centered, narcissistic type individual. So dad pulls up in the carry all with us kids. The house was a ranch style with a basement and a Spanish type tile roof. The inside was very elaborate and decorated with Italian marble and French provincial furniture and antiques everywhere. There were clay statues at the door way. There was decorative tile flooring, and water fountains in both front and backyards. The welcome we got from his new wife was not quite what dad had expected. She was very cold. She said; "we were not expecting you guys or I would have prepared something nice". My father said; "that's okay, I'm just here to see my uncle Sam and then I'll be shoving off". She just stepped aside and let him through to see his family. She did not know any of us and did not have anything to say to us. Us kids just looked at her with pity and stayed outside until it was time to see uncle Sam one at a time because he was sick with the gout. So one by one we each went into the house to see him and he was very frail and ill looking. He did not recognize any of the kids except me and my oldest brother Robert Jr. His memory was leaving him too. It's funny; with a disease like the gout he still put down hordes of food, and ate like a pig. It was disgusting. I myself really had to try to reach up to give him a kiss good bye. I felt sorry for him but not for the things he had done to my Auntie Emma. Mom told me stories of the horrible things he had done to the family and how he destroyed everything over money, beat –up auntie Emma, poor Auntie Emma she raised those kids practically by herself, without a dime from him and she suffered through untold amounts of physical beatings and mental abuse. It seems that this type of behavior is rampant on my father's side of the family and pretty much accepted as the norm. How sick. Our family only stayed about one hour then we left. We decided to drive to Kansas City Kansas to visit Auntie Emma. It was a real shock to see Auntie Emma. She struggled up from the couch and almost fell. She had gotten so old and frail. She was short in stature, she could not have been more than four foot seven inches, and her hair was silver gray tied back with a handkerchief. Her skin was lose and wrinkled, her face bared the years of pain and suffering but her eyes and smile still lit up the room to see me and my brother Robert Jr. She held out her shaking hands and arms to beckon us to come to her for a hug. Mom and Dad were shocked to see her in her state of deteriorating condition even though she had not yet reached her seventies it was because it was of the treatment she received from my Dad's side of the family. In my opinion she dedicated her entire life to raise Uncle Dan's kids and was left with nothing but this little two story wooden shack. We stayed for a couple of hours while Auntie Emma made a chicken dinner then we ate and we left. Dad stayed on I-49 and headed into Arkansas. We didn't need any gas so we just drove straight through. You could sense by his mannerisms that he was getting upset and irritable. We drove through Louisiana and Mississippi, Dad decided to stop for dinner in Alabama. We went to a chicken place I cannot recall the name of it and mom went in to get dinner for the family. Dad was in the truck telling us kids who was going to get a beating and for what reasons after dinner. We were all terrified and quiet when she came back. Mom looked around and then she knew, he must have threatened us again. She could tell by the look in our eyes. After dinner, dad went to go and find a tree limb off one of the trees and one by one he would beat the boys. Then I got my beating for laughing too loud and instigating trouble as he put it. I had welts all over my legs and arms and back, he even missed and hit my face once. My mother screamed;" Stop, that's enough, stop!" I hated him I wasn't allowed to be a kid, only in my mind. Later on that night I got a jar and asked if I could catch fireflies. Mom said yes. I caught one in a jar and starred at it for a long time. I asked God Why does it have to be this way. What have I done to deserve this? Are you really up there? God is it really wrong to laugh, or be a kid, why must I endure this treatment with this man. He beats my mother, my brothers and me for no reason at all. I released the firefly and it flew away freely and somewhere deep inside I wished I could go with it. But I find myself back in the vehicle headed east toward Georgia. We stopped at a KOA camped to bed down for the night. Sometimes at night I dreamed that I wasn't there. I would dream that I was a beautiful fairy princess, that I could go anywhere, soar the highest mountain, nothing to fear. That I could pet all the animals, that I could do whatever my heart desired, and I could laugh as loud and as long as I wanted to. It was a beautiful world that was a gift from God and all we had to do was protect it.

Note: I constantly have to ask myself, why are the men on my father's side of the family so mean and cruel and seemingly without any remorse whatsoever, especially to their own family? The only

thing that I can summarize from this is that my dad is in someway feeling guilty over his mal treatment to his fellow man and that would explain why he chooses to make himself as hateful and as obnoxious as he possibly can. He wants to be punished.

RETRIBUTION

Dad decided to head North towards Tennessee. Now one thing you have to understand about Tennessee is that those people down there don't take too kindly to people who abuse children in front of them and dad learned that lesson the hard way. He decided that he was tired and wanted to stop at a KOA campground for the night and for mom to go shopping at the nearest store for fixings for a campfire for a cookout. He mentioned to get him some beer also. We unpacked the truck, set up the tent, and cooked the dinner and everything went along just fine. Then as dad drank his beer he became more inebriated. He started to look for something to beat Charlie with as he tied him up with rope first. I knew this was very wrong. I also knew that doing this in public even at night would surely get him into trouble. He tried to keep his voice low but, he kept hitting Charlie as much and as fast as he could. My other brothers tried to intervene, but dad would hit them too if they didn't back off. Then all of a sudden this group of men with guns started to approach my dad in a circle like formation and wanted to know what he was doing to my brother. My dad said; "It's none of your business, I'm correcting my kids, now go back to whatever you were doing and leave me alone". "I'm real sorry Mr. But, I can't do that. You see here in Tennessee we don't treat children like that, and we don't take too kindly to beating on or tying them up. What I'm trying to say is you're not in wherever you come from anymore, you're in Tennessee. Now you got one or two choices, either, untie that boy and quit beating on him, or I could just blow your head off and then call the police and notify them of what you're doing, do you understand. Because all these witnesses will back me up in a court of law with your body dead in a casket" This man was serious he had a double barrel shotgun pointed at my dad's head. My dad was silent. He looked up made a face walked over, untied Charlie, and decided to stop doing what he was doing because these people were Southern Folk and they were serious and they would have killed him and he knew it. I think for the first time in my life I wanted to say thank you to those people so I ran over and yanked on the guys pants and smiled; and he knew what I wanted to say and he said; "Your welcome baby girl".

NOTE: The group of people that confronted my dad could be considered hillbillies in every sense of the word. They were all dressed in worn, tattered and soiled overalls and wore black leather boots some wore torn tee shirts while others wore plain flower sack pattern long sleeve or short sleeve shirts. A couple of them even wore long johns, they were all smoking corn cobb pipes or chewing tobacco and spitting on the grown. Their hair was un kemp and in disarray and all of them needed a bath. They all carried riffles and shotguns. The spokesman of the group had a double barrel shot gun. While the above visual observation is certainly demeaning to most it does not pay homage to the true nature of the character of these men. But these type of men are usually the first to answer the call when help is needed in any type of crisis. They seem to have some sort of fire that burns from within that drives them forward when there fellow man is in need. My dad was no match for this kind of a man.

WE CONTINUED NORTH BUT DAD FORGOT HIS LESSON

We drove through Kentucky and Ohio with dad's moods becoming meaner and fouler. As time passed, the trip became extremely boring and everyone was becoming restless and irritable especially dad. He was becoming extremely short tempered and quiet and you could feel his tension. Dad then headed east toward Lake Ontario and you could feel the mist and change in the atmosphere as we got closer to the lake. As soon as we arrived we all got out of the vehicle to stretch our legs, and dad took pictures of the beautiful Lake and its surroundings. It was so beautiful it was mesmerizing for the kids because we have never seen anything quite like this before. I walked around collected a few shells and rocks, for safe keeping, the other kids all went in different directions doing their own things. Then dad decided to stay awhile to have lunch here. So the family found a nice picnic area type bench for lunch and we rested for a while. The breeze was real nice here. I looked at my father's eye's looking out over the water reminiscing about the things he had done and where he needed to go. He started yelling at the boys again and myself and I knew he was his old self once again, I guess he forgot his lesson learned. I knew deep down the rest of the trip would be hell with him, but I had no choice I was a kid and was under his rule with no- where to go, so I suffered in misery with the punishment he dished out as he saw fit. Anything at all seemed to set him off. For example, if the laughter was too loud in the back seat or if one of the kids accidently kicked the back of his seat, he would become extremely upset. He would wait until we would reach a KOA campground then go and look for a tree branch of his choosing and start beating the kids until he felt that they had had enough or he became tired. Sometimes my mom would intervene when she felt he was going too far with the beating, and then he would go after her and beat her. Sometimes he would do this before dinner or after dinner depending on how he felt at the moment. We visited all the southern states and stayed at all the KOA campgrounds along the way, and pretty much received beatings in every state and campground in the nation. The only states we did not visit were Alaska and Hawaii. Our family finally ended up in western Colorado. That's the beer dad always drank, and he always said; "Someday I want to work for that company". Sure enough, we stayed by the stream in western Colorado while he filled out his application, then we stayed at a KOA campground until he was hired. At some point during our stay at the KOA campground, we were getting ready to bed down for the evening when a strong wind came along and ripped through the tent. The tent was completely ripped from its tie downs and blew the tent end over end toward the busy highway below the campground. Inside the tent, the kids were left screaming and yelling for help. My brother and I along with my other siblings, my Mom and Dad were outside the tent getting water when this happened. I was the first to notice the blowing tent and notified the others. We all began to chase the tent as fast as we could. We finally caught the tent but were afraid at what we would find after opening it. Luckily there wasn't too much physical damage. Tim was the only child who really got hurt and his injuries were just minor. He received second degree burns because the propane camp stove was left on to make a pot of coffee. Lilly and Marsha were all in sleeping bags and were protected from the tumble which included all the flying debris inside the tent such as stoves lanterns suitcases personal items, etc. Tim had second degree burns on both of his legs so we took him up to the cold water spigot and kept it on his legs for a while about thirty minutes until all the heat was completely gone and his legs were very cold. He felt great. Then mom applied some Neosporin and clean bandages with tape. It worked well because I would say within two days his legs were better. But we soaked them every day in cold water for at least thirty to forty minutes a day and would apply the same treatment to prevent infection. Then after that, we stayed in a mobile home park in a very small two person airstream trailer in western Colorado and went to school from there. It was really cramped living quarters, I mean really cramped, but it was a roof over our heads. We stayed for six months. It was the longest six months of my life.

Note: There are two very important lessons to be learned here, first, never leave a group of children alone without adult supervision and second never ever leave children exposed to dangerous chemicals or fires.

NO PLACE LIKE HOME

Dad finally got on with the brewery and decides to buy a home up in the mountains in western Colorado to be closer to his job, all he had to do was drive down the mountain each day or night or whatever shifts it happened to be because it was rotating shifts at the brewery. The home was up above 10,000 feet. It had two bedrooms on the main floor one bathroom then stairs to the basement with two bedrooms downstairs with a bathroom. It had two living rooms, one fireplace, two car garage, and beautiful deck for sunbathing. Dad even had a guy named Marcus come out to sandblast the place to get the green and yellow paint off the house and surrounding buildings and poles which enclose the property and put it back to its natural state then Shellac the wood so it would stay nice and beautiful. There was also a guest house on the property. It had three bedrooms two bathroom, a kitchen, Livingroom, but it needed to be renovated inside and dad never did that so all of us kids got to play in it all the time. The property also had rabbit cages, a real live kid size dollhouse which me and Marsha enjoyed a lot and spent many hours in away from dad. We really fixed that place up. It was our dream house you could say. The boys had lots of room to run and play and make noise away from dad. But Charlie always found a way to get himself into trouble, he was just one of those kids that somehow trouble always found him poor guy. I remember one day it was the weekend and Charlie and Tim walked down to the gas station and convenience store just down the hill from our house. Charlie always checked the phone booth for money or change left over so he could buy candy at the store. Well this time he found $1,600 in cash in an envelope and quickly stuffed it into his pants so he could buy candy. He walked into the store and bought bubble gum a whole bunch of it and handed the lady like a $50.00 bill. The lady questioned him and wanted to see his pants for more money. She found the $1,600 and called the cops and Charlie told the story and returned the money. He wasn't even given a finder's fee for it. When Charlie got home he still had the bubble gum and my dad wanted to know how he got that gum. Charlie explained what had happened and my dad was furious. He said;" why didn't you just come home with the money, then we would have had $1,600 dollars not the cops stupid". My dad knocked Charlie around a couple of times then demanded the gum and threw it all away. Charlie watched where he threw it, and went to the trash and retrieved it later on that night and hid it under his mattress. Another thing my dad decided to do was to fill up the kennel outside with a Doberman Pincer. He went down and bought a puppy, then he had surgery done to his ears and tail and then he named him Blue. Blue grew into a big dog. He topped out at 130 lbs. of pure muscle and the boys were constantly teasing him, which made him meaner and more aggressive. Blue was no good for children. Every night dad would come home from work and would stop at the butcher shop to pick up saw meat for blue he would instruct me to cook it up and mix it with his dry food and take it to him in his cage with fresh water. The cage had to be cleaned out with a water hose daily. Blue was a good dog but dad was way too rough with him and abused him too. He would punch him, and correct him whenever he felt that he needed to and I don't think the dog liked that at all. I felt sorry for blue because this was making the dog meaner and would result in a horrible death for the poor dog.

I also remember my mom telling me one day after school that she was pregnant again, and that this would definitely be her last child. This news was very upsetting to me because I knew that I would have to raise this one totally on my own. As the days passed mom grew weaker and weaker

Note: I am an avid dog lover and have owned many, many dogs, and my favorite is a German Shephard. These dogs are amazingly intelligent and their only desire in life is to please their master. The only downside in having a German Shephard is that they don't live that long and when they finally leave you it is truly heart breaking and yet I keep doing it over and over again because their love is truly a blessing.

BIGGER THAN A HOUSE CAT

ONE THING THAT STICKS out in my mind about where we lived is there were mountain lions in the area so you were supposed to be on the lookout when you went outside, especially up in the trees where they hide. When we came home from school we traveled up a mountain after getting off the school bus. Well, I remember we lived in kind of a cul-de-sac situation and the twin boys lived directly across from us. Robert Jr. was walking home with the twins when suddenly a mountain lion came down the tree and landed on one of the twins back and put its claws deep into his shoulders and clawed him all the way down to his waist line, then the lion must of saw Robert pick up a large stick and became scared and quickly ran away. The twin was only fourteen years old. Robert Jr. immediately rushed the twins over to our house and called mom and myself to help. We immediately got the first aid kit and took off the kid's clothing, to examine his back. I told him not to move. He was bleeding profusely. Robert called 911. There were three claw marks on each side of his back, both extended from his shoulders to his waist. They were deep enough to expose his rib cage and several of his internal organs. I never forget this horrible sight. I went to get some warm wet towels to put those on those terrible wounds. Then we tried to hold the skin together, and then we put sterile dressings on the wounds with normal saline and wrapped them up with sterile tape until the ambulance could come. We gave him all we had. Then the twin passed out. Mom turned him over to start CPR until the ambulance arrived. The twin woke up, they immediately gave him CPR, then morphine and looked at his dressings and redressed them, and put in I.V's and thanked us for our bravery and service and for saving his life today. I will never forget the look in his eyes as he turned back to look at me, and my bloody hands. He smiled and shook his head in approval. Then they took him away. I wonder if he still remembers us as he looks at his scars today and how we intervened to save his life. Someday I would like to see him again.

Note: I felt this wonderful sense of comfort and warmth that enveloped my entire being and I wondered if saving lives was to be my ultimate purpose or if it was a calling that all human kind was suppose to answer and what about my dad?

DAD WANTED TO TEST THE STRENGTH OF MY MOM'S C- SECTION STITCHES BY VIOLENTLY SHOVING THE KITCHEN TABLE INTO HER STOMACH

Mom was in her late thirties when she gave birth to Jimmy her last child, Jimmy was delivered by C-section, and in those days it was not a bikini line it was a vertical line all the way up the belly. It was an incision that measured at least twelve inches long so mom was in bed for a long time healing and I was twelve and was given more responsibility to care for Jimmy. Mom would breast feed Jimmy then give him to me to care for all his other needs. Plus I had the other kids too, along with house work, cooking, and keeping the kids safe. My fun time is when mom decided to bake pies. You see fresh rhubarb grew right outside the front door beside the front porch, and we had strawberry plants too. So I would go and pick the strawberries, and pluck the rhubarb and put everything into my basket then mom would carefully wash all of it and boil it all. Then we would start making the dough for the pies. Boy they were delicious. After baking I would put the pies outside on the deck in the cool breeze and the entire neighborhood could smell them! With the left over dough we would make cinnamon rolls. Sometimes if we had enough change mom would send me down to the convenience store down the road to get some vanilla ice-cream for the top. This was just heaven. Strawberry/rhubarb pie with vanilla ice-cream, really doesn't get any better than that. Dad could smell the pies as he walked in the door and he knew she had been busy. It was his favorite. Mom always made fresh cinnamon rolls because the kids needed something to keep them distracted and this seemed to work until he got home. The winters up in Slow Creek Canyon were very harsh. Getting up that last patch of road to get home was the worst. My dad drove an old 1949 ford I am not really sure of the year, all I remember is the hood was round and he named her; "old Nelly", because she never made the last stretch of road home in the winter time and he always had to park her at the gas station and convenience store and walk that last mile home. By the time he got home he looked like he was frozen solid. So he would just stand by the fireplace for a half an hour or so to thaw out. We would get him towels to dry off with, but boy was it sad. Then one day as I recall it was in the evening after supper my dad got into an argument with my mother over something and I was in the living room holding Jimmy rocking him to sleep. My dad became very violent towards my mother and grabbed the table and shoved it into her C- section incision in her belly which popped it right open. I immediately put the baby down in bed because my mother's insides were hanging out. So I went to get a warm towel to put her insides back inside her the best I could and tried to calm her down because she was in shock. Luckily, it was springtime so old Nelly was just outside and I helped mom into the truck carefully and explained to Dad to take her directly to the Emergency room so she does not bleed to death. He reassured me that he would. I received a phone call later on that night that she was going to be okay but would be in the hospital for a few days. He would pick up some formula and bottles for me to feed the baby myself. Inside the truck they must have invented a story to tell the nurses before they got to the hospital. They questioned both of my parents at the hospital; both came up with the same story saying she fell down the stairs. Again, these lies of hers were just getting worse and worse. I thought to myself how could she do this to herself and to her family? But I was very young but I knew that the violence would never stop until my dad got some sort of treatment. Now I felt that my mother could use some sort of help. It had gotten to the point that his anger had drained the very life out of each of the family members and the fact that we were all still alive is just by sheer luck alone. When dad came home from the hospital he would not help out at all he was still belligerent towards me and mean. I never knew what to expect when he would walk through that door. I was just quiet until he spoke to me with his requests and needs. Then when he wanted a report on the kids and how things were doing I would just reply with; "Things are just fine, no problems". I did not want my brothers and sisters to be beaten up or hit for trivial things that they did doing the day or night, besides he wasn't there and as long as they were okay and in good health, and the house was in one piece and nothing was broken, hey I thought forget it, don't sweat the small stuff. That's why the kids loved me to take care of them I never told on them or anything like that; I protected them from that monster. We all knew when he was coming home from work or from wherever he was to get the house spotless and get things in order and to get the kids cleaned up. I had it down perfect. I knew the drill. Sometimes it really wore me out, but I kept on going, not only for the kid's sake but for mom, as well. Mom finally came home from the hospital. She wobbled through the door and said; "hello, I'm going to bed now to rest". I gently kissed her on the cheek and put Jimmy down beside her to breast feed. They both went to sleep I was relieved for a while. Things got sort of quiet. It gave me a chance to sit and reflect for just a few moments. As I looked out the living-room window it had a beautiful view of the valley. At the time I was only twelve and half years old or so, but I felt that I was pretty mature for my age and could handle pretty much anything that came my way. At least I hoped that I could. The only difficult thing is that I had to start taking on more chores and more of my mom's stuff, so I could no longer be a kid and play as much as I wanted to. But I still managed to sneak in my play time with my sister Marsha in our dollhouse outside and play with our rabbits in the guest house if I had time. Dad was demanding and very strict, he was the kind of a guy that always made you take off your shoes before entering the house. Yep he was a mean lean Italian and it was his way or the highway. If those cupboards weren't waxed, and the floor wasn't waxed and clean and the kitchen was not spotless you would not eat and that was that. We had a buffer but it was old, and the wax was old too for the cupboards. But it still worked. The only thing that was not working was me. I was so sick and tired of his out bursts and his yelling, and screaming, and whenever he felt like it he would just hit me for no reason what so ever. Or maybe I missed a spot on the refrigerator, or maybe I forgot to dump the trash, or not clean out the dog kennel. I felt so sorry for my brothers and sisters and all the beatings they had to endure on a daily basis for stupid shit too. Yes, it was all unnecessary. He was the meanest man I knew. I remember how it felt around him almost like I was walking on eggshells all the time, and if I stepped out of line, I would get another beating. I was very fearful of him, throughout my entire life and even today. I guess maybe it's the tone of his voice, or maybe, his demeanor, or maybe just what would happen after he spoke to you. His words were penetrating and hurtful, and mean and ugly and painful right down to the bone. But because he was my father I learned to obey him and respect him because of my mother and because I had nowhere to go I thought. I did know that as soon as I turned eighteen years old I was leaving the house never to return, I could hardly wait for that day to come. But until then I would have to suffer under his rule.

Note: My dad's unpredictable nature made him a very dangerous man and I wanted so desperately to call the police on him, but if I did I knew that my mom would be very upset with me so I decided to keep quiet. I'm sure that if I were a little more mature at the time, I would have made a different decision.

THE SPIRIT REFUSED TO SHARE

My dad decided he wanted to move and explained to my mother that he wanted to buy fifty acres of land somewhere close to his job and stay in Colorado. My mother agreed, she said we need to get out of this house. I suspected that dad's real reason was that he was afraid of the spirt but didn't want to admit it. You see this house was haunted by the son of the previous owners. The son which I will call David was coming home one day after completing a shift at the brewery. He was traveling up the winding mountain road that leads to the house. Without warning a large boulder became dislodged from the mountain side, rolled down and crushed David's car killing him instantly.

David's spirit found its way home and lived in the same room that me and my sister Marsha lived in. One night I woke to see the spirit standing in the doorway to our bedroom. He was filling a duffle bag with some of our figurines and various collectables while smiling and staring at me. I am not a real firm believer in ghosts and spirits, but that particular experience has left me wondering. While watching the spirit, I wanted to tell him to put the stuff back because it didn't belong to him, but I was totally spellbound and could not talk or move. I made a mental note of what the spirit was wearing and told my dad about this encounter along with the spirit's full description. My dad, for some reason believed me and arranged to have a face to face meeting with the original owners. When the previous owners arrived at the house, dad let me tell my story and after I described what the spirit was wearing, they broke down in tears and said that's exactly what their son was wearing when he died. After hearing this, my dad became very irate and accused them of everything in the book and asked them why they didn't disclose this information at the closing of the sale. He then cussed them out for about 20 minutes and finally threw them out. After throwing his parents out, in the last three months the spirit became more and more active. For example; the spirit pushed my mom down the stairs. He started locking the kids in their rooms, not letting them out until I arrived. The spirit created big explosions in the fireplace. He tried to kill me. He tried to suffocate me during the night and I could not speak because he took my voice away, and he was right in front of me scaring me while talking to me all night. I and Marsha slept in his old bedroom and some of his furniture was still there especially his custom made gun cases. But when the spirit pushed my dad in the back real hard and scared him to death that was enough to convince my dad that there was something in this house that he could not compete with. Then the final blow came when my dad was by the fireplace thawing out after work and the spirit tried to push him into the fire. The kids found out that dad wanted to move and they were extremely happy to get out and away from that spirit. Today as an adult, when I talk to people about this experience they look at me kind of funny and ask a question, "Emily you don't really believe in ghosts do you?" And all I can say is; "The situation that I experienced sure seemed real enough to me"

So we sold the house with no problems, put the furniture in storage, took the kids and the dog blue and moved to a house in western Colorado. This is where dad and mom looked every day in the paper for their dream. Dad wanted at least fifty acres of land which he would use to put a large modular home on. It was summertime so I watched the kids while they went land shopping daily. When myself and my oldest brother Robert were at home with the kids we had this game we created with the kids that was kind of fun it was a made up game of course which we liked to call;" leap kid". The way we played it was to lay on our backs on the floor me and Robert Jr. of course the oldest kids only because we were the strongest and could hold the weight of the child on our feet. While laying on our backs, we drew our knees to our chest to form a human catapult, then we put our sibling on the bottom of our feet while supporting them with our hands, then we counted down to three and pushed the sibling as hard as we could straight into the air toward each other in turn and the objective was to catch the sibling without harm. We played this for hours and hours and days and days on end and we invented many games similar to this. This was one of the more physical games and one that dad would have absolutely hated and would have probably given severe beatings for if he would have known.

Note: This is a very complex world that we live in and all of us have a lot to learn, Whether or not spirits really exist, I can't really say for sure, but this experience has left me with questions that I can't answer and if there are spirits, they can't be all bad, not if they scared the hell out of my dad. Someone please give that spirit a medal.

TO THE WESTERN HOUSE

THEN MOM AND DAD decided to move out and rented a house in or near the western area of Colorado for a short while. This was a small house with mom and dad still looking for their dream. We had all those kids to watch and at times it became a real circus. The kids were young and energetic and I was too so I guess it all worked out. But one day Charlie and Tim went to the park just a few blocks down the street and went to play and Charlie who was two years older than Tim, Charlie was 10 years old and Tim was 8 years old at the time I believe and decided to put Tim on one of the swings on the swing set. Charlie pushed Tim really hard on the swing and Tim went flying in the air and off the swing and onto a huge rock below that split open his mouth and knocked out his two front teeth. Charlie searched for both teeth but only found one. Then he brought Tim home to us and in the door they came. Me and mom grabbed towels and first soaked them in cold water to hold his face together and dad happened to be home and asked what had happened, then rushed Tim to the hospital as fast as possible to fix the damage. Dad said he would need plastic surgery probably to get everything right and he was right again after the surgeon finished, he would see a dentist to put in permanent front teeth and to make it look like nothing ever happened to his mouth. My dad had real good insurance, so it was only the best for his son. Today you cannot even tell that it ever happened. They did a real good job of covering it up you would never know that he had this accident at all. In this house I also remember getting one surgery it was a surgery to get a cyst removed from my right wrist. Nothing big, I just remember wearing a sling around my shoulder to hold my arm up for one week and couldn't use my hand or get my right hand or wrist wet. It was no big deal it was just something I remember every time I look at my right wrist I still see the scar and can recall the memory. From this house we rented another house in northern Colorado. In this house I was fourteen years old and my brother Robert Jr. would graduate from high school he graduated early at 15 years old. After my brother graduated from high school he went to work immediately at a restaurant called Gung Ho. He could not wait to get out of the house. His friend would come over every-day to pick him up and drive him to work and sometimes he would just walk. We rented another house in northern Colorado. This would be the last one before we moved to the trailer park. In this rented house I can remember that I watched the kids 24/7 and missed a lot of school. This was the year my mother had surgery done to her legs. She had varicose veins in both legs and had over two hundred small incisions and had to rest both legs for weeks upstairs in this house with no furniture. So, every time Jimmy needed to be breast feed I had to climb those stairs to get him to her so he could be fed, then bath him, and then put him down for his nap. Also, I had a lot of other chores to do. I had Marsha, Lilly, Charlie, and Tim to look after too, Robert was off to work so it was up to me to get things done now before my dad came home from work. Then I had to feed the Dog Blue, and I had to wait for my dad to come home from work, he would usually hit the butcher shop for his saw meat so I could cook it up to mix with his dog food and serve it up at night. It was all just extra busy work for me. By the time I got to bed at night I was exhausted. One incident that does stick out in my mind was one day I was watching the kids and somehow I was playing with the kids I think Jimmy was about twenty two months old or so and he managed to get out the screen door and crawled out onto the sidewalk and down to a busy road on the side walk called Parkstreet we lived in

Colorado. A trucker noticed a small baby crawling down the street in a diaper and t-shirt and picked him up. He called out on his CB radio and called the police. The police told him to meet him at the bowling alley and to wait there for them to arrive. Meanwhile, my mother and I walked up the street calling his name Jimmy and the trucker noticed us from his truck and waved us down. We all went into the bowling alley and the cops arrived. Jimmy recognized mom right away and the trucker handed him over to his mom. But the police wanted to see some I.D. and some explanation for this incident. Mom explained that she just had surgery on her legs and showed the officer and explained that I was watching the kids and I am fourteen but that I was overwhelmed. The officer understood. There was a lady in the bowling alley and she wanted to hold Jimmy because he was so cute, with his blond hair and big blue eyes I said sure. Jimmy's diaper was full of poop and when she held him up it all came running out through the sides of his pamper down the front of her shirt. How embarrassing. We all just laughed. Mom said; "That's a breast feed baby for you". Mom really thanked that trucker for saving her son's life that day and I did too. That is one day I will never forget. Just think if Jimmy would have gone into the street like that he would not have stood a chance. It's one of the busiest streets in Colorado. Blue the dog had a cage in the back yard so I would go out and feed him daily, clean out his cage. It was really too bad the way the boys teased him and the way my dad treated him by punching him and correcting him like he did. He treated Blue way too rough. Blue was a good watch dog and did serve his purpose as a matter of fact we did have a burglar one time and blue actually saved us. I remember the guy was in the backyard trying to get in through the glass door of our living room. Blue greeted him at the window. Boy was he surprised. He never came back and we never had any further problems after that. The dog was really a good animal; it was not the dog that was bad it was us the kids and my dad who mistreated the dog. That's why I just wanted to give the dog up for adoption before the dog did something that was real bad to one of these kids. I would always suggest to dad to maybe give him up for adoption to a family with no children who could give him the care he deserves. But no, he would not have it. He said he had too much money invested in Blue to give him away, and he belongs to him. I just could not get through to my dad, but he had no common sense what so ever. Dad was still beating up all of us kids this of course never changes. I still panicked whenever he came through the door never knowing what to expect, or how he was going to react. Because he worked at the brewery a lot of times and he came home drunk, so he would just throw the saw meat at me eat a little dinner and go to bed. He would look around to see that everything was in order, on these nights he was sarcastic to me, so I did not say much and let him eat and go to bed. When he was on his days off I tried to stay out of his way and to keep the kids with me as much as possible. But as hard as I tried, he still managed to beat the kids for dumb shit, or for anything he could find wrong. He was a raging manic. I had a hard time second guessing him, and I never knew what he would hit the next kid for. He would yell and scream from day to night when he was home. That's why I loved it when he went to work, or when he had to work over time.

Note: Saw Meat is residual meat or left-over meat from all the cuttings from the various cuts of meat such as steaks, roasts, lamb chops, hamburger, etc. These cuttings cannot be used for anything else other than scraps. They are ground up along with bits of bone and packaged and sold to customers as saw meat and used as such things as dog food.

PACKED LIKE SARDINES

Mom used to say Emily; "You're my right hand man, could not have done it without you". I would just turn around and smile back at her in return. While growing up, me and my mom were inseparable. We went everywhere together, we had to. We had this 1976 red Volkswagen bug that we used to go everywhere in. I remember one time when the family was moving, we actually fit all seven kids and my mom in that bug, crazy huh. Let's see we put the small kids in the space behind the back seat; there was, Tim, Marsha; then Robert Jr., Charlie, holding Lilly in the back seat, then me holding Jimmy in front seat with mom driving how about that! That Volkswagen was truly an amazing car. Dad used that car every day to drive to his job at the brewery back and forth. It was cheap on gas, it was very reliable, very fast, and did a great job for everyone. My brother Robert and I used to get in the car at night and turn on the radio to listen to the music, and news. Mom and I used to go shopping on a daily basis in that car, and then we would go to the laundromat to wash clothes and bring everything home. This car was our little cherry lifesaver. Gas back in those days was cheap too so it was easy to fill up and it only held maybe what ten dollars' worth if you were lucky I'm really not sure if it held that much fuel. We loved that car. My mom and I made a lot of great memories in that car.

Note: One of the very few things that I really love and cherish from the farm was the little cherry red Volkswagen. It gave me more comforts and enjoyment than my mother or father combined. On cold nights when there was no electricity or heat we could find refuge in the warmth of the little red VW where we could turn on the AM radio lay back and be entertained by Alfred Hitchcock's radio program at 6:00 p.m. Unfortunately this comfort was only temporary because our little red Volkswagen was the only transportation that the family had and was also used for shopping, and to transport dad to and from work. But I could dream that someday the little red VW would be mine. But this was just a dream.

BLUE RETALIATES

Mom and Dad decided to move out of the unfurnished house in Parkridge so the move would be easy, and move into a furnished trailer in a trailer park that was closer to Dad's job. The mobile home was furnished and it was cheaper to rent. This would be our last stop before dad found his dream home. The boys were getting older and their fights were getting worse, they would tease the dog more and more and as a result, blue was becoming meaner and more vicious. One day while I was watching the kids Blue got out of his cage which was located outside the trailer and somehow he got inside the trailer, where the kids were. Jimmy was sitting on the floor in the living room after his bath in his diaper when blue spotted him. I was standing next to the couch watching blue's every move. All of a sudden Blue started to growl and snarl and he opened his mouth while showing his teeth at jimmy. I immediately jumped in to save Jimmy. Without hesitation, I jumped on his back and tackled him like an alligator I had no fear I only wanted to save my brother. When I look back I shiver at the fact that Blue could have easily ripped my arm off because I only weighed 75 lbs. and Blue weighed 130 lbs. of solid muscle. The dog slammed me to the ground which turned me over grabbed my wrist bit into my wrist with his teeth and would not let go which pissed me off so I started hitting him with my other fist as hard as I could in the face. Then He put his paw on my chest making it hard for me to breathe. My mom ran over with a stick and shoved it down his throat and he quickly released his grip on my bloodied hand and wrist. When my dad came home from work that day he announced to the family that he would be putting Blue down when he goes to southern Colorado to get an Elk this winter for fresh meat for the family. He said;" can't have an animal around my children that's going to attack them and try to kill them ". We all just shook our heads in denial because we knew it wasn't the dog's fault that he was like that, between us kids teasing him and dad beating him is what made him mean. We were all so sad for Blue because deep down we all loved him so much and after all, he was our dog. I don't know if it was wrong but deep down inside I wished that Blue could have reached Dad before my uncle Andy shot him. Winter came along and dad and Robert Jr. went hunting and took Blue with them to his Uncle Andy's house to help him shoot the dog. He told us he took one shot and missed and blue came at him with his right shoulder bleeding, then Uncle Andy finished him off before he got to my dad. Then they all went elk hunting and brought home a six pointer elk with fresh elk meat that lasted the entire winter. Dad paid a small fee to have the elk packed and stored in a locker in town. Then once or twice a week he would bring home fresh roasts, steaks, and ground meat. It was a good year for us kids we had plenty to eat for sure. My oldest brother Robert Jr. worked out daily and ate that meat and his body became really huge. The boys all grew that year. My mom and Dad searched every single day after work and on weekends to look for that special piece of land so that they could put a modular home on it. This scenario went on for months on end. Back in those days we did not have cell phones so she had to get change to go to the phone booth to make calls out of the paper. It was very tiresome for both of them and very hard on us kids. Day in and day out they would come home with no news in that little red Volkswagen. Mom would say;" Well we looked all over today, but still nothing, not yet, maybe tomorrow will bring something good to us." Then we would all just start getting ready to fix dinner for the kids and get everybody ready for bed. This routine kept up for months. I was just glad we had a bed to sleep in and a table to eat at. In the last two rented houses we had no furniture it was all in storage, so we had to make do with what we had which was nothing but blankets,pillows and paper plates with a few pots and pans to eat out of. I realized that this was just a mobile home but in comparison to the previous two homes in which we lived, it was a castle. We finally had our own beds to sleep in we had a fully equipped kitchen that mom could prepare quality meals for us kids. We had two bathrooms so there was no fighting over the shower or toilet area. For the girls this was a necessity and for the boys it provided the time to do whatever they needed to do. It was absolutely wonderful. It had a nice fenced in back yard that made me think of Blue and I cried every time I looked at the empty dog house and this made me hate dad even more and I'm sure the rest of the kids felt the same way and I wondered if he realized if he knew that he was doing the same thing with us as he did with Blue and that was to increase our hate and dislike for him.

<u>Note:</u> There are other ways of parting with an unwanted animal such as a dog. There are no kill shelters that are always willing to accept new animals and work with them and help them get prepared and ready for adoption. Blue's disposition was a direct result of my dad's mis-treatment and the dog should never have suffered for the short comings of a man like my father.

THERE'S NO PLACE LIKE HOME

MOM AND DAD CAME home one day and told the family they had finally found a piece of land in northern Colorado with a beautiful view and wanted to put a small trailer on it as soon as possible. It had no water or electricity, so we would have to make do for a while until dad could figure things out. I can remember the first time we all drove up there in that Volkswagen with all seven kids inside It. Let's see, we put the small kids in the space behind the back seat holding Tim and Marsha, then Robert and Charlie holding Lilly in the back seat, then me holding Jimmy in the front seat with mom driving. How about that! Anyways, I can still remember the dreaded feeling I got in my stomach of how much work and how awful life was going to be up there with him. All of us kids just got out of the car and looked around and saw nothing but work and misery ahead with a tyrant for a father. I knew deep down we were all in big trouble because this was his haven and our nightmare. From the minute we arrived to the minute we went to sleep at night he made us work. We had very little to eat because we lived paycheck to paycheck many times we went to bed hungry because we had no money for food. We had no electricity or running water in the trailer, so I had to walk to Scott's place which was at least a mile's walk away. We had his permission to get water whenever we wanted.

He was a big farmer in the area. I carried the buckets of water on a daily basis to our home. Sometimes I would have Charlie or Tim both go with me so we could get more water home at one time. During the summertime since the ditch ran right in front of our home we decided to take baths in it. It was just all the runoff water in the area that the farmers were using to water their crops with. It was hot outside so we kids kept clean that way for a while. We had no indoor plumbing so we used a bucket and a porta–potty to sit on and Charlie would still dump it every day. Dad instructed us to put all the toilet paper into a paper bag so he could burn it outside along with corncobs and other trash. All the farmers had their own trash holes, so dad decided to do it too. I can remember how skinny we all got that first summer all us kids were skin and bones, however dad looked perfectly healthy so I suspect that he was feeding himself from somewhere, but to question him was just asking for a beating so we keep quiet. Dad had us literally picking every weed on that fifty acres and putting it in piles, how stupid. This was before he got his tractor. We had a lantern for light at night or when a storm came, and sleeping bags for the floor with blankets and pillows. I can still remember that long winding dirt road that lead up to the farm that was full of rocks and bumps which made it very difficult and uncomfortable to get up there anyway when you finally got there you had to cross over a small wooden bridge which covered the ditch that held the water during the summertime for the farmers to use to irrigate their crops with. Then right after you crossed over the bridge you would pass by something called a pump house which was located right behind our trailer. It distributes water to various water outlets to feed crops for the various farms in the neighborhood and provide water for general use. Dads always told us kids to keep away from the pump house because it's dangerous and you could get electrocuted and die because its electricity, it's electricity mixed with water he explained and it could kill you in seconds. Besides that, there was a warning sign on the pump house door to; "**Keep out Dangerous**". The kids were still curious and at times we really had to keep an eye on them especially the boys. Note it turns out that dad was absolutely correct about the pump house and this will be discussed later on in a following chapter. He did decide to purchase a pot belly stove for the kitchen because we were freezing to death in that trailer. He had to go and get wood to fill it and that helped out some. Life was very stressful in that trailer all day every day we had to live in it. We also had to go to school from there like that. No baths. Just fix your hair the best you could. Put on deodorant, brush your teeth, and go walk down this long cold road to the bus stop then wait maybe twenty to thirty minutes to get picked up by the bus for school. It was hell. I had to endure this all through my high school years. Plus put up with a father who did not understand at all, and was mean and hateful and now thought he owned the world. Then depending on what shift he was on had a list of chores for you to do when you got home plus your homework before the lights went out. He was impossible to live with. He would beat you if he didn't like the way things were done or if it wasn't done to his satisfaction. He was always beating one of the kids up on a daily basis or my mom. I have nothing but bad memories of that place because of my dad, it was like a plague. It seemed like he started to drink more of his product, the beer that he made, which was changing his personality and his thought patterns. Then my dad went around the area to get to know all the farmers in the area and to ask them if they would help him to plant his fifty acres that year. He was successful and one farmer came over and planted corn for him and instructed him on how to irrigate it and left. Dad paid for his services. Then after that, dad bought a small engine tractor from him for his own farm which helped out a lot. By this time I had turned sixteen and my oldest brother was now eighteen and he went to work at the processing plant in town. Robert Jr. bought an old Chevy Impala car to drive back and forth to work, but the rest of us kids were left alone to fend for ourselves while still under dad's rule. I do remember one time me and my dad got into this fight one afternoon about something I don't remember what, but it led to a fist fight in the kitchen with him hitting me in the face and stomach, I punched him in the face once I think, and tried to defend myself with my arms, he pulled my long hair slammed me into the refrigerator, then told me I have to sleep in the corn field for the next three days with no food. Eat the corn if you're hungry. Then he threw me out the door. My mom brought out a bottle of water for me to drink and a blanket to keep me warm, but it was late June so it was hot outside, but still, my dad was a very cruel man and he didn't care if it was June or January. After three days I came back inside the trailer and he asked; "Well did you learn anything"? I answered yeah; "It gets real cold out there at night, and those corn cobs are very uncomfortable to sleep on". He just laughed an ugly laugh and walked away. I was very upset and very mad at him. My whole weekend spent in his lousy cornfield was for nothing and I was all beaten up too and all for nothing. I was going to need some of mom's make-up to hide the bruises on my face for school tomorrow, how sad. Well, he beats the boys up the same way, except he beats them all over their bodies so their clothes hide most of their bruises. He does this on a daily basis. He still beats my mom up on a daily basis too. We were all afraid of him and we knew what time he was coming home from work and to try to stay out of his way if at all possible at least until he fell asleep then we knew we were in the clear at least for a while because he had to sleep to get ready for his next shift. He worked rotating shifts so that really kept him on his toes. Even with all that, he still managed to find the time to beat us kids, work the farm, beat mom, yell at everyone, and just be mean all the time. His frantic outbursts got worse and worse. My dad drank beer a lot and since he had his own beer card which allowed him so much beer per month at a real cheap price, he would bring home what-ever he wanted and put it in an ice chest with ice to keep cold for him-self or mom or if you were thirsty your-self. He put no limits on anyone having a beer, which I think he should have because two of the kids turned out to be alcoholics because of that policy. He was very lenient with his alcohol, and that I thought was wrong. He was teaching the kids that it was ok to drink, and it's not ok. It's really ruined their lives. He did not know it but the kids looked up to him as a role model, the same guy that yelled at them, the same man that beat them, and let them drink alcohol, these kids were picking up all his bad habits along the way. What he was doing was molding a bunch of misfits that would not fit into society. Every day up on the farm was hell for us kids we had a routine but it got old too. Mom and I usually had to wash the clothes down in town on the weekends at the wash house, and then go shopping, it was our routine. Upon returning home mom and I never knew what we would find and hopefully dad would be sleeping for his next shift and not beating one of the other kids when we got home. At times we would try to take the little kids with us so nothing would happen to them unless he instructed otherwise. He was always there with his instructions before we could go anywhere or do anything and how many kids we could take with us. Then we got home we would question the kids as to what happened. Then they would tell us if they were yelled at or beaten or mistreated or whatever he did to them that is why he kept them behind to mistreat them or to make them work the whole time with nothing to drink and to wait for our return. It was pretty sad. I would immediately go to my brother or brothers to see what they needed and how I could be of help. He would look at me with disgust. This sort of thing went on all the time. Then all of a sudden he would eat his lunch and change his clothes get ready and go to work like nothing ever happened. After the summertime was over all of the kids were enrolled into schools, including myself. I sure was not looking forward to this at all. My tenth, eleventh, and twelfth grade years were all ruined because of that farm and my parents. I guess the only good thing about going to school for me, as well as, the rest of the kids was we did not have to work hard out in a field all day in the hot sun with nothing to eat or drink and be supervised by a maniac that yells at you every time you move out of line or beat you if you did something he did not agree with. School gave me a chance to be with people my own age and with teachers who teach you something and all you have to do is listen and take notes and participate and be part of a group and it's fun. It gave me a chance to open up a little because I was shy and being a late bloomer, I did not even start my periods until I was seventeen because my body did not produce estrogen, weird huh. Well it happens. So my mom took me to the doctors and he said to start me on the birth control pill which contained estrogen and I would start my period very quickly with no problem at all. Otherwise I was healthy. He was right; I started right away, three weeks later. Mom and I were very happy. The family had to make a lot of sacrifices in order to keep that farm working the way he wanted it day by day. But we as a family did it. Somehow we managed to take care of all those kids on a daily basis, dad traveling to work back and forth to the brewery every day in that VW on that dangerous highway I-93 to Colorado daily in all kinds of weather. With my oldest brother now at the processing plant full time and now me since I was sixteen and one half almost seventeen I managed to get my first job at a place called the Skylark Buffet next to a Safeway grocery store in town not too far from the farm. It was a part-time job as a waitress serving drinks to the customers after they sat down with their meals. Then I would get paid every two weeks and give my paycheck to my mom and dad to help the family and bring home left over food from the buffet to feed the family, it worked out great. The only problem was sometimes I had to walk all the way to work, and all the way home and by the time I got home I was worn out. But at times people would offer to give me rides or mom would use Robert's old impala to take me and pick me up it just depended on the day of the week and if my brother Robert Jr. was home from work or not. I never had time to attend any parties or anything like that, because I was too tied down with homework and kids and chores at home. Also, my dad was very strict and would not allow me to date anyone as long as I lived under his roof. He made this very clear to me saying that I was to have no boyfriends up at the farm, no friends at the farm what so ever, no guests at all ever no one period was allowed up there at all ever. So, what was I supposed to tell all my friends at school and in society and everywhere I went? I told them Just what he said. You are not allowed to go up there period, I am sorry, and then I would apologize to them and walk away with my life ruined because of him. All those potential beautiful relationships, down the toilet because of him. Hell, I can even remember one time in particular while attending High School and this Quarterback from the other High school gave me his letterman's jacket which had the "D" on it to wear home. Of course, I thought he was kidding when he came over to my locker over at High school and asked me, Mrs. Nobody to wear his letterman's jacket I thought it was a joke, right. He said; "Wrong, wear it really Emily, I'd be honored". He threw the jacket into my locker and I had no choice but to take it home with me and he knew that and this is exactly what he wanted because he wanted to get to know me better and take me out for a cherry coke but like I told him before you cannot do that my dad does not allow anyone to date me until I am eighteen years old and out of his house. That QB would not take no for an answer and just walked away saying;" I'll see you tonight Emily". I knew he was coming because he needed his jacket back for the game against Smashers VS the Defenders on Friday night so; I was upset all day long because of him and his forceful tactics. So around 6:00 p.m. that evening I heard this truck come rumbling up the road to our trailer and unfortunately dad was on dayshift. Dad waited for all us kids to get home from school and saw me with this letterman's jacket and questioned where did it come from? I told him that this QB came out of nowhere from the other high school over to my High School and had apparently heard a lot of good things about me and wanted me to wear his jacket, I think this was my theory. My dad said you need to give it back right away and do not wear it. I told him I agree, and would do so tomorrow, but right now Dad, he's almost up to the farm and I can hear his truck outside if you could be nice to him I would appreciate it and I will give him back his jacket and make everything good. What do you think? Dad became furious. He said; "What? He's here now? On my property? No, no, I don't allow anyone on my property, especially QB's"! I said; "Dad, please this will ruin my reputation at school if you could just be kind and pleasant for just five minutes he will get his jacket and go away". I ran to the door with the jacket which was red and white with a big D on it, Dad grabbed it and waited for the QB to come close to the door then my dad let him have it. As he walked up the steps and reached to knock on the door dad opened up the door and said; "Who the fuck do you think you are coming to my door asking my daughter out for a cherry coke? You mother fucking cock sucking mother fucker get the fuck off my property before I blow your head off. Oh, here's your stupid letterman's jacket mother fucker and don't you come back here if you know what's good for you." Then he took the letterman's jacket and threw it in the dirt and jumped and stomped all over it with his feet. The QB tried to explain himself that he wanted his jacket back and to maybe see Emily if possible, as he spoke, my father was talking about getting his shotgun out to kill him and saying; "Fuck you get your shit now mother fucker before I have to use force you ugly mother fucker". But after hearing these words from my father he just grabbed his dirty jacket and skidded his tires in the dirt and left. My reputation was ruined I was crying inside with mom and asking why did you marry this monster, he is a nightmare he's horrible. The next day at school everyone treated me like I had the plague. No one said one word to me not even at my locker, and I expected this outcome because of what happened last night at the farm with that popular QB from the other High school I guess word travels around pretty quickly. So, I just went to my classes as usual and paid no attention to the other kids, I was shy anyways and did not have too many friends except for my popular cheerleader friend and a few other close friends that knew of me. I kept my head down and did my work and went home. My algebra teacher did notice that I was upset and asked if I was okay. I responded; "There was something bothering me but I should be okay". She responded; "Let me know if we need to talk okay?" I said;" okay". Things were very quiet around my school for me for about a week or so then it wore off and started to go back to normal the kids went back to their old selves and got back into their old routines again, thank God. I got tired of being the center of attention, that really stinks bad I mean it hurts your insides and you cannot breathe with people staring at you all the time watching your every move and whispering behind your back. It also hurts and it feels like you're being bullied by the whole school. No really, all because of this dumb QB and my Dad and me put in the middle of this stupid scenario. I hated it then, and I still hate it now. I never went back to that school for any reunions or anything like that. I never wanted to see any of those people again. I still remember all the hell they put me through. The teachers there were very good, and taught me well, but other than that I have no good memories of my High school.

Note for the reader: After reading the section just presented and hearing and listening to all the related advertisements presented by all the experts on how to raise your children or even intervene when they are having problems at school. What do you do with parents who are totally incapable of understanding their children

at all or who don't even care about their physical needs let lone their psychological needs. Professional intervention directed at freeing the children from their abusive parents is sometimes the only option.

MARSHA BROUGHT HOME A GIFT
THAT NOBODY WANTED

ONE NIGHT I AWOKE to find my mother pacing with baby Jimmy in her arms around 6:00 p.m. The pot belly stove was going because it was wintertime and very cold outside. Dad and my oldest brother Robert were sleeping side by side on the floor in the living room floor in sleeping bags and the rest of the children were in sleeping bags in other rooms. Mom had a Baby Ben clock that she kept wound up to keep good time because this is all we had. I woke up and could hear her pacing asking dad;" Robert, Jimmy is burning up he needs to go to the hospital now, I don't know what's wrong with him, but he's burning up". Dad replies;" Katy he'll be fine put a cold compress on his head, and go to sleep, I need to get some rest, I have to pay the bills around here now leave me alone". So with that, mom kept breastfeeding Jimmy and putting cold washcloths on his head it was now 8:00 p.m. and mom was becoming frantic because Jimmy was not getting any better, he was getting worse. Mom once again attempted to ask dad; "Robert I really do need to go to the hospital with Jimmy he's burning up his whole body is bright red, and he's becoming unresponsive, please let me take him to the hospital" Dad replies again;" Katy don't Fuckin bother me again or I'm going to get out this bed and kill somebody, I've got to get some rest, I told you what to do, to break the fever, I am sure he is going to be okay if you would just fucking listen to me for once in your fucked up life bitch". Mom was panicked now and waited a few minutes until he went back to sleep she then came back to the bedroom where I was and came and got me for help. She said;" Emily quick get up I need you now get Lilly put a diaper on her and a shirt, wrap her in a blanket and let's get out of here fast, Jimmy is burning up with a fever. I have the Insurance card from dad's pants and took your brother's keys. Get dressed now we will go out the back door." I told mom;" Mom I'll put Lilly in the back seat with her blanket, and put Jimmy in the front seat and you can drive while I push the car down the hill half way, until it starts because I don't want dad to hear the engine fire up okay?" mom responded;" Good idea Emily". So mom got in, put the keys in the ignition and I was in the back of the impala pushing it in the snow covered roads with only my tennis shoes on no socks until we were about half way down and then she started up the car but I had to run real fast to catch up with the car and it was pitch black outside no street lights just trees and lots of snow on the lonely dirt road that led up to the farm. Well we made it to the stop sign at the end of the road then we got stuck a little, so I had to get out and push the car and rock the car back and forth until it freed itself and it worked and finally by this time it was around 12:10a.m. And we were off to the Hospital. We arrived at 12:30a.m. We immediately took Jimmy into the emergency room and the surgeon ran up to us saying; "what's going on here"? Mom says;" I don't know my baby is burning up and has been since 6:00 p.m. tonight, please help me". The surgeon ran off with Jimmy in his arms and did not come back for an hour and a half. The surgeon yelled; "get a tub of ice ready stat"! The surgeon finally came through the doors around 2:00 a.m. and walked up to my mother and said;" well Mrs. Pandora I have some good news and I have some bad news. First of all, how many children do you have? Mom responded; "Seven children, one in high school, one in middle school, and two in elementary school and two still at home and one working now. Why?" The surgeon responded well did you get a memo from the school a few weeks back that the German measles were going around, do you remember that at all?" Mom responded;" No and if I did there is always so much going on in that trailer you know we have no electricity, no running water, no facilities at all but we will soon, my husband is contacting his father for some money to put piping up there for a water line to the farm". The Surgeon replies;" Well the good news is you can have your baby back now we inoculated him for the German Measles, the bad news is because his temperature was over 105.6 for so long that your son is sterile and he will not be able to have any children because of this. I am very sorry, you waited too long to bring him into the hospital. If you would have brought him in at let's say around 8:00, or even 9:00 p.m. We could have inoculated him and brought down the temperature and he would have been fine, but because you waited, it affected his testes and he became sterile, I am truly sorry Mrs. Pandora." The surgeon wiped his head twice and with a tear in his eye he just walked away in sadness. My mom broke down in tears and started to cry out loud and me too, I felt so bad for her and the baby Jimmy. Then my mom grabbed me by my face real hard and pinched my cheeks together and said;" Emily you must never repeat what you saw or heard here tonight never because I do not want your father to ever know about this ever do you understand? I am never going to tell him about this because it will just tear him apart and there is no way to fix it or undo it. It's his fault, but let's just forget it and time will just make it go away. I responded;" Hey, that hurts my mouth when you pinch me like that after all I did for you tonight, don't worry about me telling that son of a bitch anything ever you can count on that, but don't you ever pinch my face like that again, I mean it, that hurt real bad mom. Give me the baby, so we can go home I am very tired, your secret is safe with me."

Note: Any normal family would have a tough time raising seven children taking care of all their needs and making sure that they don't get into any trouble and that they are met and that they are always well fed taught right from wrong. But if there are obstacles in place such as an environment which has a mentally ill parent or worse yet, two mentally ill parents a situation becomes almost impossible and the ones who suffer the most at their current state and throughout their entire lives are the children.

DAD SHOWS SIGNS OF HUMANITY

As I DROVE UP the dirt road like I usually do, I noticed that there were police cars and fire engines and an ambulance right in back of our trailer. I immediately spotted dad sitting on the back staircase of the modular home. Dad was covered in black ash from head to toe and was not wearing any shoes. I asked him to explain what had happened at the pump house and why all the emergency personnel people were here and why that guy was in the middle of the road covered up. Dad explained that about an hour ago while he was watching T.V. he heard a loud boom come out of the pump house and he immediately ran outside and he always had his phone in his pocket for emergencies only but forgot to put his shoes on. So he ran to the pump house to see what all the commotion was. He found a man lying flat on his back on the ground covered in black soot not breathing with his backhoe still running and the electricity still on in the pump house. My dad noticed that the ground was completely saturated with water with one small dry spot which allowed him to place his feet in such a fashion to allow him to reach the on and off switch to the pump house. He cut the power which neutralized the electricity on the ground which allowed him to move the man on the ground from the water to safety then he administered CPR for fifteen minutes. He had no idea if this was effective and called 911 during the CPR process. When the Emergency medical team arrived they took over life-saving efforts, but unfortunately the man expired. This really devastated my dad as he just sat on the back porch in shock and buried his head in his hands and started to cry. His entire body and uniform that he wears at the brewery every day which is white, except for small circles around his eyes and lips were completely covered in black soot and even his feet. There were white streamers running down his face left from the tears and I thought to myself, how can a man that is so brutal to his own family be so emotional in the face of a tragedy in which he is personally involved?

Note: The fact that my dad is such a mean and brutal man is probably because of the schizophrenia and dual personal issues. But if he were to receive effective treatment for these diseases it would probably benefit him and everyone else immensely.

DAD SHOWS NO MERCY

DAD WORKED IN WESTERN Colorado every day seven days a week rotating shifts days, swing shift, graveyard shifts depending on the week and day of rotation. He worked inside the brewery to help make the beer. His job I know was very physical and he had to wear hair nets on his beard and his long hair for his job so it would not get into the beer. He had a special uniform and gear he had to put on too. After every shift he would return home most of the time inebriated. He never used to drink his product that much he only tasted it after work and brought it home from the brewery in cases for his personal use, but it seemed like the last ten years or so things for my dad started to spiral down-hill for him for some reason or another. He became obsessed with overworking himself to the point of no return, and on top of that trying to do too many things at once, plus if you add alcohol to the equation this spells disaster especially if there's seven children involved who are innocent to what's expected of them from this Narcissistic autocratic tyrant. Dad seemed to be in a world of his own and only he could understand this world and no one else could see the beauty that obviously surrounded him. Dad's earlier life in California consisted of working at enclosed environments while interacting with a lot of people and developed a lot of friendships. My dad and mom made a lot of friends and attended party's and company sponsored events on a regular basis. In Colorado it was mostly all work and no play with very few company sponsored events at least none that dad talked to us about. I feel that dad's entire focus had been shifted to our new home in Colorado. To him our new fifty acre plot with a modular home was like a five thousand acre spread in his mind and he treated it as such. He referred to it always as a farm, even though the only thing he ever raised was a few acres of wheat, alfalfa and a little corn. However, there were a couple of profitable years which were the result of the family's hard work and intense efforts we made a great profit off the alfalfa crop two years in a row with a little help from our friends. We were all so proud and happy at the end of those two years I can still feel the feeling inside myself, how it felt, to feel the achievement with the work completed and everyone benefiting the rewards. Then at night we all sat around the campfire talking about the day's work and how we all worked together to achieve this great feat. Dad had the check in hand and was so happy so pleased with all of us kids, mom was happy too. Unfortunately this was short lived and dad reverted back to his old self again the next day. I think if I remember correctly, my father became more aggressive with his beatings of the kids the second summer because I remember he really did something bad to my brother Charlie one day which I will explain now. As I recall I was out getting the water buckets filled up for the evening for the family and just about to come home. My oldest brother was at work at the processing plant and would be off work shortly, good thing too. The other kids were out on the farm playing in the ditch in the water, or on the farm picking weeds. Mom was in the trailer with the baby Jimmy. Dad got really mad at my brother Charlie for some reason I cannot recall for what, anyways, he then decided to tie his hands up to this metal pole so he could not move while he beat him to a pulp with his pants down. He used a belt, then he used a large stick, both items broke on him. My brother was barely breathing. I stepped in and told my father to stop. He immediately attacked me. My older brother Robert drove up in his old car and helped out and wanted to know what was going on. Dad told him to, "Fuck off, stay out of my business when I am trying to correct my children, or your next Jr". "Robert replied, dad I don't know what in the world is going on here but it looks to me that you are beating Charlie to death, and you need to stop, now". Dad said, "Are you threatening me, Jr?" "Robert replied, no, I just want to help Charlie and to make peace and for this to be over with, I do not know how it started, I was not here but he does not need any more punishment, please he's bleeding." Then I stepped in and said; "Dad you need to stop hitting Charlie he's in real bad shape right now, he can't take any more beatings, he's done". I untied Charlie's hands and took him down from the pole and helped him pull up his pants and told him to go inside and get cleaned up and get some fresh water. Dad replied;" You fuckin bitch now you're getting in on the excitement too, get the fuck out of here you mother fucker, you fucken cunt". Then he started to chase after me, but he could not catch me I was too fast for him. He chased me for a while then he stopped and I stopped he was too drunk to keep up with me, besides I knew he would forget. I was worried about Charlie and Robert and how much worse my father was getting with his beatings and abuse. My brother Robert was much taller than my dad and when dad poked him in the chest he just looked at him with real wide eyes and a big stare and was tired from working all day long in a very cold environment and did not want any more trouble with his father, he just wanted to go in, have something to eat and go to sleep. So, he just remained quiet and if dad kept up his "wild thing" he would have to get physical which he did not want to. I guess that my dad really decided that he did not want to test Robert so he found a lawn chair grabbed another beer and sat down in the chair and fell asleep in the shade. Robert went inside the trailer to get a bite to eat and get some rest. Charlie was already inside the trailer and resting. I took care of his wounds and my mother did not offer to help.

I found out later that day that dad had a really rough day at work. It seems that dad's boss complained about the length and scraggly condition of his hair and beard. His boss required that he either cut off his beard or stay home. My dad refused and replied to his boss; "no way, the beard stays". Dad thought about what he had done and returned to the brewery the next day to beg for his job back. Dad's boss and Human

Resources decided to compromise and let dad stay if he wore hair nets to cover his hair and beard.

Note: I would like to mention here that my dad and mom, for one reason or another both held some sort of hatred for Charlie and if you were to ask them about it, they would both agree. All of my siblings needed help and counseling, including myself, but Charlie was in desperate need for some sort of intervention and my dad's answer to satisfy his needs were constant beatings which my mom supported. Life can be a beautiful and wonderful thing, and each of us has the power to make it so much more beautiful for ourselves and each other. We can also do harm by doing nothing for our brothers and sisters. When my brother Charlie was being abused by my ruthless father, I was surprised at the reluctance of my mother to try to help. She just stood by and let it happen. My mother did not even help me dress Charlie's wounds. I can only summarize that my mom didn't really love Charlie or she feared for her own safety. My honest appraisal however, is that all the years spent with my maniac father and being severely abused all those years has driven my mom totally insane. But later in life, my mother did admit to me that she hated Charlie and she could not explain why, she just hated her own son. I lost all respect for my mother.

THE DAYS WERE LONG THE NIGHTS WERE COLD

THE FIRST FEW YEARS on the farm were extremely rough for most of the family, except of course for dad, this was his dream. We had no electricity, no running water, no bathroom facilities, no heat, and nothing to eat most of the time and an extremely violent father with a temper that could be set off with just a drop of a hat or a word that he found distasteful and we unfortunately had seven kids and now a dog dad found wandering around and had no home and decided to tie him up and called him "Tag" and left him outside all the time next to the ditch with no shelter for a while until he built him a dog house and put this make shift rug if you could call it that inside for him to sleep on. He was just a stray Australian sheep dog but a good dog and dad mistreated him too. I really felt sorry for him. When the kids got real hungry, especially Charlie, he would eat his dogfood can you believe it? Well it's true. We only had one loaf of bread between all of us kids and mom and it wasn't enough, especially for the boys. We were literally starving to death that year, except for dad. I think I went down to eighty five pounds and my older brother Robert went down to one hundred and thirty. We were all so skinny you could count our ribs through our skin. It looked so bad that mom decided to take a picture of this to remember it because we looked like the kids that were starving to death in Africa.

In addition to starvation, our bodies were burnt from working all day in the hot burning sun because of picking weeds in the hot fields all day long and every day so all us kids were burnt to a crisp and horribly skinny. We looked like blackened sticks and we could hardly be recognized. Dad would usually drive up and say;" God job, kids, this place is really starting to take shape I mean it looks great". Then he would walk to the trailer to get a drink of water and go to bed. He would not offer to feed us or nothing. Mom told him the kids are very hungry and need to eat now they have been working since this daybreak and need something to eat.

Dad gave her a small check of $10 to feed 7 kids and herself. She quickly ran down to the store and got what she could with the money, and it wasn't much but I remember we ate all the food she got and she was hungry too, it was very sad. I just wonder why dad wasn't hungry he must have eaten somewhere else before he came home and really didn't care about us at all. But if this was a Saturday night and the weather was nice, it was a happy time for me and my older brother Robert. We would sneak off to the ditch where the VW was parked; climb inside and jamb out to disco tunes for several hours while dad was asleep in the trailer. Sometimes we tried to scare each other by telling spooky stories while listening to the rushing water in the ditch and the strange sounds of the night. The winter times were usually the hardest because all we had were sleeping bags for blankets and we all slept on the floor we had no furniture because all the furniture was still in storage from our move from the mountains. Dad did not want to bring it out of storage until we had a permanent home for it all. The trailer was very cold inside and at times there was a built up of frost all over the walls inside. So dad decided to buy a pot belly stove and install it in the kitchen and place an open vent in the top of the trailer to vent the smoke. It worked out pretty good. Then he went and purchased a cord of wood every other month to keep warm and to cook with and to heat water, etc. the stove really came in handy for a lot of uses. The lanterns were used a lot too. We used them at night to do homework, to go to the bathroom, to go outside to check the property, check on the dog, just about everything you can think of they really came in handy we did not use flash lights too much. What I especially hated about the winter time was going to get the water, it was a real tough chore. I had to take my brothers with me because it was too hard for me through all that snow I really needed help and the boys were definitely stronger now and could carry more and we needed more water so I took both Charlie and Tim to help me and it worked great plus we had more water. The shit pot was a tedious job for Charlie but he somehow managed to find just the right spot to dump it every time. I swear that kid was a genius at that. He knew just where and how to dump that thing and rinse it with fresh water and bring it back in and put it back in the bathroom like nothing ever happened. Dad really liked that.

NOTE: The act of taking a picture of me and my siblings for comparison to a race of people who were starving for reasons which they had no control was absolutely ridiculous. I thought that she was seeking evidence to support a child abuse claim. This act should speak volumes with respect to my mother's sanity.

DADDY'S GOT A GUN

My brother was about eighteen years old when he started working at the processing plant. He worked in the freezer as a packer and wore a white suit and brown boots with a hair net and white glove because he wasn't allowed to touch the meat with his bare hands. He worked eight hours a day. Every day we packed a lunch for him it was a peanut butter and jelly sandwich with an apple also included in the paper bag for his lunch and he went to work. He drove an old Chevy impala for a while, but then traded it in for an old jeep, a 1952 jeep I think with no top on it. He worked for forty hours a week and they paid him about $250.00 per week and when he got home he gave his check to dad, and Robert would ask dad how his job application was coming along at the brewery. Dad would reply; "I'm still working on it I haven't heard anything as of yet". One weekend however, dad must have been in an extremely bad mood Robert came home from work and then the problems began. Robert came into the trailer handed dad his check as he always did and asked him about the job at the brewery. Dad exploded. He yelled; "Mother Fucker I'm trying everything I can to get you on, but these things take time, why do you keep asking me this every day I won't forget about you but I can only do so much". Robert replied; "Dad I'm just really tired of this processing plant and the very cold environment and they work me real hard for such little pay, that's why I just want to remind you because I can't wait to get out of there". Dad replies;" I know, I know, but this constant needling, prodding and asking is ridiculous I fucking cannot take it anymore. You're giving me a Mother fucking headache you bastard! Now get the fuck out!" Robert got real nervous because dad became very agitated and started to rush around the house and was cussing up a storm. He really did want him out of the house now for some reason. He said; "Get out now I'm getting my gun mother fucker and I mean it". Robert ran out the back screen door and to his jeep he got his keys out mom ran out the door too, I was right behind the trailer watching the whole thing. Anyway, dad brought out this 12 gauge single shot shotgun and started to shoot at my brother's jeep. My mom spread her arms out from her body and said; "Robert you'll have to go through me to get to my son" So dad did shoot at her and just missed her abdomen by one hair and it went through her shirt. It was amazing because God must have been with us that day. Wow, I still can feel the chills of that afternoon how my brother was spinning his wheels in the dirt trying to get out of there. He was really desperate while trying not to get shot. It was really frightening and sad at the same time. I was very scared and yet I told my dad to; "Stop it before you kill someone for real". Dad replied;" Fuck off and mind your own business daughter dear". So, with that I watched my brother finally get down the hill in the jeep to safety and mom sat down on the stairs with me as we looked at each other in dismay and confusion. We sat there for a long while just being quiet, then I spoke these words to her, Mom I said;" you came pretty close to getting killed today did you know that? Just look at your shirt, look at the hole next to your abdomen what if the bullet would have hit you, you might have died today did you know that? How much more is it going to take until you realize that this man is no good for any of us he's real dangerous mom why do you still stay?" Mom replies;" Emily this farm is all I have I have no job and seven kids to feed. Your father has a good job at the brewery and provides well for this family I have nowhere to go. What can I do? I have no skills the kids are still little and he knows that. I am trapped here." I went around and picked up all the bullet shell casings and put them in my hands so me and my mom could look at them for a while. My mom and I just sat on the porch together real close and she put her head on my shoulder and started to cry then I started to cry with her and we wished that someday this would maybe be only just a memory. I do know that god was with us today because both my mom and my brother's lives were both saved because my dad is a bad shot. Remember earlier on in the book when I spoke of Blue our other dog well dad took a shot at him and didn't get the job done he had to get his uncle Andy to do it or otherwise the dog would have killed him which I wished would have happened.

Note: As I am sure what most readers must be thinking and wondering. I too am wondering the same thing and am questioning my mom's decisions to stay with my mentally ill father. Granted, he was a good enough provider but, he was also a very dangerous and unpredictable man who was capable of killing any one of us at any time with absolutely no remorse or so it seemed that way to me at the time and to this day. Self-preservation for herself and her children should have been her primary concern. She was gambling with her life and our lives, as well.

TWO FACED

My Dad had gotten off a little early and was outside sitting in his lawn chair holding a beer twirling his fingers when I walked up and asked him;" How's it going dad, you're in a good mood today, is something good happening, or about to happen?" Dad replies;" You'll find out pretty soon, as soon as Jr. comes home from work, I have a big surprise for him". I reply;" Oh I know what it is dad, it's…." Dad replies; "No don't you even say it, now I know you know but let's just wait he'll be here shortly and I want it to be a surprise he's been waiting for this for a long time". I replied; "Okay, no problem, I'll just go into the trailer and wait for him to arrive". I went inside and told my mom about the news and she was so excited for her son. She has been waiting for this moment too, this is what she has always wanted for her oldest son to be self-sufficient and not to ever need anything ever again. You see, the Local Beer Company provides everything for their employees and only the best insurance and benefits, and pay especially brewery employees. The Local Beer Company is a Family owned and operated company and makes the best tasting beer in the world. Robert came driving up the dirt road a little later in the afternoon he had to work a little late to clean up. When he arrived Dad was there to greet him with a smile and a beer. Dad said; "Son I have some good news for you. He handed him an ice cold beer and said these words; Jr. I spoke to Tom and Jerry from the brewery today and they okayed you're getting on at the brewery." I was by the back door outside listening so I overheard everything they said. Robert said; "Dad; Oh my god you're kidding, thank-you so much, this is what I have been waiting for forever! I am so happy. You really did it. Thanks dad, for all your hard work, I really appreciate everything you've done for me, thanks, oh God, thanks. I still cannot believe it! Wow. "Dad told Robert he would need to go down to the car lot and trade in that jeep for a good car to make it to and from the brewery on that highway I-93 every day for rotating shifts. Robert Jr. immediately went down and traded his jeep in for a yellow Hornet which had a yellow and green interior. I swear that car could go back and forth to the brewery on one dollar's worth of gas. He said he got a real good deal on it and the car was spotlessly clean and paid in full. It had a great heater and it did amazing on gas! It had an AM/ FM radio and was a three on the tree it was really fast. So Robert was ready for work on Monday morning. Mom made his lunches as usual and he was off to the personnel office to start his life with the brewery. The Brewery was his dream job always and has been and still is to this day after forty years of service he still works there. I felt alienated inside. I went back into the trailer and talked to my mom about Robert Jr. and why did he get all the good things and I never got anything good happen for me when it was me who was always by her side doing all the work saving the kids all the time putting up with that monster of a father, and his beatings, and never getting any recognition for anything around here for anything, why? Mom replied;" Emily your older brother Robert Jr. took a lot of beatings from that bastard for you and all of us, plus he put up with all of his shit too. Robert Jr. has been through a lot with that man and if any one deserves that job it's Robert. Your Brother has really suffered under his rule and now he's free to go and make his own way, and to be his own man. He'll be around, but he will be distant now. I'm so happy for him this is what I've always wanted for my son. I am so proud of him now." I replied;" Mom; that's all fine and dandy, but what about me and the other children you had seven you know? I will also need a job, and security. What am I supposed to do? Because I am a woman I am supposed to suffer? You know I just don't get it, I feel like I have been used to the max. I have been raising these kids, taking care of you and what do I get nothing. Gee, thanks a lot!" So I met with my oldest brother Robert to congratulate him on his new job and ask him what were his plans now. Robert replies;" Well I'm going to get the Fuck out of here as fast as I can save every penny, and try to enjoy life a little. I replied;" What am I supposed to do? I have no-where to go, I have no job opportunities, I am a woman, I am in northern Colorado, I have a bastard for a father and a mother who doesn't care". Robert Jr. replies;" I don't know, you'll just have to do the best you can, I feel sorry for you but there is nothing I can do for you, you'll have to find your own way, I'm sorry Emily". I just looked down at the ground and walked away and knew I was completely fucked. This situation was really a hard one for a girl of seventeen to swallow because I had no one to counsel me at all. I had to try to figure things out on my own and I did not do a good job of it. I really messed my life up and this is how I got my-self into a lot of trouble which I will cover later on in the next chapters.

Note: 1 **When reading the above section it is easy to see that the favorite child in the family is in fact the oldest son. The other six children were born probably as the result of a distorted religious belief system of not being able to use contraceptives, so therefore the love for the remaining six children is probably mostly lip service and given for fear of not being accepted into heaven. At any rate, this is a very sad situation and these people do not deserve to have children. Each affected child is concerned with self- preservation and only the stronger child will be able to help their siblings while most will go their separate ways. In addition to these observations, we must all maintain an awareness that the males in our society still hold the priority positions and the females must work harder than ever to achieve the same or equal status as their counterpart males. My parents were especially neglectful of me and my potential mental situation associated with the prior sexual abuse that I suffered at the hands of my grandfather.**

<u>Note 2</u> For you younger readers, three on the tree is a vehicle with a standard transmission with the gear access located on the steering column. The gears are clutch controlled and consist of the standard Reverse Neutral And Three forward Gears. The Pattern Is configured as an H.

THE LITTLE HOT BLACK BIKINI

As I RECALL I think this was the second year on the farm when I was working at the Buffet as a waitress and was in my second year of high school. I decided to buy a little black bikini for the summertime to celebrate with my small paycheck so I could sunbath in the lounge chair out in the sun with my tanning oil and be nice and tanned for the new school year coming up. Then give the remainder of my check to my parents like I always did. I found this cute little boutique in town and found the perfect black bikini and tried it on and boy it fit perfect! It felt so good and the material was so smooth and soft, I think it was silk, yes it was silk the lady complimented me and she said I looked beautiful in it and it fit perfect on me too. The bikini was expensive for me it cost at the time I think, $35.00 plus taxes and back in 1978 that was a lot of money for me. Anyways, I was happy and my girlfriend drove me home with my black bikini and my paycheck and some food from the buffet for my family we were always hungry and never had enough to eat so I always helped out that way and mom really appreciated it because the boys were growing and really needed the nourishment. Sometimes I brought home chicken and mashed potatoes and gravy with rolls, or turkey, or pork chops, or hamburgers with French fries, it just depended on whatever was on the menu they would scrape up and give to me for my family instead of throwing it away. The crew knew my family was going hungry and wanted to help me out, so every night they would give me containers of food to take home and I really appreciated that they were a great group of kids and I will never forget them forever for doing that. Then after work we all decided to celebrate a little bit. One of the kids brought in some vodka for everyone to share and invited me to the party in the back. The cook was busy getting my big white containers full of food and asked me if I wanted dessert too I said; "Yes fill it up because it was cherry cobbler, and everyone loved the cobbler". So he did with a big smile on his face and was happy he did not have to throw food away any more. Then after everything was cleaned up we had a small party to celebrate getting paid, and just being together as friends. Boy did we have fun. We all had shots and were jumping up and down, and for one reason or another we were playing like little children in the back with the pots and pans and weighing our-selves and god only knew what ever. It was the most fun I've had in a long time until I threw up all over the floor. I guess vodka doesn't sit too well with me I was too young to be drinking anything like that it was my first time drinking and my body let me have it big time. At the time, I had a boyfriend named Steve and he had to carry my containers to the car, his car of course and help me out. I guess I was a bit rude to him, and belligerent to him. He asked if he could kiss me earlier when I was sober, and I said; "only on the cheek". I didn't really consider him a real boy-friend, at least not yet it was way too soon I had just met him a few weeks ago, he would have to wait for those pleasures. This pissed him off apparently, oh well I thought, too bad. After my episode of throwing up, Steve helped me to the bathroom, I cleaned up he helped me to the car and drove me home. When we got up that dirt road we started to talk. Steve said;" I never knew you cussed like that, but man when your drunk you can cuss up a storm". I responded;" So what; Steve everybody cusses once and a while and it's not a crime to cuss I'm sure you do it, you're just careful not to do it in front of me. You know what, my father is very mean to me, he beats me up and cusses at me all the time and I'm not allowed to date anyone did you know that? He's a strict Italian and man he's real mean. So If you don't want to see me any-more I understand completely, let's just part ways now I'm sorry about tonight, and goodbye". Steve responded;" Yeah; we better just call it quits now because I don't think your right for me, so I'll see you later, goodbye". Well at least I got my ride home thank God. I brought the food in and the kids and mom just loved it and were so happy to see me. The weekend was here and I was so excited because I was getting ready to put on my black bikini this afternoon to sunbath in the lounge chair out front by tag's doghouse next to the ditch where you can hear the roaring cold water going down the ditch all the time to feed the crops in the area. That was the good part. If you wanted to cool off, all you had to do was get in the ditch and it came up to your waist and it was really cold and refreshing and it was really hot out and the combination was terrific. After I got out of the ditch I put on some Tropicana sun tanning oil all over my body then proceeded to lay down on my lawn chair. Everything was going just fine the sun was out and I was feeling great. I was just about to enter a state of total relaxation when I heard mom calling; "Hey Emily, would you like a tall glass of Hawaiian punch with ice, it will cool you off while you're tanning?" I responded;" Boy, that sounds great mom, thanks a lot, could you bring it to me?" Mom responded;" Sure, but it will be in a few minutes. "I responded;" That's fine, I can wait." After a few moments my mom brought out the punch and crossed over the ditch using wooden planks that my dad had previously laid down for people to access either side. The punch was welcome refreshment and I immediately drank about half of it because my mouth was so parched. I was laying on my stomach and I had barley closed my eyes when suddenly I was startled with the sound of a high revving engine off in the distance and coming my way. I raised my head to see where it was coming from and was surprised to see that it was a truck fast approaching my location on our private road. I was startled and scared so I yelled for my dad and I screamed for help from dad. Dad immediately opened the curtains in the trailer and seen the boys in the pickup truck that was harassing me and going around in circles while I was in the lounge chair helplessly holding to the chair and not able to get out of the chair because they were holding me hostage with their truck by going around in circles and not letting me out of my chair and creating a lot of dust so no one could see what was going on. My dad screamed;" Katy give me the gun and the bat." My mom immediately gave him the gun and the bat and he went out-side he told the boys to;" Get the mother fuck off my property now." The boys saw him and immediately put that truck in gear and went down the public access dirt road with my dad in tow and he purposely rammed the back of their truck with his Volkswagen on the way to the trailer-park. According to what my father told me he pulled them out of the truck and gave them a physical work over with the bat as well as busting the windshield of their truck. As a final statement to the boys he grabbed each one of them by the hair and pulled them towards his gun which was in the back seat of his Volkswagen, and said;" I want you to stay away from my property, my family and my daughter, if not I will put a bullet right between your eyes with that gun do you understand that?" The boys replied; one at a time, "Yes Mr. Pandora I do". My dad added emphasis to each statement to the boys by pounding them in the chest with the bat after he finished talking. When dad finally came home he explained to me and mom exactly what went on and what was said to those two boys and he was pretty sure they would not be bothering me ever again. The bat he was holding in his hand looked pretty beat up so I could only imagine how many times he hit those boys and how he smashed out their front windshield. I was really proud of him how he defended me that day. Then after he was done talking he addressed my bikini. He said;" Emily, I'm afraid we'll have to burn the bikini tonight at the bonfire with the corncobs". I responded;" what, why". Dad responded with a giggle and a horrible laugh; "Well, because it attracts too much attention to the wrong types of crowds and that's not what this family needs right now, you can understand that right honey?" I responded;" No, absolutely not! Dad I paid a lot of money for that bikini, I just wore it one time, and it wasn't me who instigated the trouble, it was those men who came up here to the farm, I had absolutely nothing to do with any of it. So no, I am not burning it; I'll just take it back and get my money back if anything at all. This whole thing is really blown out of proportion it does not have anything to do with me, they came up here to harass me I did not go to them." Dad responded again laughing real hard now; "Daughter dear, I know your upset, but taking back the bikini will only make you sadder and will make things worse but if you burn it then you can be free of the bikini and the memory see it's that simple." I responded; what, you're crazy you know it, this will haunt me for the rest of my life, in fact, I'll never forget it, ever and I hate you. My beautiful bikini, my silky black bikini gone all because of some backwards hicks from the trailer park and a father who is in sane. Perfect." So around 7:00 p.m. that evening my dad was handed over my little tiny black bikini after he had a wild bon fire going out by the road with the corn cobs and as I handed him the bikini I started to cry as I handed him the bikini one piece at a time. I watched the top burn first then he asked for the bottom and I reluctantly gave him the bottom half, actually he had to pull it from my hands as I screamed and cried; "Why, why are you doing this to me"? Then I just stood back in horror and watched it burn and fizzle away just like my life with him as I stared off into the distance I cried for a long time I walked down the road and sat by myself and looked up at the stars and asked God why am I being punished by this man as I held my legs together towards my chest sitting down on the ground in the dirt on the road on that hot June evening and I felt like I just wanted to die. I knew that somewhere down deep inside that this would surely all come to pass, but knew that this horrible memory would always be with me throughout my time on earth. Then as I kept looking at the stars I saw a shooting star go by and made a wish for my eighteenth birthday. I repeated these words;" Star light star bright shine for me tonight"; and I cannot recall the whole verse now but I had it memorized back then, as I made that wish on the shooting star, I wished for my birthday to come as fast as it could so I could leave this monster and try to find my own way in this cold world of ours. Anything would be better than this.

Note: My father lives for the excitement of conflict especially when he is guaranteed to be the winner. I have never seen my dad pick on anyone who is on equal footing. My dad is a born bully, but he takes it to an extent that most people would not believe and my dad has no remorse for those he hurts, especially his own family. My dad

could have called the police on the two boys who were harassing me but, he chose to handle the situation on his own. Why do people who are like this exist? I don't have the answer but I can definitely feel the effects of his wrath and I still have nightmares about my burning bikini and his hideous laugh as he watched it burn.

I FELT THE HOT DEPTH OF HELL AS I LOOKED INTO HIS DEEP DARK BLACK EYES THEN HE FEARED I COULD READ HIS MIND.

As I GREW OLDER and stronger my desire to protect my siblings from the wrath of my monster of a father also grew. As a result, I volunteered to help my mom with all her trips to town to buy the groceries and do all the laundry. I did this to protect my brothers and sisters. I did not want to leave them alone with that monster father of mine. I always took the smallest children Marsha, Lilly and Jimmy because they were the most vulnerable and would be the first to be beat. Their young bodies and minds could not tolerate the severity of his punishment and they would be left with severe mental and physical scars. So, I always put them in the VW first then I would put the laundry in second then tell my mom to go ahead and get in the car and get it started and I will go and get the check from my father and ask her to wait for me in the car. Then I went back inside the trailer to get the check from my father which usually took a while because he wanted me to inspect his handwriting and to make comment on how pretty it was and how you don't see this type of handwriting anymore. So, I just went along with what he wanted me to say and agreed, then he would hand me the check, and off I went. But before I went I would usually ask;" Is there anything special you would like from the store?" and on most occasions he just answered;" No, but Thanks." So with that I just turned around and went straight for the door and ran to the VW which was running with mom and the kids and laundry on board and off we went. This whole adventure usually took about oh let's say a good two and half hours to do the laundry and about thirty minutes to do the shopping. That's why we left early in the morning to get everything done way before noon especially if dad had to work the swing shift because he had to leave for work early in the afternoon in order to make it on time for work at the brewery. Every weekend was a big chore for me and my mom but even though it was a lot of work I still enjoyed it, because it gave me a chance to get off the farm and gave the kids a chance to have new surroundings too. They really enjoyed it believe it or not that one soda pop and that little bit of candy I bought for them was really cherished and they loved me for that. I found some small Dixie cups in the trailer and brought along three of them so that I could split one soda between three kids because that was all the money I had. Pop back in those days was .50 a can and the candy from those small machines were .10 cents so the kids were in heaven for a while. While the kids were occupied with the candy I was washing and folding clothes, which worked out perfect for me. I instructed the kids to go and wash up before they got back into the car so that dad knew nothing of the pop or the candy and for them to keep quiet and to say nothing to him about it. They all agreed not to say a word to him and ate all the candy and drank all the pop before we left the wash house. Everything worked out perfect for me. The kids were very quiet and sat and played amongst themselves. I was so glad I brought them with me and so was mom. Mom sat and read the paper then helped me with the clothes. Afterword's, we put all the clothes in the VW, then we cleaned up the kids, put them in the car and then we were off to the grocery store. I really loved going to the store because it was so nice and cool inside. All the kids loved it too. They were actually very well behaved children, I guess because of all the abuse they had suffered at the hand of my father. They would just walk through the store without a word said just looking around and smiling and sometimes just looking down at the floor. I would, at times, put my hand on one of their shoulders and look at Jimmy or Marsha or Lilly and smile back at them then I would look away with a sad look of reflection and could feel their pain with no words spoken. Sometimes when you look into someone's eyes along with their facial gestures that's all it takes to feel their pain. After we were done shopping we went home and he was there and asked;" How did everything go?" I replied; "Fine It was a lot of work as usual, but we managed". Then mom and I brought in the clothes and put them away, I put away the groceries. I told the kids to stay outside and play quietly and reminded them what to say if he questioned them about today. The kids all agreed they would do as I said to do;" We sat quietly at the washhouse and helped with the clothes". They memorized it and just as I was putting away all the clothes, I noticed dad outside the trailer talking to the kids about their trip to the washhouse. Just as I suspected, he was questioning them about their experience and what they did down there at the washhouse but it was too late for him to get any information out of the kids, because I had already prepped the kids on what to say and to not be afraid and to look him straight in the eye when you said it because if he sensed any hesitation at all, he would know you were lying and we would all get in trouble over a little bit of candy and soda pop, so please just tell him like I told you to and you'll be alright. So I watched nervously out the curtains in the trailer as the kids told their stories and they did just fine because they knew how evil and mean he could be over just the littlest things and kept to the story I had told them thank God. Then I slowly pulled the curtain back and went into the kitchen before he came back into the trailer for lunch. Mom was making lunch so I told her I would go up to Mike's farm to get some more water for tonight, she agreed we needed more. But before I left I asked the kids how it went and they said;" It went just as you said Emily and he questioned all of us, but we kept to your story and it worked". I just smiled and hugged them all and went on my way, but took my brother Charlie with me to help carry the water it was too heavy for me in this sweltering heat with temperatures well above 95 degrees my body just could not take any more punishment. Another reason why I liked to take my brother with me was for protection. He was starting to get bigger and there was a lot of farm workers around and I was young and with big water jugs to carry and no protection or any help but myself out there all alone, I knew deep down that it was better safe than sorry so if they saw a male with me they were likely to leave me alone because it was a long walk on those dirt roads by myself in that blistering heat at least I had someone to talk to and protect me along the way. At times I noticed men would just come right out of the corn fields at us and surprise us and say; "Hello in Spanish" which was kind of scary, I guess. But we became accustomed to it and learned to speak Spanish from those families that lived on that farm. But still, I'm glad I had my brother with me at times like that. On this occasion, I also had the opportunity to ask Charlie if dad beat him and Tim while me, mom and the younger kids were shopping and doing the laundry. Charlie did not hesitate with his answer, "of course Emily, in fact, he told me and Tim to go have fun. It's as though he wanted for us to get into trouble so he would have an excuse to beat us." "Me and Tim went to Delmar's barn to play on the tractors and 5 minutes later dad walked right up behind us and dragged us both home and beat us both for about an hour with a leather riding strap." Charlie then showed me the bruises and bloody strap marks. After hearing this from Charlie I hated dad even more. Dad was not only an opportunist when it came to beating the kids and his wife, he had to create situations that provided the opportunity for him to exercise his sick craft. In other words dad is not satisfied with a happy environment where all the kids are well behaved. Dad is happiest when he gets to beat the kids. My dad is a very sick individual. After reflecting on this I needed to get my mind back to the task at hand; Being all alone would not have been a good idea, because you never know when someone has something evil on their mind no matter who they are. I've learned that through life's lessons. So Charlie and I brought the water jugs home each was a five gallon jug which was pretty heavy and yes I developed some muscles during those years. We carefully brought them inside the trailer one by one for my mom. Charlie and I thought to ourselves well that's it for today it will start all over tomorrow. I thanked him for going with me today and he said;" No problem Sis, I'll go with you every day if I have to or if you need me to, I'm your brother". I responded;" Thanks Charlie I love you, thanks for what you did today, they all saw you and knew you were there for me, so thanks". Charlie responded;" No problem, I got your back". Then Charlie just went off with his brother Tim and played in the ditch water. I just looked down at the ground and at the fields of corn growing all around us. Wondering and waiting for the nighttime breeze to come and refresh us. As soon as night fell I went outside to sit on the steps with an ice cold glass of fresh water. I sat and starred up at the heavens for the longest time. Looking, in wonderment, at the beautiful and unique formations of all the stars and experiencing the cool crisp and clean night air, which creates a tranquil environment that is in total contrast to the hell that my father has introduced to the family by virtue of his mere existence. **How can something so beautiful be so close at home to something so morbid and tragic?** Dad had a street light installed on the property so you had a light to illuminate one side of the trailer. Now if you go to the other side of the trailer it was very dark and you could hear the water rolling down the ditch with a soft breeze caressing your face along with the night time sky and all those stars, it was a beautiful place to be right around midnight. Sometimes you could hear a coyote off in the distance, or the horse out front bedding down for the night. It's a different world at night that's why sometimes I like to stay up to experience it all alone without the yelling, screaming, or antics of the family to see what this place was really like.

<u>NOTE:</u> Being alone and able to reflect inward, I was puzzled and asked myself, with all the beauty and tranquility and possibility of universal love which was controlled by our being, why is there so much hate and ignorance allowed to exist as a form of pleasure for one individual designed to control and hurt so many and to overpower the common good with fear.

HIS FATHER THE MAN WHO MOLESTED ME!

My Father was less of a man than anyone could have possibly imagined as he announced to the family that he was receiving money owed to him by his father to support his new modular home.

IT WAS A SATURDAY afternoon and I was getting ready to take the kids outside to play. My mom and dad were in the trailer and very busy getting things done and ready for our new modular home. Dad said that he was getting ready to put water on the farm finally but in order to do that he needed $10,000 and did not have the cash funds to cover it. So he was going down town to make a call to his father to get the money to start the work on Monday morning. I just turned around and looked at him with a frown because I thought he had lost all contact with his father after his father molested me. I did not say a word to him but I was feeling disillusioned so I just turned away from him and walked out the door without saying a word. I was disgusted with him and my mom. She had nothing to say which meant to me she must have known about it too. So both of them have been in contact with that horrible man over the years and I did not know anything about it until now. How horrible and for some reason dad emphasized that his dad owed them money. I thought for what? I started to put 2 and 2 together, but I was too young to fully understand the implications of everything that was going on at the time, and when I think about it now I truly understand the whole thing. So his father did wire him the money and the water line was installed in the farm. Then next came the foundation for the modular home, which by the way did not pass inspection in Butte County because they put the septic system in the wrong place so they had to come back out to re-do that. At any rate, things finally all came together and the modular home was put on its foundation finally after all those years with no running water or electricity. But for some reason dad still would not let us flush toilet paper down the septic system, he insisted that we wipe ourselves and put it in the paper bag next to the toilet so he could burn it out front. I guess he became accustomed to it. He said; "I don't want to have to replace that septic system any time soon so just put the toilet paper in the bag please". Which I thought was pretty off the wall because all you have to do is get rid X or something like that and then have your septic cleaned out maybe twice a year is all but he did not want to do that. It was his way or the highway, always. Then he finally got all his furniture out of storage and put it in the modular home. It was weird seeing all that stuff after all these years, it was all still in pretty good condition, it was all just old and as I walked through the house I remembered sitting in front of that RCA victor TV set and I remember all that furniture, my mom's bedroom set, the kitchen table was the same, everything that was in storage brought back memories from the past. Even the kids old toys that Jimmy played with up in the mountains were there. I bent over to touch the toys to see if I could remember anything, then I opened the barn house to see the toys inside and smell the smells and they were the same which brought back a few old memories for me.

NOTE: If I had not of been born to this set of parents I could not have believed that such ruthless and heartless people existed, but unfortunately they do. I had no way of knowing that my dad accepted money from his father to keep quiet about molesting his own daughter. I don't know exactly how much I was worth, but it was more than $10,000. Even more surprising is that my mother knew about the scam.

NO HAPPY BIRTHDAY FOR ME

IT WAS MY EIGHTEENTH birthday and I wanted to make the best possible impression on mom and dad that I could because they usually had a birthday party for me so I visited my hair dresser Jerry to get my hair done and put on my best clothes. When I thought I was ready I presented myself to mom and dad for their approval. It was a happy day for me and I felt that maybe mom and dad would be happy for me. I should have known better. I walked into the kitchen and saw my dad sitting at his table with a chocolate cup cake and pink icing with one single pink candle stuck in the top. It was placed in front of him with his hands folded around it and my mom was in the kitchen walking around being very withdrawn and quiet. I said;" Hi dad, Hi, mom how's everyone going? I wanted to celebrate my birthday with you." Dad responds; "Well, Happy fuckin Birthday Mother Fucker." My eyes grew real wide, I responded to my mom by saying; "Mom what is this, why is dad so upset with me, did I do something wrong, have I said something I should not have said or what is it? I'm lost. Dad responds;" What you are is a half breed, and you don't think right before you do things so you do stupid shit and then regret it later on. Now if you were a full breed Italian you would really have your shit together. But since I married your dumb ass mother, it makes all you kids all half breed mother fuckers you're all fucked up, every single one of you!" I responded;" So that's how you feel I never knew that about you dad, I thought you loved all your children unconditionally no matter what or how we were we all came from you and mom so how can you call us half breeds?" Dad responds;" You fuckin Bitch, get the fuck out of my house and don't let the door hit you in the ass on the way out!" I responded;" No, I am not a half breed I am part of you and mom and I've never heard of such a thing where did you come up with this ridiculous insinuation." Dad responds;" Get the fuck out of my house now before I kill you bitch, now!" Then he took the chocolate cupcake and threw it at the door behind me and screamed to never come back. As I walked to my car I got in and was crying I drove down the dirt road very, very slow looking back at the trailer thinking to myself what had just happened and why did he have do this to me today. Out of all the days in the year he choose this one and it hurt me deeply even to this day I remember it all and every word he said cut like a knife. So I went home and got ready for work and worked the night shift with no lunch and cried through all of my breaks, then went home and cried myself to sleep. I prayed to God that night that somehow that he would punish my dad for all the hurtful things that he's done to me and my family.

Note: My father has no communication skills whatsoever. Cussing and humiliation are the only skills that he has and he would never admit that he is wrong or even that he is even capable of making a mistake. The underlying message that he was trying to convey with his extreme childish tirade was actually trying to tell me that it was time for me to leave his house and that I was no longer welcome. His ultimate objective was to live alone. Unfortunately however, my father took great pleasure in hurting and abusing people, especially those who cared and loved him the most. For my dad, this was an enjoyable experience.

AM I REALLY HIS DAUGHTER, I TRIED WITH MY ENTIRE BEING BUT I COULD NOT MAKE IT HAPPEN

SHORTLY AFTER BEING THROWN out of the house, I saw my mom one day in down town Colorado on my way to work and I asked her how things were going at the farm. She told me that Dad recently had an accident with the tractor and injured his ankle and back and would be out of work for the next three months and she was not looking forward to that at all having him at home full time with the kids watching their every move. My mom really didn't trust my dad at all and feared for the children. She told me he was on some heavy pain medicine and drank constantly throughout the day and he was always in an unpredictable mood. I was concerned for the safety for my younger siblings so I decided to pay mom a visit. At first, I was a little reluctant to drive up there, but I was really concerned and worried about the family. As I drove up dad was sitting in his usual chair in back of the trailer where the shade of the morning usually hits just right before midday so it's nice and cool and he was having his usual beer sleeping with his head tilted back. As I walked up you could see his crutches lying beside him in a state of readiness and his ice chest on the other side of him filled with ice cold beer of course. As I approached him he was sleeping, but I think he did hear my car pull up out front. It was really hot out so I greeted him with a usual; "Hello dad how's it going, I haven't seen you for a while and wanted to check up on you to see how things were going and how you were feeling?" Dad responded; "Well I'm doing the best I can considering this broken ankle and this sprained back. Actually dad says I shattered my ankle it has pins in it to hold it together and I fell flat onto my back off the tractor so my back really took a turn for the worse. This back of mine is really a bitch. On top of everything else they have me on Vicodin and valium for the pain and that does not even begin to even help out a little bit with the pain. The pain is just excruciating." I responded;" Dad I'm real sorry to hear that, it sounds like you're really suffering. Dad responds;" The kids have been very noisy and hard for me to be around right now they never fucken mind my orders or instructions, they don't listen, your mother is all fucked up in the head she complains all the time the fucken bitch gives me more headaches than she's worth". I responded;" Dad don't you think maybe that all the medication you are on combined with the beer might be making you say those things, because I don't think you really feel that way about your family do you?" Dad responds;" That's exactly how I feel about the whole fucking mess of you mother fuckers. You're all fucking half breeds, all of you! You're the worst of them. You mother fucker. All you are is a blood sucking mother fucking bitch and that's all you will ever be! I responded;" Oh really, boy you really do change your tune awful quick. If I would have known you were going to talk to me like that today, I would have never come up here to see you today at all, besides I didn't really come to see you I came to see mom and the kids to come and check up on them to see if they were all right". Dad responded;" You mother fucker!" He immediately got up and put his crutches under his arm pits and started to chase after me yelling," You fucking bitch, when I catch you, I'm going to kill you!" I responded;" Good luck with that because you never will I'm twice as fast as you, I'm not on drugs and I have two good legs!" He finally gave up and went to go sit back down in his chair he had been defeated. I did not go into the trailer to see mom or the kids I left immediately because this was one battle I had finally won. I thought to myself it was about time he was not able to abuse me physically at least not this time and it felt good. As I drove down the dirt road I looked in my rear view mirror to reminisce about past events with him as they flashed in my eyes in the mirror but thought to myself, hopefully the future will be different maybe just maybe things are starting to change.

Note: I think back at the trip I made to the farm and wonder, was the purpose of the trip to check on the safety of the kids and mom or was it an attempt to regain my self- respect that this monster had took from me? His vulnerable state would certainly give me an advantage, but how would I feel being totally out of my element and would my victory prove to be short lived? This would still remain to be seen. But I do know that this victory certainly did feel great and as far as I was concerned the trip was well worth the effort.

DAD FOUND A WAY TO EXPEDITE THE REALIZATION OF HIS DREAMS BY DESTROYING THE DREAMS OF THOSE WHO HE CLAIMED TO LOVE SO DEARLY.

WELL DAD HAD FINALLY put his modular home in the condition that he wanted it. The kids were all back in school and things pretty much went back to normal for the moment. But dad had other ideas on his mind. He was his usual self and was continuously beating up the kids on a daily basis because I would go up there and check on them from time to time. He was also beating up my mom a lot too. His temper was going from bad to worse it seemed and mom was frustrated and had nowhere to go. I would counsel with her about what to do but she was afraid and did not want to make a move just yet. So, I left things alone until she became desperate as I knew she would be very soon. Then one day I ran into my brother Charlie in Colorado and saw him in the street and asked him why he was not in school right now. He explained; "Dad just lost it a couple of days ago and threw me out of the house at gunpoint with a fully loaded gun! I had to beg for my life, I had to put my hands in front of my face and slowly back out the door and run down the dirt road as fast as I could to social services for a place to stay and something to eat. It was pretty sad and I didn't even do anything wrong, I mean it was for something stupid like forgetting to burn one bag of toilet paper in the back bathroom. That guy is off his rocker. Anyways I'm leaving this state Emily and I'm never coming back. I will always love you, you are my big sis, but I can no longer take his abuse and threats and now he wants to kill me." I started to cry for him, and just hugged him and said; "I will always love you and miss you forever". What a bad man and bad father who could do this to his son. I guess my biggest question is why? I mean pulling a loaded gun on someone is the worst thing I could think of and then to point it at your son's head and threaten to kill him. Since that incident, I haven't seen my brother in thirty seven years to be exact. I miss him and would like to get in touch with him after completing this book to get back together with him again. I miss him and I love him very much. I think the horror and torture that my father put us through was totally unnecessary. In fact, I believe that Charlie might have suffered severe spinal injury from all the beatings that my dad gave him when he lived with my dad. Dad got rid of all of us one by one. As me and my brother parted ways I knew someday we would see each other again but I did not know how or when I just wanted to see him again no matter what. I do know in my heart that my father, if there is a God, will pay for these horrible things he has done to our family and the deep seeded scars he has left on each and every one of us kids and my mother who let this go on for far too long has challenged her reality to the point that she could probably be considered insane. But she still does recognize the value of money and she believes in her mind that staying married to this ruthless and vial man will someday bring her great wealth.

<u>NOTE:</u> Through the years my father has gotten away with so many horrible things and the injustices that he has performed against others, especially his own family, are beyond understanding and reason. Today he walks free where others who are equally or less guilty are behind bars or are somewhere in their graves. The only explanation for this is my mother's constant protection. She either

truly does love him or is sure that one day she will inherit a ton of money from his yet to be realized fortune or an entirely different explanation altogether; she is totally afraid of him and afraid of the possibility of retribution that might pose a threat to her whether he is free or not.

JIMMY KILLS THE HORSE

MY FATHER HAD MADE a barn one year to house a horse he had purchased to put on the farm which was located in front of the home next to the ditch in front of the property. It had a covered place for the horse to rest in the wintertime and a place for the hay and a watering troth in back with a water spout. It was perfect for her with lots of room for exercise. My dad really loved this horse and he bought lots of grain for her and gave Jimmy specific instructions on how to feed her the grain and how to mix it with the hay and especially to provide plenty of fresh water in her bucket every day before going to school because she cannot digest her food without lots of water. He also instructed him to not give her too much grain because it will kill her, it will make her go belly up. Only give one to two cups then give two or three slices of alfalfa and mix thoroughly because this way she gets everything in correct proportions. Then, she will get her water and exercise and nap later on. Jimmy nodded his head yes he understood all the instructions and gave dad the okay to go to work. Little did dad know that Jimmy was not listening at all, his mind was on something else entirely different. What Jimmy did was fill up her feeding troth with all grain and did not give her water in her water tank.

Then he left for school. By the time he had gotten home from school the horse was belly up in the corral, just as dad predicted. When dad came home from work and saw this, he was furious and knew Jimmy did not hear a word he said earlier and questioned him why. Dad responds;" After all the Instructions I gave you and you said you understood and look this is what I get"? Jimmy responds;" Dad I'm sorry I didn't mean to kill the horse, I just wasn't thinking clearly, I was in a hurry, I'm very, very sorry for what I've done". I'm not exactly sure what transpired that day between Jimmy and my dad because I was not there, but I do know that the horse was removed from the farm immediately and a few days later both my brother Jimmy and my sister Lilly were taken in to the nurse's office at school and asked to remove their clothing to search for bruises and reports were filled out. Both of the kids were taken away from my mom and dad that week. Both kids were placed in social services until my mom was able to prove that she was capable and willing to take care of them again. The children were not allowed to go back to the farm ever again to be with or near their father. Timmy and Marsha were the only kids left on the farm with mom and dad. Social services went over to their schools to have them checked out for bruises on their bodies as well. Again, both kids had bruises and both kids were removed from the home and placed in foster care. My mom packed up her stuff and decided to go get a job but to keep close ties with my dad because after all it was her farm too. So my father had finally got what he wanted the farm all to himself. With my mom visiting all the time and letting him know all the details of things. He seemed to enjoy life on top of that hill, all alone with that dog still tied up on his chain to his dog house, poor tag he'll die there I thought. My mom and I managed to secure a townhouse in town and together we paid the rent. I was working two jobs. The kids were spread out all over Colorado and she kept trying to get them back. She got a job as a live in Nurses Aid. We were suffering trying to pay the rent and buy food and trying to manage everything, but still she wanted her children back so I did everything in my power to help her. She applied and was approved for food stamps so that helped a little, but things were still pretty tight.

Then she would go visit dad at the farm and get money from him and that would help out also. Somehow we just managed to get by.

NOTE: If we really care deeply for something and need to entrust its welfare to someone else on a permanent or temporary basis, we need to provide specific instructions on how to care for its well-being. Not so much as a long drawn out set of verbal instructions, but a written set of easy to understand directives fashioned in such a manner that the reader will be fully capable of understanding. In addition to a written set of directives, a recorded message would also be more than helpful. Follow up with a phone call and have the recipient read back the instructions to insure understanding.

MY MOM'S MOTHERLY INSTINCT IS STILL ALIVE

As RESULT OF OUR tight work schedules, my mom and I did not have much time to communicate. But While I was at home from work one weekend we had a chance to share some thoughts regarding the kids and it seems that mom still had a strong desire to get the kids back. I told her that I would keep my promise and do everything I could to help her. There were several problems that needed to be resolved before we could do this. First of all, the kids were located all over Colorado. Secondly, my mom needed to get approval from Social Services in order to do this. There were other related issues of course but these would be dealt with on an independent basis. Mom got her children back. First it was Jimmy and Lilly then a few months later it was Tim and Marsha because they were attached to the people they were living with. Things went well for a while, but mom had her hands full. As time went on, the kids were getting into a lot of mischief and throwing parties while she was at work and mom lost track of the kids. They were basically out of control. I was usually very tired when I got home from work, but one day I noticed that it was unusually quiet around the apartment so I looked for Jimmy and Lilly and found that they weren't there, I woke mom and asked her where the kids were, she said Jimmy had taken a job at Taco Bell down the road and Lilly had a job somewhere as a waitress.

Mom gave me the addresses of the kid's jobs so I could go and see them to check up on them to make sure they were all right. Mom was tired from working so she went back to sleep for the afternoon. What I found was something really shocking. First of all, I found my brother Jimmy sleeping in the trash can at taco bell and asked him why. Jimmy responded;" Because I have no way to get to work every day on time and mom sleeps too much, so I just stay here punch in and out and stay in the trash can overnight". I responded;" Jimmy you cannot do that, it's not safe, healthy or legal. If the police catch you, you will go to jail that's it. Now get in my car were going home". Next I headed off to see my sister Lilly and she was at a strip joint. I thought, perfect. Some waitress. I walked in to go see my sister and there she was doing her thing, so I waited, until she was finished then I said;" let's go I need to talk to you." "Mom said you were a waitress, but as I see you're not." Lilly responded;" Emily I had to make fast cash and this was the only way I knew how". I responded;" Well I guess there could be other things that could be worse than stripping. As long as you're not hurt or anything like that, but Lilly this is a dangerous business and you need to stop. Get in the car with Jimmy. I'll take you both home." I had a discussion with mom and informed her of what was going on with the kids and she seemed very concerned. Mom decided to drive Jimmy to work and was going to talk to Lilly and not allow her to do that anymore. Mom also discussed the bus routes available for Jimmy to take to his job if she was unable to take him to work. Lilly got a job as a Nurses aid it's a live in job for the elderly. Then a few months later Tim and Marsha decided to come back so mom really had a full house now. Her apartment was really full. Mom was working full time. But unfortunately the workload of taking care of all the kids was just too much and her desire to sleep more than most people normally would, inhibited her effectiveness. This extra time could have been used for taking care of her kids, but mom kept on sleeping and as a result, the kids grew up in an environment with little or no guidance and practically no supervision.

NOTE: If most of us try hard enough, there is little that we cannot achieve. If we have the mental ability to support us, all we need

is a positive attitude, belief in ourselves and a continued effort to never give up, we will certainly win. But after achieving our goal, is it really something that we truly need or in fact really wanted in the first place. Reality can sometimes be a rude awakening. What if holding on to what we thought that we wanted in the first place requires constant hard work and vigilance? Are we prepared to make the required sacrifices?

DEJA VU

MORE AND MORE THE conversations that me and my mother had, was about marriage. Mom thought it was about time that I started looking for someone that I could possibly start a family with. She was suggesting that I get out on my own. The idea became implanted in my mind so I started talking to my friends and one day one of them said she had someone she would like for me to meet. I went over to his trailer to attend a party and meet with him and he seemed like a nice person. He talked a lot about himself, told me all about his farm and what his plans were for the future. It seemed like he had a lot of friends. But I really was not too attracted to him. I felt like the girls at the party were drawn to him because he had money or claimed to have money. But I wasn't turned on by this. So I excused myself and went home early, I was tired. He was disappointed to see me leave, I told him I had to work tomorrow so I cannot stay up too late. He understood. I went home. Mom asked;" How did things go" I responded; "okay, I could not stay too long I have to work tomorrow, He was nice enough but really not what I expected. We'll talk more tomorrow goodnight". When I got home from work mom was more curious even more so than the night before. She kept talking to me about this man who had a farm and desperately wanted to know more. So I told her his family had a lot of land and oil and tractors and that this was their only son. They had two daughters and their daughters had daughters. My mother was so thrilled she started to scream and yell and was so happy. She exclaimed;" Do you know what this means Emily, if you marry him and have a son for him your son inherits everything, do you know that?" I responded;" Mom your full of shit". Mom responds;" No really, I've seen this sort of thing a thousand times before, throughout history this is how things have always been the father always hands the land down to the son who has worked the land all his life the boys are strong and can carry on the name". I responded;" Mom if you think those people are going to give me anything you're crazy, because they are not, they don't know me I'm just a stranger. Those people are locking down their money and protecting everything they have I'm sure and making sure I cannot get any of it no matter what. My mom kept disagreeing with me and told me to marry him as fast as I could, but I disagreed with my mom but gave in to her wishes. So with that, I went after this man. We dated for a while. Then he asked me to marry him, I accepted and we got married in Colorado. What a mistake. I felt it was wrong that night, but what could I do. So I hung in for a while, until he became violent. He drank and did drugs. In fact, he did drugs and alcohol 24 hours a day 7 days per week. He even got a DUI on his tractor one night and was thrown in jail. That night I had to drive the tractor home, and then I had to go pick him up in Garfield the next day. His outbursts of violence were becoming worse and he was hitting and beating me more and more. The bad part was he was not remembering hitting me because he had blackouts after the incident so it became a nightmare. I got tired of all of this and I was pregnant and decided to go visit my mom and dad for a while. While I was there my dad and I got into a verbal confrontation which soon got physical. He shoved me into the truck and then I reached out and grabbed his beard, then dad grabbed my hair, punched me in the face and slammed the truck door into my stomach several times and I was seven and one half months pregnant. I was screaming for help but my mom did nothing until I said;" please help me and your grandchild now". I had bruises on my face and stomach and he pulled all my hair out by the roots. Mom reluctantly went down to call the police dept. The police came and took him away and took me down town to file a report. My dad was placed in jail for two weeks and his fate would be determined by me and the judge in Butte County. I will never forget that day as I stood up to sentence my father on attempted second degree manslaughter of me and my unborn baby. The judge wanted to sentence dad to ten to twenty years that day with no chance for parole which he deserved. He had kicked my mom in the stomach eighteen years earlier with Tim until she almost bleed to death on the kitchen floor in front of me. It seems like he has come full circle. He has now done it to his daughter with my unborn child and his unborn grandson in my stomach. When the judge said rise I did, and my mother begged me please not to put dad away because she would lose her farm and everything she had worked for all her life not even caring for what dad had done to me or my un born son. I just looked down at her. The judge spoke to me and requested an answer. The Judge asked; "Emily do you wish to press charges on this man today, because if so I would love to put your dad away for ten to twenty for this crime. Your dad has caused unnecessary harm to you and your unborn child. What would you like to do?" The court room got real silent, then I said; "No your honor I am not going to press charges today". Everyone in the courtroom went; "oohhh noo". The Judge ruled that the defendant be let out on bond the next day with all charges dropped. My dad did not even look back at me in the court room dad just walked out and that was that. I told my mother: "I hope you're happy because dad almost killed my baby and your grandchild.

NOTE: Sometimes we need to listen to that still small voice within us and disregard the advice of others because their motivation could come from a totally different place than ours. Happiness for me meant love, sharing and friendship. Happiness for my mom was simply money and that's it. My mom was willing to endure suffering, pain, abuse and belittlement all in the hope of someday receiving a small amount of money after my dad dies. For myself, I wanted happiness now without the abuse, is that too much to ask? Besides, the farm was nothing more than a modular home placed on 50 acres of land and at the time was not that valuable. When

they sold it however, the land had appreciated considerably and was worth more than a million dollars of which my mom was awarded almost half, but my brother Robert managed to steal that from mom and she was left penniless anyway.

DAD WAS DIAGNOSED WITH PARANOID SCHIZOPHRENIA

DAD WAS PLACED ON a 72 hour hold but, he must have done something to upset the staff at the facility and they decided to extend his stay to two weeks. During dad's two week incarceration with Butte County Jail correctional facility, the staff decided that my dad needed to undergo extensive mental evaluations. It was determined that dad was suffering from Paranoid schizophrenia. The Judge warned me to be very careful around my dad because, in her estimation, he is a very dangerous man and frankly she is surprised that he has made it this far in society without getting into serious trouble. As the Judge was counseling me on dad's situation, I reflected back on dads interaction with various people associated with the farming industry. He had a lot of acquaintances who included; owners of farming equipment, land management experts, and neighbors who owned adjoining farms. He would use these people to gain information on how to establish his farm and moreover to grow the crops that he was interested in and with their help and assistance he learned what type of equipment to purchase, what type of seeds to plant, how to plant the seeds, when to plant the seeds, and how big of a yield to expect from his crops. After he learned what he needed from these individuals he really didn't have too much to do with these people anymore and his personal interaction and communications with these individuals either diminished or came to a halt. My father was a very stubborn man and in denial of the fact that he just wanted to forget what was told to him back at the Butte County Jail. He knew he had Paranoid schizophrenia but never attended counseling classes or obtained the medication needed to help him overcome his disease process or anything to help himself. He just ignored it and acted like nothing was wrong and went on with daily life and his work schedule and work on the farm as usual. He was as mean as can be to my mother and beat her up on a daily basis or whenever he got the chance I am sure of it. He was always in a foul mood and no wonder the disease was getting worse he needed medical attention immediately according to the Judge, he was really sick and needed constant medical attention and I'm sure what they put in his file reflected this. It seemed like every time I went up there he was very quiet and withdrawn and drinking a beer out in front of the home in the shade and he never smiled, he was never happy about anything. Even after I had my son Adam he never seemed like he wanted anything to do with my son or me or my mother, why I do not know. I think his disease process, on certain days, was real bad. Other days it seemed better but at other times he seemed more focused. All of these memories that I have of my dad and of these individuals who helped my dad get his small 50 acre farm off the ground and especially those who physically helped him with their labor scared me even more than what the Judge told me about my dad's disease. Because if my dad in fact, was suffering from schizophrenia it was totally uncontrollable. This realization made my father much more dangerous than the Judge predicted which simply means that my father is a walking time bomb and his outburst could occur at any time without any warning whatsoever.

Note: The man that this book is written about still walks the earth. I spoke with him last year over the phone and to my amazement, he has not mellowed at all, in fact, he has gotten worse and he seems to have forgotten my husband's name entirely. He just refers to him as Motherfucker.

FOLLOWING IN MY MOTHER'S FOOT STEPS

DROPPING THE CHARGES AGAINST my dad was certainly not the biggest mistake I made during my younger years and it would not be the last. Trying to stay married to a violent man that I should never have married was one of my biggest ones. This man was not only physically abusive, he shot at me and my family members as well. For example, I remember one time we were having some kind of an argument or disagreement over some trivial matter that started one morning when my sister had spent the night and we were in the kitchen and I was in the process of preparing breakfast for Henry who was also present and instructing me how to prepare his meal along with a list of other things that he expected me to get done during the day. As Henry continued speaking at the table, his loud voice woke up my sister because her room was located right next to the kitchen. So, my sister woke up and came into the kitchen and sat down at the table to listen to the drama. Her hair covered her face because she was still half asleep. Henry continued to talk as I gave him his breakfast and his coffee. He gave it back to me saying; "Emily these eggs are not done correctly, can you re-do them and make these eggs more runny, and fix this coffee and make it just black with sugar and no cream" which meant, I had to throw away all this food and start all over again. Upon hearing these demands and seeing what I just did with the food, my sister Marsha slowly lifted her head and raised her eyebrows and gave more attention to Henry because to her, Henry's actions were totally unheard of in the Pandora environment. She was raised to appreciate and be thankful for what she received. Returning a plate of food for corrections begins with severe beatings from her father. She knew that Emily had married a spoiled brat and she was sickened by this proposition. She would not let this happen to her sister. Marsha decided to take action. Meanwhile, I fixed Henry's eggs so that they were perfect and runny and his coffee was to his liking. I set the plate and coffee in front of him. Henry said; "Emily this is just the way I like it, it's perfect". He took one sip of his delicious coffee, and just as he cut into his runny eggs my sister threw her hair back looked over at me her eyes grew real wide our eyes meet, then she looked at Henry, then she reached over just as he was ready to eat a piece of his runny egg and she took the plate and grabbed the end of it quickly and with one smooth move she threw it in his face. It was an absolute mess, the perfect runny eggy eggs were attached to his eyes to his eye glasses and running down his cheeks, one piece of bacon landed on his ridiculous looking work hat, the other bacon and toast landed on his cheeks and his chest. His chin was dripping with yellow egg yolk. His eyebrows were completely coated in yellow. His face was totally frozen. His mouth was wide open and he could not see because his glasses were completely covered with egg residue. Finally, he managed to say; "You fuckin bitch". He took off his glasses and tried to clean himself up the best he could with the napkin I gave him with his breakfast. He then got up from his chair and stood there. Marsha stretched out her arm and pointed her right finger toward Henry and yelled out;" You deserve what you got you spoiled bastard the way to treat my sister Emily. You should not be giving back plates and giving her orders that take up her whole day and treating her like she's your slave, because she is not. You should treat her with respect and that is something I am not seeing here at all Henry. You're a spoiled brat and you need to learn that life is not handed to you on a silver platter you have to earn it. But you see life differently and I can tell you've been served, well that won't happen here with us you have to eat what we give you or nothing is served at all. Like it or lump it Henry." Henry quickly went for my sister and Marsha quickly jumped behind me and I had my hands on a pan full of hot grease and told Henry to "back up or I would throw this in his face and he would be disfigured for the rest of his life I also said to him that he could take his orders and he could shove them up his ass and do them himself and that I was tired of being his slave. Henry then tried to get to my sister to hit her but I intervened and had that hot grease and told him to ;" Get out now before I regret splattering this all over your face". Henry backed down and said; "I'll be back later ". I responded;" I will be waiting and ready for you Henry I am not afraid of you now or ever mother fucker ". Henry went to the back room to clean himself up and went over to his mom and dad's trailer to have breakfast. Then later on when Henry returned I had a discussion with him and told him that he needed to step up and start doing more around the farm and to stop his drinking and stop doing so many drugs day after day with his friends there every day and night it was really getting old fast and driving me crazy to the point that I could just not live there anymore. I mean really, every day his friends would come over never give me a break, then on the weekends there were crowds of them in the shed partying and I could hardly stand it. Henry was becoming more and more uncontrollable. When Henry and I were outside talking my sister Marsha intervened because Henry said something derogatory to her first which started a dominos effect type of an argument that lead into something very dangerous. Then my sister and I were joking with him but we found out that he didn't have a sense of humor and he told us to stop or he would shoot us. I really didn't think he was serious, but the next moment I looked around and there he was with his huge revolver. My sister yelled, "He's got a gun". My sister and I ran into the trailer to hide in one of the bedrooms and put our heads down and luckily we did that because the bullet went right through the window and just barely missed my head. Then about four months later around midnight when I was sitting on the bed which was located in the back bedroom nursing my baby, my husband approached me and demanded that I make him a bacon, peanut butter and lettuce sandwich. I replied; "You got to be kidding me, I just got done feeding the baby and I'm tired, go make your own damn sandwich" I carefully put my baby down in his basinet and he threw my water glass at the wall it splattered all over and he slugged me in the face. I quickly grabbed my baby, I yelled; "You stupid son of a bitch, you really did it this time, you stinking drunk" I raised my arm and pushed him forward and he stumbled backward because he was too drunk to stand. I kept moving backwards and I walked through the glass in my bare feet and held Adam tight against me, we were in the hallway and Henry was in front of me threatening me asking me; "Just where you do think you are going"?" I told him I was leaving him, you just don't hit a woman with a baby". Then I backed up towards the front door until I felt the doorknob and turned it with my left hand and opened the door up it was pitch black out because it was around 12:30 A.M. now and it was getting kind of cool out doors and all I had on was my night gown and a thin robe and no shoes. So I ran towards one of his trucks I knew there were keys in all of them so I choose the first one I saw and tried to get in but he stopped me. My husband grabbed me by the back of my long strawberry blond hair and started to yank on it real hard. I told him to let go of me that I had a child in my arms and was afraid I might drop him. But he insisted on pulling my hair out by the roots so I took my hand off his and freed my hand so that I could grab the door to slam it on him and it worked because he fell down to the ground that's when I took my shot and ran away as fast as I could down that cold dirt road with my baby in my arms and never looked back. I ran like lightning and knew that I had to reach the road so that I could hitch a ride with someone that could help me get a ride to my mom and dad's farm in Colorado. At the time I was very scared and very cold and very sorry I ever listened to my mother I should have listened to myself but it was way too late for that now. The damage was already done. Adam was here and I'll never regret giving birth to him. I just regret meeting his monster of a father I did not deserve this horrible treatment after what I had been through with my own father. But anyways, as luck would have it I made it all the way down that dirt road which was about or at least 2.5 miles to the pavement with the baby. Then when I got to the pavement I took a breath and looked back to see if my husband was out looking for me but there was nothing. So, I started to walk up the paved road in the middle of the night hoping and praying for someone to come by and pick us up that could help us and not kill us so I knew I had to be very careful and choosey because my son's life was on the line. So I walked for about 15 minutes then I got lucky, this trucker came along and saw me and my new born baby and immediately stopped. He said; "Mam looks like you're in trouble, can I be of assistance"? I said; "Yes me and my new born are in trouble my husband has beaten me up and threatened me and I'm trying to get to my mom and Dad's farm can you take us to Colorado"? He answered; "Well as a matter of fact I'm on my way to Colorado so I'll take HWY 287 and drop you and your baby off there you'll half to walk the rest of the way, think you can make it?" I responded; "Yes that goes right in front of their farm it would be perfect sir. I really appreciate this. It's still a long walk, but I'll be okay." The driver asked me how old my son was and we made some small talk. You could tell he felt sorry for me and at the time I was just worried to get to safety. After he pulled over he handed me my baby and I thanked him for all he had done for us and I told him that someday God would bless him for this moment in time and that I would never forget him for what he had done for me and my son. At that moment I reached up to shake his hand and he kissed the back of my hand and said; "It's ok baby you take care now YA hear". I responded;" Thankyou I will. At that moment I stood there for just a second to watch him pull away in his big rig I think it was a Kenworth and thanked God for sending me this perfect angel that I so desperately needed in the middle of the night with my little one. I thought for a while in perfect silence, "Why couldn't I have met someone like that?" Then I started on my long walk home to the farm and I knew I had to be careful because there were wild animals out here at night especially this time of night but I was ready to fight if I had to I would pick up a stick and use it and I knew how to fight to protect my child. As I approached the door of the house I was really tired and thirsty but I held it together. I gently knocked on the door. Dad answered. He said; "Emily what are you doing here at 2:00 A.M. I responded; "I got in a fight with Henry and he was drunk again and beat me up real bad and I had to walk in my bare feet all the way up his dirt road, then when I reached the highway a trucker picked up me and the baby and brought us to hwy. 287 and dropped us off on the hwy. Then I had to walk all the way from the tree farm to your farm." Dad responded; "Your feet are all bloody and your face is black and blue, you wait until tomorrow morning I'm getting out the shotgun and if that son of a bitch even shows his ugly face I'll kill that cock sucker". I was very scared and my feet were bleeding. I stayed there with the baby until things calmed down.

Henry came over to the farm the next day and my dad came out with his shot gun and told him; "To get off my property now before I blow your head off your shoulders". Henry left abruptly while spinning his wheels in the dirt. I told my mom that we were wrong about this guy, he is a total looser and she agreed, but it was too late. I ended up going back to this monster a few more times and he beat me up some more, then one day he came up to me and said;" Emily If you don't divorce me I might just kill you and not even remember it". Well that was all it took for me I went down and got the divorce papers we both signed them and agreed on joint custody of my son and a meeting spot once a week. Henry had a severe drinking problem combined with drugs and would black out and not remember things the next day. So this was dangerous and he knew that if he did not divorce me, he might just accidently kill me, but he was also threatening me and did want to kill me but I honestly could not figure out why, maybe money. He did not want me to be around any of his family's fortune with his grandmother getting so close to dying things were going to change soon and Henry did not want me involved in any of what was coming up next for him. What happened was they got into my son's head and told him how bad of a mother I was and it seemed my son was becoming more distant every day. It seemed like every time I seen my son he was more and more grown up. I knew being around that drug addict and alcoholic father wasn't good for him but I could not convince the judge otherwise. I tried to tell them what kind of person his dad was and how he was no good for my son and a bad influence on him but no one would listen. The Judge still awarded Henry half custody of my only son even though I told him about Henry's drinking and drugs. I suspect the judge was paid off because that boy should have never been with his father at all. My mother used to take Adam up to the farm all the time when she had to run errands, and she would leave my son with my father. He was so abusive towards Adam. Adam used to tell me how he would treat him while he was up on the farm with him and how grandpa was mean to him it just made me sick to my stomach. I felt so sorry for Adam. My mom knew better but she had other more important things on her mind most of which were money related. Both Henry and my father were abusive and no good for my son and Adam grew up with their teachings and way of life imprinted on his mind. I just wished I could have been there to rescue him and teach him the right way to live a normal and happy, drug free life and away from these bad people and bad experiences from ever happening to him and maybe his life would have been a little different, who knows? I do know this, the people who made my son suffer will pay a price for what they did and it's not me they have to answer to it's a higher power, a power that rules over all of us no matter what or who we believe in.

NOTE: **Being young, single and free is a gift, a gift that is given to each and every one of us just once in our lifetimes which no amount of money on earth can buy. You might say that we are all wealthy at least once in our life and how we treat our gifts will shape our lives until the day we die. There are no rules written that says that we must have kids or get married or live or act to please others. We need to reach that happy place in life that makes us happy while promoting a universe that is free from hate and promotes universal love for everyone and if we do choose to get married and have children, we should not hasten our decisions because time is on our sides. A union between two people whether it be between man and woman or otherwise should have a common goal of love and continued happiness. The world is a wonderful and exciting journey that waits with new adventures that can only be realized by those with a pure and open heart so look around, let go and learn to love.**

And especially learn to appreciate your own uniqueness and love and accept who you are.

MOM'S MOTHERLY INSTINCT IS OVERCOME BY REALITY

As MY SON ADAM grew older and older my mother started to complain more and more. Some of the things she complained about were: congestion in the apartment, not getting enough sleep, too much babysitting, too much noise. These complaints really hurt me deeply because of the sacrifices which I had made when I first moved in to help her. I gave up a lot of my freedoms to help her raise her kids which obviously she had totally forgotten about. So we moved to Colorado with the kids and I continued to pick-up my son on the weekends until one day Adam's grandmother called and said Adam was starting school that September and he would be turning five years old. So I could still pick up Adam on the weekends but sometimes he would need to stay home for his school plays or whatever came up as needed. I understood but was unhappy, but I felt that I could negotiate extra days sometime in the future if I had the opportunity. My live in relationship with my mom and siblings ended within 5 years after we started living together. One day mom approached me and said, "Emily I found a new apartment and there is no room for you and Adam." I was devastated, but, "I said OK." I made a call to a friend that I had met at a local health club and he decided to help me and I have been happily married ever since. Thanks mom. My husband and I have been married for over twenty eight years now and going strong. When I first met my husband I did not know he would end up being my soul mate. It turns out that Tim is. After all this time Tim and I are still together and will be throughout time I believe. Tim came to my rescue without any questions asked. What happened was when my mom told me this information, I immediately went down to the health club because I had met Tim about oh, three months earlier and he was very nice and friendly to me and had asked me out on a date. But at the time I had two boyfriends, whom both worked for Big Bell they each worked in different departments, and neither one of them were worth a plug nickel. At any rate, Tim was working out on a piece of equipment when I walked in to the gym and I just walked up to him and he was upside down lifting weights. He then stopped immediately. He saw me standing there in my trench coat with my high heels on and my long red hair and dress because I had just gotten off work earlier at Big Bell and he was really aware of my presence. I said;" Hi Tim; How are you.?" He wiped the sweat from his brow and said;" Hello, how are you have not seen you in a while." We talked for a few minutes, then he asked me out to dinner. Tim said; "Let me go take a quick shower, and I'll be right out". I said; "Sure, I'll just wait in the front lobby for you". So, with that Tim ran off as quick as he could to shower. In a short while Tim appeared in the lobby with his workout bag he was dripping wet I noticed and he had a left pocket full of pens and such and complimented me on my beauty and said that I smell good all of which made me a little bit leery of him. Tim said; "Where do you live." I reluctantly said;" Do you know where Parkstreet is"? Tim replied;" yes, I do. I think there is a Chilies over there not too far from the Blvd". I replied;" Yes, your correct. I know, why don't I just follow you over to Chilies in my car, and we can have a quick dinner and then I can go home and get ready for work tomorrow and see what happens from there. Sound good"? Tim replies;" Yes that sounds good to me"." I replied, what kind of car do you drive"? Tim replies; "I drive a black Beretta, its right out front". "Okay, I said, I drive a black tracer". We were on our way to Chilies, and then on to a long lasting relationship and marriage. My Oldest brother Robert's marriage ended in divorce because of a drug related issue so he invited my mom to live with him in a spare bedroom to help take care of his children in exchange for her living quarters she would not have to pay rent but could work if she wanted to. My mom continued to work as a live in nurse's aide for extra money for clothes and food and whatever she wanted plus I'm sure my brother Robert gave her money too. My mother took care of Robert's children until they were all grown up. She stayed there for over twenty years in his home. She never really earned an excessive amount of money; mom just kept his house clean and watched my brothers Robert's kids, and helped out with my son too at times. I would take Adam over there on weekends to go swimming in his pool and the boys. Robert my brother had two sons, David and Alvin which were close to my sons age, so they all grew up together. My brother Robert continues to work at the brewery full-time and is still there after all these years. He dated some women along the way but no one seemed to suit him because every time he came close to marriage he would request them to sign a marriage contract and they all refused. So my brother Robert stayed single for a long, long time. Until one day when my brother Robert went to the brewery and was introduced to a lady who had just won the lottery, her name was Vivian. Well now, this made my brother open up his eyes, if she had money and no kids this was the one for him. So, they dated and they seemed to get along real well. I think from what I was told they dated for a couple of years before getting married, can you believe it. I did not attend the wedding and as a result I'm not sure if my brother asked Vivian to sign a wedding contract. I did not attend the wedding. I have no details other than they got married. I do know she won six million dollars and my brother Robert was not about to let that get away. My brother Robert has always been chasing the dollar bill because that's what my parents taught him. That's why my brother Robert still works after forty years at the same job. My brother Robert is also the same guy who went on a cruise to Alaska and had a portrait done of himself that hung in the Livingroom. My brother Robert is a very narcissistic type of an individual that only thinks of money and can't get enough of it. In fact, the last time I seen Robert he opened his wallet and said; "Emily look at all those one hundred dollar bills aren't they beautiful?" I just looked at my brother Robert with a frown and said nothing because I did not know what to say. I thought my brother Robert was a freak and thought to myself, "This guy really needs some serious help". My husband was with me and witnessed this little display he said; "He's just trying to upset you nobody is this crazy over money". But as the night progressed my husband began to witness more and more displays of greed and soon my husband was convinced that my brother was a serious narcissist individual and from what my husband knew of my mom he suggested that my brother Robert was a carbon copy of her.

<u>Note:</u> **My brother's love for money has matured well beyond the point of being cute and it is not funny by any means because it has been used to hurt people. Especially, those who could have used his help and support in a miniscule way. I will cover this later on in future chapters, but for now, keep in mind that his wealth could have made many in need smile with hope and gratitude. I'm not saying this because I am a jealous person but a lot of the money that Robert has earned is through the efforts of others but a great deal of it has come from receiving money from my dad's Father to keep quiet about my molestation. He also forced the sale of my dad's farm and promised the court awarded amount of my mom's share to my mom but somehow managed to keep most of the money himself and left my mom virtually penniless. The sale of the farm will be discussed later in future chapters.**

MOM RUINS A GOOD THING

MOM GETS A VISIT from Marsha. My sister was unhappy with her marriage and decided she wanted a divorce from her current husband Dexter. They had two children together. But my sister Marsha was willing to leave the kids for drugs and alcohol. Marsha could not escape her childhood and everything that went with it including her childhood sweetheart Mark. Mark was still around and still single, but some things never change. I don't know why for the life of me those two never got married. They really loved each other, but for some reason they never got around to marriage. In fact, to this day Marsha, my sister, still visits Mark from time to time in Colorado he still looks the same as he ever did just gray now. What a shame those two should have been together a long time ago, why they never married I will never know.

My sister Marsha took moms friendship opportunity that she developed with my brother Robert to try to convince her to legally take the house away from my brother. This was a terrible mistake. First of all, my brother Robert was not happy with my mother's acceptance of my sister Marsha into his home. Second, I believe that my brother Robert suspected that my sister Marsha would try something sinister by convincing my mother to follow a plan that would allow them to steal his house from him with little or no effort whatsoever. My brother

Robert was ready and waiting. My mom and my sister initiated the legal process by filing the necessary paperwork that claimed they were being mentally and physically abused by my brother Robert. In essence my brother would yell and scream at both my mother and my sister and physically push my sister around but unfortunately, there was no proof to support their claims. My brother Robert who always keeps an attorney on retainer filed counter charges that claimed that my mother and sister Marsha were just trying to fabricate false information designed to lead the courts on a poor judgement ruling against his character. At the court proceedings the judge ruled in favor of my brother Robert and my mother and Sister Marsha were ordered to vacate the house. As I recall the courts gave my mother and my sister seventy two hours to vacate the premises. My brother didn't waste a second of this time. He immediately began to toss the furniture and belongings into the driveway. He did not take time to pack or wrap anything with care. He literally threw it outside as fast as he could with no regard for damage or any kind of special protection. Needless to say, there was a lot of breakage and ruined furniture but my brother Robert was not concerned. His motivation was to get my sister Marsha and mother out of his house within that seventy two hour time frame. In the past my brother Robert has purchased and sold an apartment building and, as a result, has had some experience in dealing with tenants and I'm sure that he set a new record for vacating tenants when dealing with my sister and mom.

Note: **When my brother Robert allowed my mother to live in his house rent free, he felt that his generosity was well above what the courts expected from him. He expected mom to kneel before him and graciously accept this as a gift as good as from the gods on high. He felt like a king only to be worshipped with a special appointment only. When my mom allowed my sister Marsha to move in with her, Robert's power over her was challenged and he simply could not have this. When my sister Marsha refused to leave at his beckoned command, my sister Marsha got belligerent and threatened my brother Robert. For some unknown reason, my**

mother allowed my sister Marsha to speak for her. This was one of the biggest mistakes that she would ever make and unfortunately, she would continue to make the same continuous mistake with my sister Marsha over and over again.

GRANDPA, THE GUY THAT MOLESTED ME, FINALLY KICKS THE BUCKET

Dad had received word from his family in California that his father had passed away and that he needed to attend the funeral. His father was the same monster who molested me when I was six years old and threatened to kill me if I ever told anyone. I told my father that I was interested in going to the reading of the will to find out what type of relationship my father still had with his dad because of the molestation issue. I asked several times, but the answer was always the same, an emphatic no, but there was never a reason given for this answer. After sharing this situation with my husband, he opened my eyes and re-enforced my suspicions when he said, "Emily, at the funeral your dad and brother made arrangements to receive hush money for keeping quiet about the molestation committed by your deceased grandfather. The money was obviously promised to your dad and brother in the event of your grandfather's death. The money should be yours." After hearing this, it was like a huge dark cloud had been lifted from over my head, everything was much clearer now. The secret that my dad and his father had shortly after finding out that he molested me was probably about money. The times that my brother Robert told my husband that I was naïve was probably related to the hush money that my brother Robert and my dad were to receive. After being rejected and told that I could not participate in the funeral, my brother rented a brand new, fully equipped Cadillac and together with my dad drove off to California. The trip there and back took them a total of about 4 days. They collected their money and immediately headed back. I have no idea how much money changed hands but shortly after returning, my brother filled his house with new furniture, electronics, etc. My dad could not stop smiling and he did invest a lot of money in remodeling his house. After the realization of watching my brother and father embark on their spending sprees, my heart was broken and I was devastated because I knew where the money was coming from. I ask myself, aside from being so closely related in the same family, how could they treat me like a piece of garbage. Didn't they realize that this would leave a mental scar on me forever and hurt more than being shot dead with a gun. Most of all, my mother was part of the pay off and managed to keep it a secret, as well.

<u>NOTE:</u> Greed can cut deeper than a sharp double edge sword and the wounds that are created hurt longer and never heal. It takes a ruthless person to inflict this type of pain within their own family. I am absolutely sure that if my brother Robert wasn't there to witness the molestation, that my father would not have included him in as part of the will award process and this also applies to my mother. Greed in my family and the love of money is highly worshiped in my family and most family members are blinded from all of the other attributes such as love, respect and caring which usually serve as the cohesive element that ties a normal family together. I learned these valuable lessons, and several of my siblings are beginning to accept the values, but it is a painful process without help and support.

WITHOUT THE RINGMASTER MY MOTHER'S INSTINCTS WERE USELESS

I'M SURE THAT MOM in her own way felt she loved the kids but she just did not have the skills and talent required to raise them on her own. She had never really learned how to be a mother. Mom always depended on my dad to be the ruling entity of the family. Unfortunately dad only knew how to manage this through physical means. My mom's social status of the family was that of a brother or sister. My mom provided no guidance or supervision whatsoever simply because she did not know how. Eventually mom gave up trying to be an effective mom and I really believe she had second thoughts about trying to raise the kids on her own. I could see that the kids were not even listening to mom but mom wasn't even trying that hard. Mom's answer to confronting problem situations was to go to sleep. Now I'm not saying that I'm smarter than my mom but at least I did recognize her deficiencies and I decided to volunteer my time and efforts to help mom raise her kids. The fact that I was twenty two years old made me somewhat more mature than my siblings in addition to that, I really did love and care for my brothers and sisters and did not want to see them get into any more trouble. So the first thing I did was lay out a strategy that took into consideration the kids responsibilities and schedules on a daily basis. I then met with each child independently and provided each of them with their own personal activities schedule. This was all inclusive including travel times, work times, and any other applicable times such as lunch and play times. The schedule was negotiable depending on personal needs. I completed a one on one with each of my brothers and sisters and made absolutely sure that they understood what their assignments were all about. I let them know that I was always available for questions and concerns and I would never get mad if they messed up and if for some reason I was asleep, they should feel free to wake me up. The kids seemed to be very happy to get some structure and guidance in their life and the strategy seemed to be working out real well. Mom was real happy it gave her more time to sleep.

<u>Note:</u> Sometimes we need to recognize when a task is too large to handle on our own and we need to swallow our pride and ask for help, if we don't, we run the risk of doing more harm than good. Faced with overwhelming odds, the more intelligent approach is to seek help from others or if we recognize a situation where help is needed we should have the strength and willingness to offer our support. This results is a win-win situation.

MY DAD'S BAD ATTITUDE DID NOT CHANGE BY BEING ALONE

ANY TIME SPENT ALONE with my dad was a time to beware because of his violent nature. Every time my mom took my son Adam up to the farm my father was very abusive to him. Adam told me he would make him sit on a bucket all day long outside with no food to eat or water to drink and stay in one spot until grandma returned from her errands. Adam was crying and my father just turned his head away. Adam told me he never wanted to return to that farm with grandpa he's too mean. For the holidays at Christmas time my father had to be the center of attention. He was so loud and outspoken and obnoxious all we could hear was him. Usually there was drinking going on so, this meant that dad would get violent towards mom or someone else. We tried to have a Christmas party the best that the family knew how but it usually didn't last too long because the family all lived in Colorado and had to drive home so the family had to leave early which made it a good thing because the family did not want to over stay our welcome. My Dad's farm is located in a northern suburb of Colorado. Dad would get violent after a while and the family knew this so the family wanted to leave before dad would explode. Mom started to clean up the kitchen floor and dad started to kick mom in the back for no reason at all while she was on the floor. I immediately said; "Stop that, you're going to break her back". Dad responded;" Fuck you, you bitch, I will do what I want in my own home". I responded;" Yeah, but don't kick my mother in the back while she's cleaning your floor." Dad responded;" Go fuck your-self". I responded; "Okay Dad I'm leaving, mom you should leave too and never come back, to someone who disrespects you like this". Mom got up and her back was sore and you could plainly see that she was crying. Well dad ruined Christmas again everyone piled out the door including mom. Another holiday ruined and it's too bad. The family did have fun for a while and got some pictures taken earlier on in the afternoon before the drama started. As a Family we were able to enjoy Christmas dinner before the arguments started to get worse and intensified. But then after that, thing's went south dad got tired and I think dad had enough of the family. The family should have realized in the beginning that's probably what dad wanted and that was to be alone. Most of us were trying to have a family celebration together but it just didn't work out we had no father, what we had was a ringmaster.

Note: One of the major questions that the reader may have because it is surely a major question of my own is why none of the other siblings did not intervene to try to help mom? Let's look at the facts. All of the brothers are physically capable of overpowering my father on their own. Each of the three are young strong and muscular and quite athletic, especially Robert who is well over 6 ft.3 in, tall and weighs over 230lbs. During their young lives, they have all been severely beaten by my dad. My mother's influence in this particular dilemma weighs heavily on any intervention of help from the family. My mother has always preached and impressed on the kids the value of money and as a result, my siblings became more and more greedy as they matured. It seems that dad had quite a large bank account which was the result of various Investments and the increased value of the farm. As a result, the kids stood by and watched dad kick mom because of fear of losing their place on his will. How greedy can you get?

MY BROTHER ROBERT GETS ITCHY FINGERS HE FORCES MY MOM TO SELL THE FARM.

MY BROTHER ROBERT HAD been spending a lot of time researching the value of the farm and he would always keep my mother updated on its value and he was always in contact with real estate agents and lawyers to try to determine how hot the market was in the Colorado area. Without much difficulty using factual information he convinced my mother to force the sale of the property and to force her to initiate divorce proceedings. Soon proceedings were well on their way. My dad granted the divorce but fought the sale of the land. My brother wanted a 50/50 split for the land but actually received 40% of the sale price. While the proceedings were in progress, weeks before they were complete, my mother used to contact me on the phone to keep in touch for various reasons but she would always talk to me in a low voice she would whisper. I would say;" Mom why are you whispering, I spent years and years up there on that farm, I cared for you, my brothers, and sisters, and I took all sorts of abuse and I think I have earned the right to know what's happening and to be part of it". Mom gave no explanation she said she had to go now in a low voice and hung up. At that moment in my heart I knew that dad had physically abused her all of her life and now my brother Robert is going to mentally abuse her for the remainder of her life. As part of the secret that my mom failed to disclose to me, my conniving brother Robert promised the ownership of the house (his house), to my mother but she never got this in writing and Robert's word to my mother was not worth a dime. He did not even provide a written promise. He confronted her face to face and totally denied the promise after everything was paid off with her money. See, at the round table in Colorado when the checks were being handed out Robert had (POA) Power of Attorney over my mother so when they handed out the checks my dad took his check and the attorneys gave mom's check to my brother. The farm sold for one million dollars and it was a 60/40 split with dad getting the 60% and mom getting the 40% because dad made all the payments on the farm all those years. So, my brother took her check and deposited it in his checking account and paid off his house, his truck and all his credit cards and left the rest in his checking account. My mom was furious. She said;" This house should be mine now Robert you promised me and now you have changed your mind just like that". Robert responded; "I never said I promised you the house mom you misunderstood me". Mom shook her head no and knew she had been taken for a ride by her own son. She should have drawn up a contract beforehand. Now it's too late she will never see all her money again. I called her up and told her to try to get back some of the money because this was theft of an elderly person and that there was a chance he could go to jail for this. My brother got wind of this and gave her some money back just enough to put a down payment on a Ranch, a suburb of Colorado, but my mother still had to work hard to make the payments which I thought wasn't fair at all. To this day he still owes her approximately $150,000. I am just assuming through information I got from other family members. I really think it's sad and disgraceful the way my oldest brother Robert treats his own mother. My mother had to work very hard to keep that house for approximately one year before she had to put it up for sale because she could no longer keep up the mortgage and up keep of the house. It was just too much for her. My brother should have stepped in and gave her what he owed her so she could pay off her house. But no, she suffered and worked hard until the end. Then she moved to an apartment again with my sister Marsha who continuously takes advantage of my mother's kindness by taking everything that my mother is willing to give her which is basically everything she owns. My sister ends up spending it on alcohol and cigarettes and whatever else she needs for basic sustenance. Marsha and my brother Robert have been the two primary reasons in my mother's life that have put and kept her on the road to failure since she has separated from my father. My mother currently lives in an assisted living home and my sister Marsha is still bothering her by hanging around the home trying to sleep there at times, and still asking my mom for money and is still co-dependent on her. My sister is in her fifties.

Note: Coming from such a large family with such a variation of interests which have been nurtured from such a high degree of dysfunctional aspects makes for a unique and diverse variation of personalities. It seems that the drive for money is the strongest force that can even overcome the power of love and compassion. If you allow yourself to be blinded by this force it will eventually swallow you from within and you will live on as a very unhappy uncaring individual who nobody really loves or cares for.

FOR DAD THE DIVORCE WAS A CHANCE FOR HIM TO LIVE HIS DREAM BUT MOST PEOPLE WOULD CONSIDER HIS DREAM TO BE A NIGHTMARE.

DAD TOOK SOME OF his court proceedings from the sale of the farm and purchased a brand new three quarter ton ford pick-up truck and a brand new air stream fully self-contained trailer, to live in and travel the country when he wanted to. He did travel for a while, but quickly got bored and could not find anywhere he could call home. He came back to Colorado and parked his airstream trailer in a mobile home park in Colorado right off the major highway. Ironically the mobile home park is situated about five miles south of the location of the farm that he sold, but, loved so dearly. He lived in that mobile home park for about ten years all by himself until one day it was flooded out by rain storms and it was unsafe to live there any longer. All of the family members used to visit him there as often as they could but we all had conflicting schedules. But personally I disagree with his lifestyle I could not live like that. I need people around me all the time collaborating with me and talking to me and helping me with things and ideas etc.... My dad is different. He prefers to be alone and secluded. Whereas I like to nurture friendships, and get along with people. I enjoy learning from others and I like to teach others the skills that I have learned.

This information sharing technique of my life has enabled me to develop in most of the career goals of my life including writing.

My father was getting too old to live by himself and could no longer care for himself so he moved out of the trailer park and took the truck and airstream to Kansas to go live with my sister Lilly in her house. My sister purchased a house in Kansas before she met the man she was destined to marry and after she married, the house was left vacant and she gave her house to my dad to live in, it's just a two bedroom one bath house and its paid off and he lives next door to my sister and her new husband she married. So Lilly takes care of her new husband who is disabled and my father, it works out real well for them both. When I spoke to her a few months ago, she said she takes dad to his doctor's appointments, I believe that my dad has diabetes type two and suffers from the gout in his feet and she gives him his shots, takes care of his feet and cares for all his needs. He pays her for her work because she is a nurse an LPN and can legally give the shots and give him care as well as caring for her new husband who is disabled and needs nursing care for his health care needs. I have not spoken to my sister Lilly in a while because she has changed her phone number and I cannot call her anymore. I do not know why she did this I do know she sent me a post card in the mail several months ago letting me know she is loving the ice-cream she buys and the shopping. The post card came from Sydney Kansas that's all I know. I guess I will need to send her a post card, I do have her P.O. box thank God. She did not even give me her address. She says;" They do not deliver mail here you have to go to the post office to pick up your mail". I have not had any contact with my family at all for a while. My sister Lilly was the only open line to information about my family that I had. I'd really like to get in touch with my sister because of my dad he is totally unpredictable. He has been diagnosed as a Paranoid schizophrenia and I am afraid that he could turn on my sister and become violent at any time, but my sister Lilly is extremely religious to the point of being a fanatic and she always tells me that; "I worry too much just sit back relax and let Jesus take care of everything".

DAD DECIDES TO PAY MYSELF AND MY HUSBAND A VISIT IN COLORADO.

SUDDENLY THE PHONE RANG. I was surprised to hear my father's voice. He said; "Daughter dear I have been thinking about you and I have a little free time and would like to come down and spend a little time with you and your husband". It was Monday around midnight he rang the doorbell and said;" I remember what you said about being the second house on the right from the stop sign because at night you really can't see too much and things look totally different to you I got lost a few times then doubled back to find you". My dad does all his driving at night for several reasons: first of all his eye sight is very poor and he refuses to wear eye glasses, he always travels with his thirty foot Air stream trailer pulled by his one ton Ford extra cab pick-up truck. The entire rig is over sixty feet long and is emblazoned from front to back with all sorts of lights and emblems all of which can be seen by other drivers for at least a mile away and the primary reason that dad drives at night is simply that dad can't drive worth a damn. He rang the doorbell I opened the door and **invited** him in for a cup of coffee, but he declined and he asked for an outlet to plug in his trailer. He said he would stay in his trailer tonight then make different arrangements tomorrow. Dad and I and my husband went out to the garage to find an outlet for his trailer so he could have electricity. My husband provided an extension cord but the electrical requirements of the trailer were too much for the extension cord but luckily we had a larger cord in our utility shed which worked out ok. The next day dad came over with all his dirty clothes and I washed them for him and made him a nice breakfast. Then we took him to Walmart to buy groceries for the evening meal. We planned to have burritos because that was dad's favorite. After dinner we all settled down to watch several movies on T.V. around nine O'clock dad said he was tired and he said;" I want to go outside to go to sleep in my trailer". I did not think he would accept but I offered him to stay in my spare bedroom, he accepted. Everything went well for the next three nights but on the third night everything went to hell. I just returned home after a visit from the hairdresser. I got a new color I wasn't really happy with the new color, my husband liked it but my father really hated it and he didn't hesitate from voicing his opinion in fact, his condemnation was so intense that it made me feel like shit and it upset my husband to the point that he was defensive and told my father to ease off. Things between my husband and my father became heated. My father physically threatened my husband and my husband responded and they were just moments away from a fight and I intervened with a shout and yelled ; "Stop this Now"! While standing between the two of them you could see my husband's hand on the rolling pin and ready to smack my father in the head with it, and my father's fist was just inches away from his face. It was nerve racking to say the least. I knew inside that my father had tried to ruin yet another relationship of mine. He had called my husband every name in the book including: Motherfucker, (Dumb Mexican), he is a racist, he is constantly embarrassing me in front of other people and I do not know why, I guess it's his way of saying he does not love me anymore, but then again, he really doesn't know how to show affection anyway.

Dad prepares to leave the next day as he was cleaning up around his trailer he asked for assistance with the hook-up of the trailer to the truck. My husband and I were happy to assist him. My husband told my dad to get in his truck and to back up to the trailer hitch. As soon as it was lined up properly, my husband signaled my father to stop the truck to let him know that the truck was properly aligned. Then my father exited the truck to complete the coupling process. My husband showed him exactly how to do this. My father realized that he had been incorrectly doing this on past occasions and he was grateful to me and my husband for showing him the correct way to do this because if he continued to do this the incorrect way he could have lost the trailer. He said he was grateful. He informed me that he would be leaving around midnight so he would be spending the rest of the evening in his trailer he did say he would keep in contact with me no matter where he is and gave me his unlisted phone number. I hugged him and did give him some presents some shirts, socks, and a new coat for the winter that did in fact fit him I was surprised and very happy too. He took the gifts quickly and hung them up he said; Why Emily you didn't have to do that, these types of shirts are my favorite too". I said; "It's okay, I wanted to dad, I know how you never buy yourself anything so I did it for you". He was so happy he had a small tear in his eye there for a moment which really surprised me. At that second I sat on his small couch and time stopped for me to see that I will never forget it I just looked down with a grin, it was worth every penny to see that especially for me. You see, I have been through hell with this man and everything he does to me really cuts deep and bothers me for some reason or another I guess after fifty or more years with an insane individual the little things really start to bother you. I went back into the house for a while and my husband and I talked for a while until I became tired and I went to bed. My husband stayed up to see my father leave. The next morning my husband was very excited and couldn't wait to tell me about the experience he had of watching my father leave. He said; "Emily I didn't really want to wake you up because you were so tired but you missed a good show last night it was better than the fourth of July. Your dad managed to light up the entire neighborhood. It was around twelve o'clock midnight. Your dad started up the engine of the one ton Ford pickup truck and I'm sure the engine is loud enough to wake up the entire neighborhood, but oh boy, when he hit those light switches it was like God opened up his hands and unleashed the most powerful lightning display that he ever could in all of humanity. It went from pitch black to twelve o'clock daylight

I could see every house for two miles in every direction I could count every tree and every leaf on every tree for two miles, all the little birds left their little nests and flew south for the winter. The little rabbits scurried off in droves. The night owls were so confused they fell from the trees". My husband was so frightened he thought there was a gas leak in the neighborhood so my husband looked out the window and his heart slowed to a normal beat when he realized it was just my father leaving the neighborhood.

NOTE: Writing this book is probably the most difficult thing that I've ever done in my entire life, not because of the physical challenges, there are none, but because of the extreme mental challenges which reflect all the physical and mental challenges. Every aspect of our lives resides within us forever and is only dampened through time and effort and help when needed. But if we are forced to remember the bad things that have happen to us, they can be just as painful and as real as they ever was but hopefully through the efforts of facing our demons such as writing this book or seeking help from others we can learn to live happy and healthy lives. But sharing with others is the key and opening the door to our hearts will start a healing process that will not be stopped.

TIM FOUGHT VIOLENTLY JUST FOR THE RIGHT TO BE BORN AND HE STILL BEARS THE BATTLE SCARS TO PROVE IT.

TIM WAS THE FOURTH child born into our family he was a boy. Tim weighed over 10 lbs. and was born on my mother's birthday. I can still remember the day my father came home from work and had an argument with my mother over something I cannot recall I was only five years old at the time. He came into the kitchen while she was cooking dinner and she was nine months pregnant and was about to deliver Tim. My father was enraged over something and started to push her around. My brother and I were too small to do anything but watch in horror as this man continued to hit my mother around the kitchen. Then she lost her balance and fell to the floor I remember screaming; "MA, MA are you all right" she could not answer me because he was still attacking her. Then suddenly he started kicking her in the stomach with his work boots on and they were steel tipped boots and he kept kicking her and kicking her and kicking her until she starting bleeding from her vaginal area and she passed out. I quickly ran over to the phone in my bare feet through the blood and climbed up the little step stool to dial 911. I told the operator to come quick my mommy is on the floor and she is bleeding with a baby in her stomach and to come quick. The operator wanted me to hold on but I wanted to be with my mommy so I dropped the phone and went to her. The cops came and an ambulance and firetruck is how I said it for a five year old. I can still remember those exact words to this day. They took my dad away and we went to stay at my mom's friend next door for a few days until things settled down. Reports were filed but my mother choose not to press charges again like she always does and was back home with Tim about four days later. Then as the months passed mom and I noticed as we were changing Tim on the bed in the master bedroom that Mom said;" Emily come over here". I did and she said; "Do you notice Tim's head it looks funny compared to the rest of his body his head is not growing with the rest of his body it's too small". I replied;" Yeah his head is way too small mom why his body is growing but not his head". After we talked it over mom decided to call her family physician and take Tim in right away. From there it was off to Children's Hospital in Los Angeles. Tim's head was not growing so they would need to open up his skull and perform major surgery on his brain right away. When I went in to see him he looked like he'd been in a car accident with all those tubes in every orifice of his little body. At home, mom wanted me to breast feed off her to keep her milk fresh for him so when she went to the hospital she could breast feed him. The first time she saw him she passed out according to what dad said. This would be Tim's new home for the next two to four years because Tim was also crossed eyed so he needed multiple surgeries for that. When Tim was released from the hospital he had long deep red hair and so we put it in a ponytail and because he was crossed eyed my dad would call him Benjamin Franklin because he would put his arms behind his back and walk around and he was a very comical kid. We all protected Tim and tried to enjoy him while he was at home because he had to go back to Children's Hospital for more surgeries and more pain. When it was all said and done Tim finally came home with perfect eyes and a scar along the crown of his head from ear to ear measuring ¾ inch in width which he still carries with him today. Then when Tim was all better he finally came home and was part of the family again. Things started to settle back down and dad turned back into his old self again. The beatings started back up and this included Tim which really made the whole family mad because after all Tim had been through he really did not deserve a spanking not now not ever. But, you could not stop dad from his habits of physical abuse and torture. But there was one time in particular that Tim actually ran away from my father just as he was ready to spank him on his bottom he said;" Tim reach down grab your ankles and look at the wall". Tim did with anticipation and then he made his get-away. I then stepped in and told Tim to; "Run Tim run, run as fast as you can". Of course my dad was furious with me and would deal with me later for my beating for this. Meanwhile, he ran after Tim. He finally caught up with Tim and asked him why he ran. Tim explained;" That he did not deserve a beating for what he did and should not get a severe beating because he had already been through enough". Dad had to think on that for a while then brought Tim back to the garage and gave Tim two swats and off to bed. As for me I received a severe beating for my role in telling Tim to run. But I didn't care it was worth it I really saved Tim's life that night from something he really did not deserve. Charlie on the other hand received a bad beating and my older brother was beaten badly too. Yes it was one of those nights to remember. My father did most of his beatings in the garage with a large wooden stick. As Tim grew up he became more and more comical and funny he was the kinda kid who you could laugh with. He hung out with Charlie a lot which got him into trouble because Charlie was into mischief. So wherever Charlie went Tim went. They were typical boys growing up doing what boys do. Every time they got into trouble dad would beat Charlie and Tim because they were together on the same escapade. Tim grew up just like the rest of us watching our father drink and smoke pall mall red cigarettes when he was young. Watching him beat everyone in the family and mentally destroying everyone's minds at the same time. Although Tim did not realize it at the time, he picked up on some of dad's traits too. The beatings continued all of Tim's life until one day Tim was up on the farm with his sister Marsha when social services took him and his sister away from mom and dad and put them both in foster care. From there Tim decided to get a job at a local Store and managed to get married he had a beautiful wife and two beautiful daughters. Tim had one big, big problem though, he was an alcoholic. This trait he picked up from my father. You see from a young age my dad used to give the kids beer to drink and said its okay a little beer won't hurt the kids. But it did. It turned my brother into an alcoholic. Tim's marriage ended up in divorce, both daughters are married now with children of their own Tim I believe still sells cars for a living or is retired I'm not sure. Tim is fifty two years old by now and seems happy in pictures I have received over my cell phone from my younger sister. I have not spoken to Tim in quite some time.

NOTE: It's really unfortunate how dad's influence ruined Tim's life and the lives of his children as well and it will probably have a negative effect on generations to come. My dad suffered from Paranoid schizophrenia and this disease can be transferred through the genes and chances are that my brother carries this gene and will distribute it with-in the rest of the family.

CHARLIE BEATEN WITHIN AN INCH OF HIS LIFE

THIS SECTION IS ABOUT my brother Charlie whom was the third born child of the family. I am dedicating this entire section to Charlie because of the extreme circumstances of his life. He had a very traumatic life under the rule of my father and to an extent my mother. When Charlie was first born, he seemed like every other child but mom was really busy with me and my brother and started to neglect my brother Charlie. She wasn't there on time to change his diapers so he started to clean out his diapers himself by smearing his feces all over the crib and walls because he was tired of being dirty. That's when my mother and I had to clean up his room for hours and my mom just hated that. I think this is when she started to hate her own son. She would change his diaper but she would spank him and punish him for something that was her fault to begin with I'm sure. Then she would leave poor Charlie alone in his crib for hours while she cleaned house. I would go in and check on him and ask her if I could watch him. Charlie never had enough to eat because mom could not breast feed him anymore. My mom wasn't receiving enough nourishment because my dad wasn't providing enough food for the family. During this time in our lives my dad's income was limited and the money he did make he choose to spend on the house and the car the welfare of the family came second. As Charlie matured the beatings became more severe. My mom could not tolerate anything that Charlie did wrong and together with my father they would display their ill feelings toward Charlie through abonnement and physical beatings. This served to reinforce Charlie's feelings of worthlessness. Charlie desperately needed love and attention but he choose the wrong path to find it and as time progressed Charlie's antics increased to the point where everyone in the family labeled him as a bad kid and he was treated as such. Charlie's status within the family was a direct result of the parenting skills of my mom and dad. But, they would never assume responsibility or accountability for Charlie. They just simply labeled him as a "rotten no good kid" and it was reflected in the intensity of the beatings my father gave him. As far as the rest of the siblings are concerned, all of them were treated equally as far as food, shelter, and clothing are concerned but the rest of the siblings are aware that Charlie received most of the beatings and they took advantage of this. Whenever they got into trouble for one reason or another they realized that if they blamed Charlie my father would easily believe them and punish Charlie whether he was guilty or not. It didn't take much to convince dad because dad really enjoyed beating Charlie. All of these beatings on Charlie took their physical toll on his weak body and Charlie's body developed several noticeable deformities. These beating's continued all of Charlie's life every day and sometimes twice on Sunday. Sometimes my father would beat him until his buttock were bloody and his back was welted it was horrible to say the least. That poor kid suffered tremendously both physically and mentally. Today his buttock is distended and he probably has serious spinal damage because his shoulders are slumped and his back is crooked and I fight to hold back the tears even just to think of him. This is what I remember from thirty years ago when Charlie was in his twenties. I haven't seen Charlie in over thirty years and wish these bad things had never happened to him and miss him very much he's my brother and I will love him forever.

<u>NOTE:</u> Charlie was forced to leave the family at gun point by my dad. I feel that this is the best thing that could ever have happened to him.

MARSHA WAS LOOKING FOR SOMETHING THAT WASN'T THERE

MARSHA WAS THE FIFTH child to be born into our family and the second girl. She had dark hair and dark complexion and looked more like my father and she was destined to be mom and dad's second favorite child just under Robert. When she was growing up we used to call her "pebbles" because she reminded us of the little girl on the T.V. show, the Flintstones. It was a cartoon popular in the 60's. Also, mom and dad used to tell her how beautiful she was growing up which contributed to all the social problems she would experience throughout her life. She did manage to win a contest when she was in her early teens at a local beauty pageant, which inflated her ego. While she was growing up mom and I protected her from dad's violent outbursts. If she did get a spanking it was a small one not too hard or too long I was there to monitor that. I always looked after Marsha and Lilly my younger sisters and told lies if I had to in order to protect them from harm. If there was a beating to be had I took it for them. As Marsha grew up she confided in her brother Tim because he was more her age and he was always there for her and he went to the same schools as her. But Marsha developed a liking to alcohol and prescription medications and fell in love with a boy she met in her teens and never really grew out of that love for him.

They never married each other and over the years they just kept seeing each other no matter where she was she kept going back to Marvin. I don't know whether it was the sex or the fact that she met him first in her life or what but he just seemed to be the right fit for her. Marsha had a beautiful family two children a wonderful husband nice home I know this because I was there. Then one day while I was visiting and sitting on her bed she explained to me that this wasn't what she wanted and she wanted her old life back. I wasn't sure what she meant by that but I told her that she could never go back because going backwards in life is no good and if you look back you would so to speak "Turn into a pillar of salt" I said meaning everything here on out would be bitter for you. She did not like what I had to say and managed to come up with some story of her husband abusing her and threatening her and she needed a divorce. She left her husband and her children were taken away from her by the judge and given to the husband. I went over to my mom's house one day and saw her with all the children's toys selling them at a garage sale. I thought that was very selfish. Marsha continued to drink alcohol and take prescription medications and still does to this day. I'm wondering how she survived this long. I blame my father and mother for this, they were both mentally ill and were unfit to be parents. Marsha, although she would never admit it, has severe mental problems and needs help. Marsha despised anyone who had a successful marriage and she did everything she could to disrupt their happiness. For example: My brother Tim has two beautiful daughters and Marsha introduced both daughters to drugs and alcohol. Needless to say this infuriated Tim's wife and caused friction between Tim and his wife. Marsha also tried to create problems between my oldest brother and my mother by convincing my mother to steal my brother's house through legal efforts of the court system, the end result was that my mother and Marsha ended up losing the court battle and were thrown out of my brother's house by the court system. Before Marsha got involved with my mother, my brother promised to give his house to my mother. Marsha also got involved with my life and my marriage and she physically attacked my husband over a comment that he made regarding the care of my mother. She physically attacked him on several other occasions. On one of these occasions he refused to accept her advances. She eventually filed restraining orders against me and my husband along with my mother. These restraining orders could have been averted because a member of the Colorado Police Department got involved with the case and found that my mother and sister were lying and trying to fabricate the truth about me and my husband, He warned them to cease and desist with any further harassing type of activity. Today Marsha is in her fifties and, does not work and lives with my parents. Unfortunately, the restraining orders were levied against me and my husband and are in effect and are permanent. The judge totally believed my mother's lies and was effected by her tears and was not even interested in hearing our tape recorded message that would have proven beyond a reasonable doubt of our innocence.

NOTE: Some people are more sensitive than others and respond differently than others. We need to be careful in what we say to certain people and especially in how we say it. Our words can either make or break a person. Words can literally kill or boost an ego. We need to always be sure of our objective. For example, Hitler controlled an entire race of people with words alone. Marsha's ego was ruined by her parents constant input of how perfect and beautiful she was to the point nothing was good enough for her and nothing could possibly make her happy.

LILLY SUFFERED TREMENDOUSLY UNDER MY FATHER'S RULING HAND

LILLY WAS BORN THE sixth child into our family and the last child to be born in California. Mom had a tough time carrying her because it was after all her sixth child and she was getting tired now. Dad was his same old self just getting older and still just as mean as can be. In fact, mom had to leave him and go over to her mom and dad's house with us kids and they could not accommodate us so we went up to Big Bear for the weekend. Her mother (grandma) drank alcohol a lot and threw a shoe at her stomach and tried to kill the baby mom was carrying so mom had to leave. At the time we had a Dachshund dog named Greta so Greta protected mom from Grandma good thing for her. After that we went home and dad seemed to be cooled off some so mom could at least carry Lilly to term. But her pregnancy was hard. I really had a lot of chores and her cravings were tremendous. Well mostly the cream pies from the ice cream truck that came around the neighborhood. Her favorite was banana cream pie, but she loved all the cream pies really. After Lilly was born things started to settle down a bit and she was beautiful. She was over 10 lbs. This was Mom's second child that was over this weight. Mom breast fed Lilly just like all the rest of us and Lilly did fine. Everything seemed to be going along just fine until the big earth quake hit in the early 70's. It struck in the early morning hour around 5:00a.m. just as dad was headed off to work it knocked over the water heater in the garage and he caught it in time thank God and it tore cracks in all the brick walls and the driveway was cracked all the way up with his marble stone in it. The earth quake shook all of us out of our beds. It was very scary. That's when my dad decided to move out of California and to a better place to live that it was no longer safe here for the family he said. All of Lilly's life was in Colorado and that is where she learned about the ugliness of my father. He would come home from work depending on what shift it was he worked rotating shifts at the brewery and the only shifts that affected the kids were days and swing shift because the kids were still up long enough for him to see them. On swing shift I tried to put them to bed as soon as possible before he got home to prevent them from getting a spanking. Lilly was very sensitive and took in all of dad's anger and violence and listened when he used his profanity almost as if she was analyzing him and you could see the fear in her eyes every time he entered the room. When dad dished out his punishment this would include Lilly and it terrified her to get those spankings and to be hit that way. Her little mind was just not capable of handling his acts of terror and unfortunately she inherited his gene of Schizophrenia I know this because I had recently spoke with her on the phone and she is now seeking therapy and on medication for this disease process. Lilly current has two children by two different men and has been married twice. She finally found a man that really loves her and has settled down in Kansas. I really love Lilly she has been through so much all because of two dysfunctional parents and other siblings whom are dysfunctional who have caused her pain not to mention her own mental problems she has to deal with on a daily basis. Still deep down I know she's still my little girl, the little girl I raised practically on my own. It's funny too, when I look at her I still see her as that little girl with those pig tails I would put in her hair every day and make sure she was clean and ready to go. Time can take away some things, but it can't erase memories I have of the kids I raised. Lilly's kids are both grown up now and gone now it's just her and her husband. I think this is good for Lilly because it will give her a chance to heal and pay attention to her therapy sessions. I wish her only the best of everything because she deserves only the best. Our life growing up was very hard and too much for Lilly to handle not to mention the rest of the family. All of us kids were broken all because of the meanest and ugliest man I know:

<u>NOTE:</u> It is truly amazing how much influence that one individual can have over another especially if that influence is of a negative derivative. Consider the power that would be available to be used to satisfy the distorted whims of a sick individual. Think about it. It's happened many times in the past and it could easily happen again now or in the future if left to go un- checked, watch out!

JIMMY ALMOST BELIEVED HE WAS IN A NORMAL FAMILY

JIMMY WAS THE YOUNGEST child of the seven children of the family. He was the last to be born and the hardest one for mom to give birth to. Mom was in labor for three days and required a major C-section. In fact dad said, she almost died according to the surgeons at the hospital. Jimmy was the first baby to be born in Colorado. Then she got her tubes tied finally, because, according to the doctor, having any more children would kill her. Instead of the normal horizontal cut they had to cut her in a vertical fashion from sternum to vagina. That was a blessing in itself for her. My dad did not believe in contraceptives because of his misconceptions of the Catholic church and he was a religious fanatic. Actually, he was a hypocrite. After mom brought Jimmy home she breast fed him then gave him to me to watch and bathe and put him to bed daily. She was very tired now and needed her sleep. I tried to keep the house clean and watch over the children and keep things running while she healed up. Meanwhile, dad still went to work rotating shifts and was mean as can be but I just ignored his threats and did everything possible to keep him at bay. Until one day about two months later he came in the door and I think he had drank too much of his product that he makes at work and came blasting in the door and was ready for a fight. I was right there and seen his fury roar up as usual. Mom was in the kitchen making dinner when he decided to pick a fight with her. I screamed at dad; "What are you doing mom is healing up leave her alone her stitches are not healed yet". Dad suddenly turned toward me and I could tell that he didn't like me to interfere while he was arguing with my mom. I sort of felt relieved that his attention shifted from mom to me because I could out run him and mom could not, I teased him for a while until he got tired and he decided that he would rather sit down as opposed to chasing me around the house. I just stayed out of his way until he got drunk and went to bed before I had my dinner. The next day things went back to normal for a while, But dad was still beating up the kids including me, on a daily basis for anything that upset him. Then one day he bought a Doberman pinscher dog and aside from having his ears clipped and tail chopped, he did everything he could to abuse the dog and make him mean and vicious. He kept him locked up outside in a wire kennel. I felt sorry for the dog. I remember him bringing home saw meat for me to cook in a pan and mixing it with his dog food every night and taking it out to Blue and giving him fresh water. But the boys teased him and made him mean. Soon the dog was exactly what dad wanted and was definitely not a family dog, especially for children. At the time, we lived up in the mountains at about 10,000 feet we lived in a beautiful log cabin with a rental house on about three acres. Dad had the house sand blasted to take off all the yellow and green paint from the previous owners and put it back into its original log cabin beauty then had it shellacked. It was amazing to look at when completed. After a while, dad decided that he wanted to get closer to work so it was time to move. We found a nice little trailer in Blue Vista and went to school from there. It was a cramped little trailer, an airstream very tight for seven kids, but we managed. Then from there we went to another trailer park this time in Parkridge. The trailer was bigger and furnished while dad and mom were still looking for a place for us to live.

The boys were everywhere running wild you could say I just had to remind them to be home before dad came back because you know how he can be. As usual dad would come home and if chores were not done, beatings were dished out. Charlie hated this but I tried to warn him and he just would not listen.

After a few more moves our family finally moved up to the farm. Jimmy at the time was still breast feeding and still very young. We had a small mobile home with no running water, electricity, no bathroom facilities. We lived off of a lantern and I hauled in water by the bucket on foot from the adjacent farm which was operated by a hand pump from the well. Usually two five gallon jugs at a time. Jimmy really looked up to my father and really soaked up everything he said. But still when my father would dish out the beatings Jimmy thought he deserved it and he was happy dad was strict with him because he thought it would make him a better person for it. What he didn't realize is that it was hurting his mind all the yelling and screaming, hitting of people it's just crazy. My father would literally beat the shit out of Charlie and Tim and Jimmy thought this was normal and just what boys needed. But he was wrong. Dad was nuts It's just down right insane to keep treating your own children worse than a pack of wild and crazed animals. My father needed mental counseling and nothing less than long term. I'm talking a minimum of at least 5 years of supervised intense one- on- one counseling I would even consider jail time if counseling didn't work. I personally recommend jail time and here's why: He would throw those boys around like they were rag dolls with his hands. Grab them by the throat slam them against the wall, pick them up then hit them again, and again, and again with his fist until they would practically start coughing and crying and screaming in pain. Then I would stand in and say Hey; "That's enough man you've proven your point". Then he would usually come after me with the usual, "You mother Fucken Bitch are you telling me again how to correct my fuckin kids". I responded; "No Dad I just don't want you to kill them". Then he tried to run after me but I was too fast for him now so I just ran away". I would come back later on when he went to work, he was really a bastard. I hated that man. At least he stopped hitting the boys for a while. He was a monster from hell. The next day he reminded me about staying out of his affairs or next time he will kill me, understand. I just shook my head yes but I really meant nothing by it. This was what Jimmy's life was like until the courts intervened when he was in his early teens and he was at school and found bruises on his body and took Jimmy away and assigned him to foster care. To me Jimmy was a naïve kid and a slow learner. I say this because he looked up to my dad and praised him for being tough on him because he felt that it taught him a lot about the world. What he didn't realize however, was that the world is not as cruel and as mean as dad taught him. It could be a beautiful place if you perceived it with a clear and unobstructed mind.

NOTE: **Jimmy had no idea when he was a baby that the lack of indecision by his father and his unwillingness to help transport him to the hospital when he was a baby and running a very high fever, would leave him sterile for the rest of his life and he would never be able to have any children of his own. My-self and my mother knew about this, but my mother had forgotten about it over the years and Jimmy didn't know anything about it at all and it was held as a secret from Jimmy until he was about 44 years old. At this point, Jimmy had been married and divorced two times and I'm sure that the question about children had probably come up so I wanted to make sure that Jimmy was aware of his sterility situation so I decided to tell him. Unfortunately, he was living with his father when I did. He received the news gracefully and several days later, he left my dad's place and I haven't seen or heard from him since.**

REMEMBER ROBERT ONLY THE STRONG SURVIVE

ROBERT WAS THE FIRST born child of my family. Robert was named after his father. His father always expected too much from him because he gave him overwhelming responsibilities and he was punished severely when he couldn't live up to his father's standards and especially when my brother couldn't understand my father's distorted ways of reasoning. During his adolescence years, Robert was an altar boy and became interested in baseball. In fact, he won several awards for home runs in baseball. Robert truly was mom and dad's favorite child because I can remember one Christmas when Robert got a bicycle with a steering wheel, a long sissy bar, and the bike was metallic blue and had all the latest upgrades. Then he received a brand new watch all of which, dad filmed on his camera. Yes, Robert had it all and nothing but the best for his number one son. I felt left out. Come to think of it, that was the same bike I rode on the back of one summer when Robert popped a wheelie and I fell backwards and hit my head on one of those many brick walls that they have in California and split the back of my head open. Then my brother had to drive me home on his bicycle so mom could drive me to the hospital to get stitched up. Yes, all there is in California is brick walls everywhere we used to call it; "cement heaven". Then all of a sudden things came to a sudden halt probably because of my molestation and Robert lost interest in everything. When my dad found out about the Molestation he immediately beat Robert and my mother half way to death why, I do not know. Then the next day I was removed from my grandfather's house never to return. Robert grew up with heavy weights on his shoulders day in and day out every day. He was responsible for all of us kids and our whereabouts all the time. He was a nervous wreck and all he could think about was how to escape the household. He used to tell me;" I can't wait until I graduate from high school so I can get a job and get out of here". He graduated at age 15 ½ with straight A's and he graduated early, he took all the hardest courses in High School: Chemistry, Physics, Trigonometry, Latin, etc. and he graduated in April to go to work at a fancy restaurant in town. The family moved a couple more times before finally settling in Colorado. When the family first moved up to the farm, Robert myself and all the other siblings worked the farm to clear out all the weeds from the fields that was the year we all practically starved to death and there are pictures of this somewhere to prove it. Dad, of course was immune to this because of his employment at the brewery, he never starved, but he never brought anything home extra for the kids. Anyways, at night my brother Robert and I would get into the VW and listen to the oldies to relieve the tension and stress with a soothing backdrop of the trickling running water of the ditch behind us. The continuous flow of the icy cold water created its own refreshing cool breeze. The following year Robert found a job at the processing plant in the freezer department packaging cold foods. It was hard work but, it was a job. He worked there for a little over a year. Then my father managed to get him on in the brewery in Colorado. While he was working in the processing plant he was staying in the trailer with no running water, no electricity, and no heat. It was very uncomfortable for all of us. We all slept on the floor and the kids and I brought in the water by hand by the buckets from a neighboring farm nearby. The lanterns provided the light and we used wood for our pot belly stove in the kitchen. Dad constantly confided in Robert for everything and it seemed like every time I would try to listen in dad would just shut me out and tell me to go away were talking and the place was usually behind the trailer somewhere behind the trailer in a secluded spot. I always just shook my head and thought to myself someday this will backfire in his face. Dad's outbursts were getting worse and his drinking was definitely getting more and more noticeable. Then when he fell off the tractor and fractured his ankle and injured his back they put him on valium and Vicodin and his beer drinking made for a horrible combination. I know the pain was excruciating but putting up with him was worse. Robert just kept going to work night and day. After Robert left the processing plant, he sold his old Impala car and traded for a yellow Hornet three on the tree and I swear that car could get him to and from the brewery on just a few DOLLARS worth of gas and back in those days that was a great savings. The car had a great engine too and never failed him. What a great car. It had a green interior. That car was really fast too. It was just what the Doctor ordered you could say. Robert was now working rotating shifts and that was really hard to adjust to and so he needed a car he could rely on and he had it. Things were going along just fine dad being his usual self, Robert trying to sleep in the back room and myself still in school. Robert did these rotating shifts for about eight months until he could afford a new car. His credit was great and he pulls up the drive way on the farm in his new Camaro. The whole family was shocked to see how pretty it was and how expensive it was. But, hard work brings nice stuff dad says. So, enjoy but be careful it's a fast car. Nice work son. Robert was proud that day you could see it on his face to hear those words come out of dad's mouth. With dad patting him on the shoulders and saying; "Good job, good job". So after my brother received his pat on the back he went in the trailer and went to bed. I wondered today if dad realized that if given the same opportunity as Robert, did he know that all of his kids could reach their own high potential or did he even care. Robert continued on his rotating shifts at the brewery until he became too tired to drive home one night and hit the guard rail on the interstate because the car was very quiet inside and he said he put it on cruise control and went fast asleep the car then went out of control and rolled onto the interstate fortunately it had a roll bar inside the car and saved his life the car was totaled. Robert woke up but it was too late to correct the damage and he had the car towed to a garage to have it fixed up with his full coverage insurance. He had a rental car in the meantime. He walked away without a scratch. It was the first time Camaro decided to install roll bars in their Camaro cars. Robert wasn't happy with the job they did on the car and would never be happy simply because it had been in an accident. Robert was way too particular and was just like my father nothing would satisfy him now that the car had been in a wreck and that was that in his mind. After the car was fixed he brought it home to the farm and it was perfect. But Robert was not satisfied, he said;" I'm going to sell this car and use it for a down payment on my first home it will be closer to work so I do not have to drive so far any more I think that's the problem. So, Robert finally left the trailer and went and purchased his own small home close to work and got an old truck to drive to work. Things seemed to work out better for him now. His drive was only maybe six minutes to work and he could concentrate on fixing up his new little home which he did. He put on a little deck on the back of his house, and really fixed the place up real nice. He seemed very happy now that he could take showers regularly, go to and from work without any trouble, and was more relaxed. He was away from the family now and was trying to forget his past, but bad memories of dad and mom and what they had done to us kids unfortunately, you really do take it with you and he was really affected from my father he had a lot of his traits deep down and did not know it. He carried the baggage around with him inside his mind and other people noticed his mannerisms for example: His handshake was a bit on the feminine side, and my husband made the comment that shaking his hand was like holding a; "wet noodle". He spoke in a very soft and low voice. He had no sense of humor whatsoever. He couldn't accept criticism at all. He was very short tempered. Robert was married twice. The first time to a woman who claimed she was pregnant with his child so he married her. Then five years later the baby did not look like him so he did a paternity test and it was ruled that the baby belonged to someone else. But Robert kept the baby as his own because she was pregnant with his baby now and would try to make the marriage work if at all possible. Robert's wife had one more son and this one was his. Everything seemed to be working out well for a while then Robert found out that his wife had been doing drugs and sent her to rehab but this did not work out so his marriage ended in divorce. That's when my mom stepped in to live with him to watch the kids full-time and clean his house plus she could live there rent free and work too. Robert stayed single for years until the kids grew up then Robert finally remarried again and has been happily married ever since as far as I know. He's been married about eight years now. A lesson he learned from my mother is her love for money. When mom moved in Robert and mother started talking about how to finagle money from dad. Robert and mom developed a plan to divorce my dad after forty- two years of marriage and force the sale of the farm and split the proceedings between my dad and my mom. Of course Robert found a way to make himself the POA for mother so that when checks were handed out he would gain a large portion of the profits. Then he promised her he would give her the house after she turned over the check. This was a promise he did not plan to keep. Shortly after the divorce was finalized, Robert kept all the money paid off all his bills including his truck his house and all his credit cards. The rest was deposited in the bank. Dad took his check and left. Robert was not going to give my mother nothing until I called and said; "Robert that's against the law you can't do that there's a penal code against that stuff you are doing and its adult financial abuse, I will report you". As soon as Robert heard this he immediately made efforts to improve his mother's financial situation and living conditions by putting a down payment on a Hud home in Sun Valley Ranch. This didn't satisfy all his monetary obligations to his mother. This move only served to help my brother Robert because my mother could not afford to make the house payments. But it did release his house so he could sell it with no problems from my mother or my sister Marsha. Marsha has always been with my mother to the point that she could be considered as a thorn in her side. She takes advantage of my mother's kindness and she hardly ever works and she uses my mother's social security funds to feed her alcohol and drug problems. My mother was finally forced to sell the house at a loss and she had to liquidate all her furnishings at a garage sale and to my surprise Marsha sold all her kid's toys at the garage sale which she stole from her own kids. After the sale was final, mom and Marsha wanted to move back in to Robert's house but Robert would not accept them as long as Marsha was there. So my mom had to move back into an apartment again with Marsha and of course Marsha picked an expensive apartment to rent, well it was more rent than mom could afford to pay on her meager social security income. Meanwhile, Robert sold his home and threw Marsha and my mother's stuff in the street. They had to go get their stuff out of the driveway and the front lawn. Robert was totally exhausted with Marsha's antics and he felt sorry for my mother but he knew that my mother would not do anything to keep Marsha from taking advantage of the situation so he had no choice but to throw both Marsha and his mother out of the house and he knew that any help extended to his mother would end up in Marsha's hands. It was cruel but he felt it was his only option. Robert finally sold the house for about 400% of what he paid for it. Upon the sale of his home he gave my mother $400.00 dollars and to this day he still owes her quite a large sum of money which I'm sure he will take with him to his grave. Robert currently lives in Colorado one of the most exclusive spots in Colorado and still to this day works at the brewery. I haven't heard or seen my brother in years. The last time I seen him was at my son's funeral with his now current wife. I also heard that his current wife did win the lottery some time ago and it was around six million dollars and she won this money before she met my brother. She has no children of her own that I know of.

NOTE: **It's a sad thing to see what a dysfunctional environment can do to people. My internal family had 6 siblings and the effect was totally different on each and every one of us. My brother Robert could have accomplished great things, he is an absolute genius. His ability for learning complex subjects and systems is absolutely phenomenal, but my father and mother never took**

the time or effort in any of the children to develop any of their potential. What a waste. If we are to improve or make the world a better place to live, we must look toward each other and try to define what their talents are and how we can combine our efforts along with theirs to develop new and higher plateaus never even dreamed of into reality.

MY MOTHER'S SENSIBILITIES WERE COMPROMISED BECAUSE OF GREED AND HER LUST FOR GOOD LOOKS.

I FOUND MY MOTHER's old yearbook from high school and discovered that she had met my father when she was in her sophomore year in high school and he was a senior. He even signed her year book saying; "Love Forever Your Husband ". Then he placed a heart with an arrow going through it in her picture then he signed his name. I do know that she went to school until she was seventeen then she dropped out. After my dad completed high school he went on to college and completed two years of mechanical engineering programs but he still wanted to marry my mom who was in her junior year in high school. He talked her into leaving high school early to get married. She went back later to earn her GED. My dad was nineteen and my mother was seventeen they got married on July 5th 1957 and had Robert Jr. in April 1958 of the next year. My dad worked as a Chef for about 4 years during the day and attending class at night in pursuit of a degree in mechanical engineering. After earning his degree, he worked for his father's dump truck company until he could secure his job at California Envelope where he used his degree in mechanical engineering. This was his first big step to his future. This was where he bought his first house in California. But before that we lived in an old house off Pike road. Mom said it was a very small house, it had two small bedrooms, one small bathroom, a very small kitchen one small living room, it was about 800 square feet and was located off a major highway. Mom shared this small story with me one day at the table and I never forgot it. Little Robert Jr. was maybe, twenty months old and was outside with my mother hanging clothes on the clothes line with clothes pins with me inside the small house sleeping in my playpen I was just a few months old when little Robert came in to check on me he went out to tell mommy;" baby tying, baby tying mommy". My mom instantly went in to check on me and said, "No Robert she fell back asleep, now let's go finish the clothes and come back inside to watch Casper the friendly Ghost". So they finished their chores and went back in because it was too hot outdoors in California and mom had no air conditioning, but she did have a good fan and there was a nice breeze that day. The house was situated off a major highway and the traffic was horrible so the noise was constant. My mom had to turn the T.V. all the way up to hear it. Then all of a sudden a large gas truck came right through the house and it was full of gas. It actually ripped the house in half. My mom and Robert Jr. were on the couch and the truck just missed them, and it separated my bedroom from the rest of the house. Then all of a sudden we heard a man outside the house with a loudspeaker yelling; "Get out of the house it's going to blow". My mother ran out of the house with little Robert Jr. in her arms but needed to go back in for me. The police and fireman were all there but restrained my mom from going back in and she some-how broke free and went back into the house which was soaked in gas and all she had on her feet was a flimsy pair of rubber thongs. She went in through the window, and got me out of the play pen. The gas had not reached me yet, and I was still sound asleep as she picked me up carefully she climbed out the window and got help I assume from the fire fighters and made it to safety. Wow, I came close that day to death as I did most of my life. Here I was just a few months old. After that, my parents had to move, I think it was to the new house on Hobart Street. This is where dad had his new job and his new life would start. I think mom said;

dad came home from work because he heard about it on the news. There were helicopters and policemen and firemen and news people there and everywhere putting my mom and me and my brother on the nightly news I think she said. So, Dad came home and put us in the car after answering a few questions to the news people, and took us over to his mom and Dad's house to live for a while until we could get our new home on Hobart Street. I think she said, his father gave him some money for a down payment on the house and dad had to pay him back. But, Dad was working for his dad anyway so, it worked out great. Then my dad used his degree later on, to get his job at California Envelope as a machine technician. To the best of my recollection the information just stated in the previous sentence is true. My mom and dad soon got tired of living with his parents so because there was no privacy and too cramped for space. Together, him and his father were complete gentlemen but as a little girl, I knew what they were really like when they were separated and alone. My father wanted out of his dad's house and the only way out was to ask for a loan to buy a new home for him and his family and that he would pay his father back with interest as soon as he could. So, his dad gave him some money for a down payment to purchase the home on Hobart Street and we finally moved out of his parent's house. Mom said; we lived with his mom and dad for about three or maybe even six months, I'm not exactly sure here.(Please don't take this as fact this is taken from my young childhood memory.) So mom and dad packed up whatever stuff we had at his parent's house, which wasn't much, and put it into the 57 Chevy and we were off to our brand new home in California. We were all excited and looking forward to the move. I think my mom was pregnant again with my brother Charlie that's another reason why we had to get out of his parent's house too. Charlie would be born in March of the next year so we had to move fast to get the house furnished to get ready for the new baby. Meanwhile, dad went out to look for a good job with his certificate, and found a job at California Envelope down in San Bernardino. They offered him a machine technician job and gave him his own machine to work on to make it faster and a full benefits package for his family plus bonuses depending on his work performance and other perks available to him which he would find out about later on. He was very happy. Mom and dad were very busy, dad was working at California Envelope now, and mom was pregnant with Charlie and cleaning house and trying to keep up with me and my brother Robert Jr. it was a lot of work for her but she was young and very energetic. She made friends with the lady next door her name was Suzie and she had four kids of her own. They became close friends and when mom needed something she always could count on Suzie. Mom told me that one day when she was out in the garage washing clothes at the time she used PUREX bleach which came in glass bottles to help clean the clothes. Well she kept the glass bottles underneath the kitchen sink to save them and give them back for recycling. Then one day, little Robert Jr. reached underneath the sink and picked up one of those bottles for his mommy to give back to the store and when he was on his way out the door into the garage he slipped and fell and landed with the full weight of his head onto the PUREX bottle on his face and split his right cheek from the bridge of his nose all the way to the bottom of his right cheek extending down to his right lip. But because of the competence of the surgical team in California, the scaring was minimal. The hospital had to report this to the product safety board and let PUREX Corporation know that their bottles have severely injured a child's face. Mom found out in the later weeks to come, that PUREX had changed their bottles to plastic and also introduced boxes to hold a newly introduced version of PUREX in a powder form. Most of the relationships that I can remember between my mom and dad were fraught with bad feelings and memories, but I'm sure there were instances which convinced my mother that this marriage and the man that she married could only be found in those beloved mid evil Fairy tales. For example: I remember one night, in particular they were getting ready to go out on a date with his best friend Tom Smith and his wife from California Envelope and dad was so happy he told my mom to hurry up so they wouldn't be late. My mom was very happy she had been setting her hair all day long. Mom started out very early in the morning by first washing her hair then she used bobby pins to make pin curls all over her head because in her young days hot rollers or irons were not available. So by the end of the day, her hair was ready and fully dry and her curls were beautiful. All she had to do was to get dressed she bathed earlier too. I wanted to watch so I asked mom if it was ok and she said yes but not to get in the way. She was so busy. Dad was shaving, then he jumped in the shower, I wasn't in there for that part, I was with mom in the bedroom helping with her hair taking out all those bobby pins for this Sunday's mass. She looked beautiful even before she brushed it out. She then put on her under clothes and nylons and that red dress, boy I will never forget that red dress and black high heels she was a Marilyn Monroe with auburn hair. Dad was a knock out too he would put on that after shave old spice and then wax his jet black hair back with one curl down the front of his forehead. Mom thought he was very handsome and that he reminded her of the FONZ he really cleaned up nice. He smoked Pall Mall reds and he had pearly white teeth. They looked like the perfect couple to look at them it's just a shame that they did not belong together, because together, it was like mixing oil and water. I can always remember as a little girl waking up the next morning to mom fixing breakfast for all the kids very early in the morning because it was Saturday and dad was home usually so he would be working outdoors fixing up the house or cleaning up around the front yard or back yard. He was always busy doing something. Mom was always busy inside cleaning or cooking or taking care of one of the kids with me as far as mom and dad's work was concerned their paths never crossed. Dad's work for example: was an extremely unique design of which brought together beautiful artistic displays of artistic embellishment created from rock, cement, mortar and beautiful floral arrangements and together they completed projects that were born to compliment and improve the natural beauty of nature itself. My mother did not possess the inherent skills necessary to contribute to this type of project and in turn my father did not have the skills required to help my mother in her world. It was a tedious job every day non-stop it seemed like. It would wear mom down and at times she just wanted to sit down and watch T.V. like bewitched, or something to take her mind off of the kids for just a moment, because it was a hard, hard job, I know this because I was there with her all the time. I could see how dad's beatings and his temper and her being kept pregnant all the time started to wear her down. I can remember when she was pregnant with her sixth child Lilly she told me; "Emily I really Didn't want this baby, but it's too late now, I can't turn the clock back, but if I could, I would have never gotten pregnant again. I'm so tired of being pregnant it's just killing me all these kids I really don't know how I am going to take care of all these kids with this man I am married to". This of course was at a time when she was again separated from dad because he again beat her up so we had to leave the house and she went over to her family's house and her mother then became violent and threw a shoe at her stomach when she was sleeping and tried to kill Lilly before she was even born, but mom had a small wiener dog named Gretta Von Curry with her and the dog attacked grandma and mom's dad took us up to Big Bear for the weekend to get away from grandma. You see, grandma was an alcoholic and when she gets drunk, she can't remember things or what she does and she did this to my mother and my mom never forgot this and hated her mother for it forever. My mom also said that her mom never really liked her she liked her sister Sandy better she never knew why but she said her mom always favored Sandy over her and Sandy's kids. After we left Big Bear, we came back home again as usual, mom was still pregnant and all us kids went back to school dad went back into his routine and tried not to hit mom for a while. Mom really had a hard time with this pregnancy she got really big and the baby was quite large too, Lilly weighed in at over ten pounds. Tim was born on her birthday he too was over ten pounds. My mom suffered postpartum depression after she had Lilly but she did breast feed her and that helped, but with my dad being so mean all the time it really affected my mom you could now see some serious changes in her, for example: she was very quiet at times and would not respond to questions when asked, she would just sit there in silence and stare out the window for long periods of time until you talked to her, she would just look down with sadness with a look of despair. She knew that the rest of her life with this ugly monster of a man was going to be a daily nightmare with no chance of escaping his physical presence but sometimes I wonder if this is what she really wanted because even at my young age, I've heard that there are people who actually enjoy being hit and I still wonder to this day whether or not my mother was one of those individuals. I say this because she even tried to pick a fight with my current husband Tim and Tim is not a violent person. It was questionable as to whether or not mom could have a normal childbirth for her seventh and last child. My mother was in labor for three days and almost died, so the doctors finally took the baby by C-section and saved my mom and the baby's life. Dad was present in the labor room with the physician and wanted mom to keep pushing in fact, he voiced it out loud; "keep pushing Katy, keep pushing". The Physician said to my father;" The only help your providing here sir is to help kill your wife and child you are going to have to leave the operating room I have to perform a C-section to save both of their lives and by the way, I am going to have to tie your wife's tubes so she will no longer be able to have any more children because giving birth to any more children will surely kill her". The Doctor then proceeded to have my father removed from the delivery room. Good thing too, because my mom and my brother almost died, they were just moments away from death she said as she passed into the ER that night. She was in labor for over 72 hours. Meanwhile, the kids and I were at home waiting for the phone to ring for some news about mom and I was beginning to get a little nervous waiting and wondering why it was taking so long for her to have the baby. I knew something was horribly wrong and could feel mom was in trouble. Then finally the phone rang, it was dad he sounded tired and weak as he slowly said ;" Your mom is in surgery right now, she had to have a C-section in order to have Jimmy, she just could not have him naturally. She should be out soon, she will probably be in the hospital for three more days healing up then her and the baby will be home. I will be back tonight to check on you guys." I responded;" ok, everything is going fine here for now, so don't worry about the kids Robert and I are taking care of things just fine". I remember when they drove up to the house with Jimmy, Mom looked very tired and worn out, and Dad looked very tired too, but happy to be home finally. Mom could hardly walk and could not carry the baby, so I took Jimmy from her, Dad helped her to bed. I rocked Jimmy to sleep. Then put Jimmy in bed next to mom so she could breast feed him. Mom was totally incapacitated for most of the year. This was the year that my mother asked me to stay out of school to help her out with the kids and the house work I was 12 years old and was really excited to start high school, but I knew my brother was into sports and he wouldn't help. As far as my brothers were concerned, they were hardly ever home it seemed like they were at a friend's house, or attending a sports event. I literally stayed home and took care of Jimmy and Lilly and helped with all the cooking and cleaning and laundry and dealt with dad's tyrant outbursts. Then there was this one time in particular that I will never forget; when he came home and he was totally drunk, and decided to go on one of his drunken rampages, he came home shortly after we had been baking fresh Rhubarb and strawberry pies from our own home grown garden we had just finished putting the pies out on the balcony outside and from experience we knew just how delicious they were. Then suddenly, dad came storming threw the door from work. I guess he was mad about something, and I am not sure what it was, but he came up those steps and in a fit of a rage he came at my mother and started screaming at her and yelling at her and I intervened and he just pushed me out of the way and went for my mom with a vengeance, he caught her by surprise and she lost her balance and fell back a little then he took the kitchen table and shoved it into my mother's stomach with enough force to pop her stitches and she was left with her intestines hanging out. She was frantically screaming and yelling in fright while trying to hold her intestines in; "Emily quick get a cold wet towel so I don't bleed to death, out of the hall closet fast, run, run, fast go". So I ran and I tripped over the baby gate for the first time breaking my baby toe limping to the closet and soaking the towel in cold water and bringing it to my mother. I carefully wrapped the towel around my mom's stomach real tight and told her to be real calm and helped her to the old truck outside. I gently helped her get up into the truck and told dad to get her to the nearest ER because this was very serious and she needed help now. Then I told my father to take her to the ER immediately before she bleeds to death. I would stay here with the kids and try to make do until he returns. As soon as dad left with mom, the baby started to cry because he was hungry. So I warmed up some milk and added some sugar to it and sterilized a glass bottle and nipple and fed him, changed his diaper and clothing and rocked him to sleep. Then I went ahead and made dinner for my other siblings. After dinner everyone watched T.V. before going to bed. I really did a lot of work every day and night around the house, in fact I was completely worn out before I went to bed at night. Then on top of everything else, at night my sister Marsha and I slept in the room of a man or boy that was killed just down the mountain from his home. He was killed accidentally by a huge rock that had fell on top of his car as he was traveling up the mountain from his overnight shift at the brewery. He was only 22 years old. His spirit decided to come home to live and this house is where he stays. I'm not a real believer in the supernatural, but while living in this house I had several experiences that have left me to question my beliefs for example, on one occasion, when my mother was pregnant, she claimed that someone pushed her down the stairs, but there was no one there, there were cold spots in certain areas of the house, a physical presence could actually be felt in certain areas of the house, I clearly saw him one morning, I saw the color of his hair, his skin, his clothing, his physical features, etc. I told my parents and my dad called the previous owners of the house and invited them over. My dad didn't tell me about the meeting but, when they arrived, my dad welcomed them and invited them in and said "welcome, my daughter Emily has something to tell you". I was totally surprised but was asked to describe who I saw to the boy's parents and after I described them, they became very saddened and emotional and they both began to cry and explained that I was describing their son. My dad was extremely upset and mad that their son's death was not disclosed. So our family had to put up with their son's antics every night until the house sold and this wasn't fun at all, it was very annoying to say the least.

Mom finally came home from the hospital and was doing much better now. This time the hospital put in staples and they were much more permanent. All of us kids welcomed her home and dad remained very quiet because he knew this was his fault and I think he knew he had over stepped his bounds. All the kids knew what he did because I had told them and I felt they needed to know what kind of man their father was. But I'm sure they already knew through their own experiences but I just wanted to make sure that they would never ever forget this incident. It didn't take too long for dad to forget because soon after he was beating the kids, as well as, me and my mother again. His police record was getting longer and longer but still my mother failed to press charges to put him in prison. She kept going back to the same old excuse, "The farm the farm, we have to save the farm". My mother was becoming very greedy and to her the farm was just a means for her to make money.

<u>NOTE</u>: **My mother is a very complex person. My mother can be a very loving person, but only when she chooses to be and only on a selective basis. My mother seems to play favorites, but again I feel that this depends on how she feels or how she interacts internally. I believe that my mother has more than one personality and I have been introduced to several different versions of my mother. First and foremost there is the masochist. No matter how many times my mother gets beat from my monster of a father, she keeps going back for more. My mother is also a very loving person and protective of her children, My mother didn't really raise her own kids that job was given to me and various foster homes, but mom did try, but she just didn't have the skills or the support from her maniac husband. As mom grew older, she seemed to become greedier as time went by and soon her and my oldest brother Robert developed a plan to liquidate the family holdings so that the two of them could reap most of the financial rewards. The rest of the family would not benefit.**

THE UGLIEST MAN I KNOW

WHEN MY FATHER FIRST saw my mother in 1956 he signed her yearbook, Love Forever your husband, then he signed his name and placed a heart next to her face and she was only in her sophomore year in high school getting ready for her junior year the following year. I guess my mom must have met my father earlier in the year because of the way he signed her year book. They married in July 1957. I don't know if mom knew too much about the monster that she just married, but unfortunately she was soon going to find out. My mom seemed to just tolerate the first few beatings and prayed that he would snap out of it shortly but, the beatings only became more frequent and more severe and dad was starting to enjoying them more as the kids were born. Now he had more people to beat on and mom never pressed charges. But she did leave him once or twice but she would return and each time she came back, my dad would be more bitter because she left him and his beatings of her and us kids just kept getting worse and more terrifying. He would always remind her of how she left him and he would sarcastically ask her, "when was she going to do it again"? I can remember like on a Sunday right before church he would say again sarcastically;" So Katy, when do you plan on leaving me again? Maybe after church, bitch". Mom just looked at him with disgust because she knew he was just trying to pick a fight with her again right in front of the children before church. Mom just walked away. Then when we got home mom brought in the groceries from the dairy and he always made fun of her for buying cinnamon rolls for the kids, herself and him. Mom thought they were delicious heated up in the oven with butter on them and the kids loved them. But dad always said; "Katy you're going to die with a cinnamon roll or a cake, or a pie on your grave do you know it, that's the way they will bury you mother fucker". Then sometimes he would actually get up rip open the package and shove one of them down her throat. He was awful. The one thing he did know how to do was work, and that was when we had some peace. Growing up around my father was like walking on eggs all the time. You never knew when he was going to crack. Even in conversations with him you had to watch everything you said to him. I can still remember all those beatings in the garage with my brothers and how they felt and how he tortured us. I can also remember how on Sunday evenings all of us kids were assigned spots on the floor in the living room in front of the T.V. and how each of us kids had to sit in our spots, as assigned by him in order to watch T.V. Before we could even watch T.V., We all had chores to complete before we were even allowed the luxury of watching T.V. with him. My job was to get the kitchen spotlessly clean plus wax all the cupboards, and buff the floor. Then he had to approve all the completed jobs to see if they met with his approval, if they did, you were allowed to watch T.V., if you failed his scrutiny, you were required to re-do the job until he was satisfied. There were times, however, when I simply just could not satisfy him and I missed my program, but I soon learned what he expected and I was able to complete my tasks a lot easier.

When my father found out about the Molestation committed by his father against me, he immediately confronted his father and words were exchanged, I am not sure what was said, but I would be willing to bet that the entire issue was settled with some amount of money being offered to my father for appeasement. After the issue was settled, we went home and my dad beat up my mom and my brother half way to death, why I don't know. This made no sense to me, but maybe my father, in his warped sense of reasoning, was trying to warn them to keep this incident a secret. The molestation incident combined with the big earthquake that we experienced sometime during 1972, convinced my father to sell the house and move. He just ripped us away from all of his family members and my mom's family member's and everyone else that we grew up with. Needless to say, all of us kids were scared to death, we had no idea what was happening or where we were going and unlike other families the excitement of a family outing was just not there with our family. This was a nightmare. He was horrible to travel with, he was very mean, he beat the kids and he didn't really have a clue as to where he was going with six kids and a one man pup tent. He just kept drinking beer from his favorite brewery and after one year of traveling on the road with this maniac he had finally had enough. He said; "Let's go to the local brewery I will try to get a job at the brewery after all I was born in Colorado this is where we should settle down". The family went to Colorado and sat by a stream while dad filled out his application for a job at the brewery he loved. Dad did get hired at that brewery so the family moved to a little trailer park in Colorado and moved into a very small one to two person Air Stream trailer because that's all they had available. So we rented it. We had all six kids at the time. Our living quarters were very cramped and uncomfortable but we just had to make the best of it. Our family moved around several times before mom and dad finally found their dream, "The Farm". This is where the family's nightmares really started to become a reality. It almost seems like yesterday I can still remember driving up that old dirt road with all seven kids cramped into the VW with mom driving and all of us looking in disbelief at that old dilapidated trailer at the top of the hill as we drove closer over the bridge we passed an old pump house and for the first time in my life, I believe that me and my siblings were all in total shock to realize that this would be our new home for the next three to four years with no water, electricity, no lights, no bathroom facilities. We had no idea what we were up against, only that this was our new home and we were forced to unpack the car. We all received the talk from mom and dad and knew that we were pretty much screwed we also knew that this was going to be hell and a lot of hard work with a man that was a monster and that made things even worse. My father was a hideous sadistic person that put all of us kids including my mother through hell each and every day of our lives. He enjoyed punishing or hurting someone for just the most insignificant things. He hardly ever smiled, and when he did it was usually to a stranger in a conversation between himself and the stranger. Most of the time you could find him with a mean look on his face looking or staring out into space thinking about what he needed to do next and always contemplating his next move. That was the scary part of my father you never knew what he was going to do next. You never knew if he was mad or not mad or what he could possibly be thinking. It was pretty scary. Living on the farm was real hard and a lot of work for all the family and with a father like this, it was almost impossible to try to deal with his moods and out-bursts on a daily basis. But somehow we survived to pull through all his hatred, beatings, and starvation, and bad living conditions. One of the saddest things is that none of the kids came through this ordeal unscathed, we all suffered some sort of mental impairment from him in one form or another. Yes, he managed to cripple all of us including my mother if she already wasn't mentally fragile before she met him he only made it worse. This man did quite a bit of damage to our family and never went to prison for it and was never charged with anything because my mother never pressed charges on him. I personally have to live with these memories each and every day and I can see how it has affected my other siblings as I have spoken about earlier in the book. All seven children especially Charlie who was put out of the house at gun point nearly 37 years ago and who received some sort of a spinal injury from all the brutal beatings. If you were to ask my mother or father today about Charlie they would both tell you; "I'm glad he's gone I hated him". Now why would a parent, any parent say that about their own child? Charlie was not a bad kid, yes he got into mischief just like any other boy but he was a kid, he needed extra attention. I know this because I was there. What my mom and dad did was focus all their anger and hatred on him for years and years until they actually convinced themselves that Charlie was the devil child and he was not, he was my brother. He was just an ordinary kid who was begging for love and attention. The poor kid received extreme hate instead, both mental and physical. My mom colluded with my dad to get rid of my brother and they were successful, I have not seen or heard from my brother since, he was forced out at gunpoint by my dad while my mom turned her back and looked the other way. I'll never forget the sad look in my brother's eyes as he held back the tears.

One of things that I truly despise about both my father and my mother is how they could hate so easily and treat family members so bad and show absolutely no remorse whatsoever. And you never knew how they felt about you. Did they love you? Did they hate you? Everything mom and dad did between them, including all decisions and plans and strategies was kept secret between them and soon the children learned to keep secrets. Sometimes keeping secrets cannot be avoided, especially when the secret is designed to protect someone, but children of a young age must be taught when secrets are appropriate. My parents didn't have a clue what the difference between right or wrong really was. Greed was the driving force behind their existence.

NOTE: I wish I knew what a real childhood feels like. I envy those who have had the opportunity and chance to live and experience the most exciting times of their lives. I know that something very beautiful was stolen from me and I can never get it back, but maybe by sharing my life with others, I can reach others who are suffering as I did and maybe shed A little light on their world. Above all, you must never be so fearful of those that abuse you that it forces you into a prison in your mind and one who is too scared and fearful to tell your story to others. Just be careful who you tell your story to. My mother and father were not good parents in fact they should never have had any children at all. As presented earlier in this book, my father could not even care for dogs. In fact, if you ever met my father, you would see that he can't even care for himself.

MEMORIES

As I TRY TO evaluate my own life and associate my childhood experiences with my family, especially my father and to a lesser degree my mother, and how it has contributed to my development, I find that I can't walk this path alone. This is my story and how I reached out for help and of those who answered my cry for help and walked my path with me.

My earliest recollection of life began when I was about 18 months old and I can remember I was always seeking attention from my mom, but after she became pregnant with her third child and with all her housework, not to mention the constant beatings she endured from my father, she just didn't have the time for me. To gain attention, I use to bang my head on the floor until my forehead was swollen and bloody. My mother responded by treating the damaged area with a band aid and verbal reprimand; "stop it Emily, I do not have time for your nonsense". After words, she would shake my arm with force, and walk away. I was really pissed so I sat there until I found something else that interested me.

After Charlie was born, my perspective changed considerably, I felt closer to my two brothers. We all had something in common, a fear of my father. He would beat all three of us when we least expected it. My brothers were punished more than I was and I felt the need to protect them whenever I could. I would either try to intervene and protect them when I could, I would lie to protect them or I would try to convince them to try to fight back. The latter usually proved to be a fruitless effort and I usually ended up getting punished instead of my brothers, but for some reason, I didn't care because I considered this a victory, especially if it meant saving my brothers from getting a beating mainly because when he beat Charlie, he did not know when to quit.

As time went on dad's disease got progressively worse and he became meaner and meaner and living around him became more and more tense and when mom gave birth to Tim, it was almost unbearable. In addition, I had just returned from spending the summer at my grandfather's house and this added to the stress. As an adult and I look back at my childhood, I've tried to analyze and reason my young life and especially what the stressors were that caused such unhappiness and what I have determined is that the answer in simple my mother and father is the root of the problems.

First of all my father is a paranoid schizophrenia. This was a diagnosis performed while he was incarcerated in Butty County Jail for battery against me while I was pregnant with his grandchild.

Second, my mother is totally incapable of caring for children. All of my mom's children, including me, were placed in foster homes at least one time in their lives. My mom's primary interest is in money and that's all she cares about. I'm sure that my mom does love us, but her love is illusive and hard to define. My mom was mentally and physically abused her entire young life and that's the only life she knows and to her I'm sure it's perfectly normal so when it comes to love, she is totally confused. Ironically however, love and understanding is the only thing that will cure my mom and heal her of her dependence on her monster of a husband.

As time progressed, my job became harder and harder because it seems that mom would give birth to a new baby every two years or so and I was expected to care for the new babies, in fact, I had to drop out of school for the entire year of seventh grade to help care for her children. In addition to missing the entire seventh grade, my mom needed my services throughout most of my teen years. I was forced to spend a lot of extra time during the evening hours to maintain my school work and keep up my grades and I did manage to maintain an A average and get on the Honor Roll for three semesters but I just couldn't quite make the fourth semester. This broke my heart.

As far as my social life was concerned, my dad was honest with me. He informed me "daughter dear I don't ever want you to bring any of your friends into this house, no girls and especially boys and no dating until you're at least 18 years old and out of my house is that understood?." I replied, "yes dad, I do". What else could I say, I had nowhere else to go and I was too young to make it on my own so I was basically screwed and my father was well aware of this. Needless to say, High School was a bad experience for me in more ways than one. The primary reason was because of the restrictions placed by my father and other related family issues. Another issue was related to a missing credit that I needed for graduation and that was controlled by the mother of one of the boys that I knew. It seems that his mom was a member of a student board of directors who maintained the integrity of the student grading system and she refused to give me a chance to make up the extra point to bring up my grade simply because she did not approve of me associating with her son because she was familiar with the reputation of our family.

If I wanted my High School Diploma, I was required to pay $250.00 for attending a 2 month camera class. The school would award me 2 credits even though I only needed 1. I completed the class and earned my Diploma.

I was really excited when my 18th birthday rolled around, I had a full time job at a local gas station as an attendant. In addition I remembered what dad said to me when I was younger and that I couldn't date until I was 18 years old. I couldn't wait to get home because I knew that mom and dad were planning some kind of a surprise for me and mom probably baked a nice Birthday cake. I drove up the hill a little faster than I probably should have and quickly exited the car and slammed the door. I ran up to the house and quickly flung opened the door. Dad was quietly sitting at his desk with a mean blank stare, looking down at a single chocolate cup cake with a single pink unlit pink candle sticking straight up and placed dead center in the middle of the perfectly round cup cake. I broke the silence and said "hi, how's everybody doing?" My dad looked up and said "how does it look I'm doing Mother Fucker?" I replied, with extreme surprise and shock, "we'll it's my Birthday and I was kind of excited to spend it with you guys". "Oh really, what were you expecting, Happy Birthday, Mother Fucker, here's your cake, I don't know what you were expecting, but this is all I got, take it or leave it. Your 18 now so as far as I'm concerned you can get the fuck out".

During this verbal exchange with my father I expected my mother to intervene and support me, but she kept her back turned toward me the entire time that I was there and did not make even one attempt to defend me. She didn't even acknowledge my presence in the room. She probably feared for her own safety.

I really had no place to go at the present time so I had no choice but to stay, but my plan was to find another job in order to save more money because I knew that I was not welcome here and I really didn't want to stay. As time went on, dad became more aggressive toward the kids and started to physically abuse them more but, the teachers at school noticed the bruises on the kids and referred them to the school nurses and then reports were made and filed with Social Services and eventually all the kids were taken away from my parents, including myself, and placed in foster care. It was determined that my father was too abusive and the kids could not be around him.

Eventually my mom decided that she wanted the kids back, but the only way that she could make this happen was to leave my dad, so she confronted him and said, "I need my kids back so I have to leave you". Surprisingly, he let her go without any problems and even offered to give her money in the future to help with expenses.

My mom found a 2 bedroom duplex in Northern Colorado and then began to petition the court system to get her kids back and one by one she eventually managed to get all her kids back. Unfortunately, my mom didn't really have too many motherly skills so most of these activities and responsibilities were given to me.

I lived with my mom until I got married, at 23 years old. My mom kept pressing me to get married and preferably to a rich man. I thought this was a ridiculous request, but getting married was a means of escape and freedom from a life of servitude. Getting married to the man that I married was the biggest mistake that I have ever made. An even bigger mistake was having a child with this man, both for me, as well as my son, He was a very cruel individual and every bit as mean and ruthless as my father to me. He treated my son with a bit more dignity, but he introduced him to the world of drugs and alcohol at a very young age, in that respect, he ruined his life. I could have saved him. My husband was even more frightening than my father because after he sobered up and came to his senses, he had no recollection of the incident whatsoever. In fact, he did warn me that if I wanted to stay alive I should divorce him and leave because he was afraid that he would kill me. That's all I needed to know. The next day I filed for a divorce. I feared for myself and mainly for my son. My husband signed the divorce papers and talked and agreed on how we would share visitation rights with our son and after that was resolved, I moved back in with my mother until I could find my own apartment for me and my son.

As my son grew older, he became more active in school activities especially football and other related high school activities. This limited the time that he could spend with me, and as a result, we grew further and further apart.

Interpersonal communications was not one of my greatest skills and this can be attributed to my childhood upbringing of my mother and father whom had no communication skills whatsoever and thus they had no skills to teach me.

If I were to break free of this mental prison that I find myself in, I knew I had to start doing things differently by establishing new goals and quit living in the past. Above all, I desperately needed to fully control my own life. So I decided to expand my horizons. In order to do this I would look toward education to help me find the answers I needed to become the person that I felt I needed to be in order to change my life and become a stronger person and fight my demons. First of all, I took stock of my skills and documented those along with some of the things that I thought I would like to do. A dental assistant came into my mind so I made note of that. Teaching was another area that interested me, Nursing was another area, I was always interested in, and finally Business Management. Next I evaluated the opportunities in each of those areas to see if whether or not they would be practical or not to pursue and then finally, I looked at available training centers.

Note: Reflecting back, I feel that I made some really wise decisions especially when I broke free from the distorted influence of my mother and father. If for example, I continued to follow in my mom's footsteps, I would have done everything possible to stay married to a man that I despised and continued to live in misery, but I woke from this nightmare and chose a different path and for that I am proud.

CALIFORNIA DREAMING

As I THINK BACK now it was around May 1986, my son Adam was 15 months old and I was 25 ½ years old and separated from my first husband and living with my mother and my sisters Marsha, and Lilly and my brother Jimmy in an apartment in Northern Colorado. My mother told me that her father was dying and wanted me and Marsha to go to California to see if we could try to convince her father, (Grandpa) to come back and spend the rest of his life with us here in Colorado. I told her I would, I had some money saved up from the nursing home and gave the nursing home notice that I needed some time off to go and see my grandfather that he was dying. They gave me two weeks off. I had just enough, with my check, I gave to my mom money for the rent plus $ 85.00 for Marsha's ticket and $ 85.00 for my ticket and I was broke. Plus the rest was for Adam's diapers and milk and whatever he needed. Mom was going to care for him while I was away not to tell my soon to be ex-husband anything at all. She kept her promise, I can say that much for her. My ex-husband was busy farming in the fields this time of year so the timing was perfect!

The California bound Trailways bus comes through Northern Colorado once a day it's a one way trip to L.A. and someone in the family would have to pick us up so we would have to call one of her family members to let them know we would be coming. Mom called her sister to let her know that Marsha and Emily are on their way out and would be arriving at such and such time, she said to her sister. Her sister was just thrilled she had not seen us girls since dad and mom took us out of California years ago, so this was a real reunion for the family!

Getting back to the bus situation, the Trailways bus was really something. First of all, I had never been on a Trailways bus in my entire life, second of all, we had no money what so ever for the stops, you know all the stops along the way the bathroom stops, where you were able to get snacks and stuff and use a clean bathroom not the one on the bus. See, the bathroom on the bus is real nasty! That's the bathroom you go to when you are desperate and you cannot hold it any longer, the type of bathroom was similar to an outhouse! It reeks, it smells especially when you are going through places like needles California hot places make the bathroom really reek and the smell almost makes you want to gag and on top of that, there was this passenger right behind our seat all the way to California unfortunately, he happened to be a black man and I am not prejudice or a racist, and what he did to us girls was the unthinkable. He would take off his shoes, and socks roll up his pants, and put his smelly feet on top of my seat, right next to my face, all the way there every day. Marsha and myself tried to put scarves over our mouth and open the window to give him a hint, we tried to huddle down in the seat and cover up with a blanket over ourselves, but the heat going towards California was sweltering and sweat was just pouring off us. Then finally one day I got brave and all the people on the bus saw what he was doing to us and they decided to defend us in our argument surprisingly enough, I turned around and addressed him and said; "Excuse me Sir, you have been harassing me and my sister this whole trip with your dirty stinky feet. If you would, please put your feet down on the floor I would greatly appreciate it." Then the man became very angry and accused me of being prejudice. He said;" You are a prejudice white bitch". Then all of a sudden a Spanish lady walked up from no- where with a bottle of foot power and said;" You need to apologize to these two lovely young girls, I have been watching you from the back of the bus and so has all those other people they all stood up with her and she gave him the foot power and told him to use it and apologize now, or she and the others would kick him off the bus at the next stop"! The man put the power on his feet first, then he wrinkled up his lips with this ugly look and said;" I am sorry girls, I will never do that again to YA all". The woman was then satisfied and the whole bus clapped and the man sat back in his seat folded his arms close to his chest in disgust turned his head and looked out the window and knew he had been defeated. Meanwhile, Marsha and I were getting low on food and supplies, so she brought a full bottle of Percocet "where on earth did you get that, I asked"? Marsha exclaimed; "I have my sources". So with that, I took one to ease my hunger and the pain of the ride, and the stench of the bathroom on the bus. Like I said, it only stinks when it's hot and it's hot all the time now, but the good part of this story, is were almost to L.A. and this ride is almost over. We finally arrived in L.A. and there was my mom's sister to meet us at the bus stop. She gave us a warm welcome and helped us to gather up our stuff and drove us to her home in California. The house was a moderate to nice house that her and her third husband had together. It was a three bedroom two bath ranch with a good sized backyard and a pretty good size front yard for California, I guess. The inside of the home was ok, nothing spectacular but just nice. It was located in a nice neighborhood a family style neighborhood, meaning it was fairly quiet. My mom's sister met her former husband while she was waitressing at Denny's and married him. He was a Truck driver that's what he did for a living. I met him later on in the day when he came home from work he had long hauls she said, but had a regular route now, so he was able to come home every night which made her very happy. Connie finally showed Marsha and myself to our rooms and showed us where the shower was because she knew we probably needed a shower after that long stinky bus ride. I told her thank-you because I was all hot and sweaty and needed to change my clothes and maybe wash a load too. Connie said; "No problem there's some Tide in the laundry room and some Downey for the rinse, go to it". So with that, us girls cleaned up and got ready for dinner. Auntie Connie said;" we are going to have a cook out with the family so hurry up CUZ everyone is coming". Everyone came to the cookout all my cousins and uncles, that I have not seen in years and it was a real reunion and felt really good to see everyone again. We talked for hours. I was able to spend time with my grandfather, Mom's dad he looked the same just a whole lot older. Auntie Connie was a real good hostess and made me and Marsha feel at home the best she could. She called mom to let her know we arrived okay, and things were going smoothly. Mom's mind was put at ease. Marsha and I visited with the whole family for about a week and a half I think. I knocked on the door and asked if I could enter and he said; "Yes, Emily come in". I entered and he was watching T.V. I think it was" Let's Make a Deal with Monty Hall", I said;" Grandpa, do you have a moment so I can talk to you about something"? Grandpa exclaimed;" Sure honey, sit down on the bed next to me, and tell me what's on your mind". I said;" Okay, well Mom sent Marsha and I down here to see if maybe we could talk you into coming home with us to live out the rest of your life in Colorado, because we know you do not have that much time left. We were hoping to take you back with us to live because we have not had the opportunity to see you all these years and have been lonely for our grandfather. So please before you answer could you consider the fact that us kids have not been with you all these years, and have been cheated of all your love while Connie's kids have had all of your love and support and grandma's too and it's always been that way. The Pandora's have been in Colorado all alone with Mom and Dad no Grandparents from either side or relatives of or from either side just us kids all alone all these years. So, please Grandpa, come home with us now, please." Grandpa looked at me with a tear in his eye and said;" Emily Put your hand up so I did and I just looked at my grandfather in disbelief not understanding what he was about to say. Emily now that your hand is up with mine, now fold your fingers over with mine together we look like we are praying right? Now, Look at me in my eyes, grandpa is dying, now they told me just yesterday I only have maybe two months or so to live with this Cancer please don't cry just keep looking at me, your grandpa I'm in no shape to travel in a bus to Colorado and even if I did make it to Colorado, I would be dead within one month. That's not how I want Katy and my grandchildren to remember me. Do you understand, I love YA kid always have, Always will, you're just like your Ma- ma, you're beautiful, you're bright, you're a good Irish girl, just look at all that pretty red hair. I love YA kid." Then me and grandpa hugged each other and I understood what he told me, he then said;" why don't you reach under the bed and get us a beer so we can celebrate being together for the moment, because this moment is all we have together". I reached under the bed grabbed the beers and we sat on the bed and watched T.V. together until supper time. I told grandpa I will never ever forget him I will always love him and honor him through- out time. He said; "Thank-you Baby". During the week and a half we spent with our in-laws, we took lots of pictures, and were given a lot of pictures from my Grandma, and Auntie Connie from years past. I carefully put them all away for safe keeping. Each picture was fully explained and was then given to me for safe keeping knowing full well that this could be the last time that they would ever see me again in their lives, and they were right. Marsha and I made the most of every second we spent with our family in California, and to this day I can still remember and cherish the moments we had together with Grandpa, Grandma, Auntie Connie, all my Cousins, and Uncles and wives, and their children what wonderful memories my sister and I made in just a week and a half. It's as if time stood still for us. Then it was time to go, it came too soon, Marsha and I were packed and ready but before we left California we had to make one last stop to see my dad's dad and his new wife, just one last time just for the sake of myself and what this bastard did to me when I was just 5 years old. He was the one who molested me for two summers taking care of my Grandmother who was crippled and in a wheelchair and unable to care for herself. My parents decided to let me go over there to help out grandma with her meals, and the cooking and cleaning and whatever else she needed. Meanwhile, her husband took advantage of the situation and helped his perverted self out to this young child who did not know anything and was happy to be away from her monster of a father who beat and starved her but was now with a pervert who molested her and threatened to kill her if she said a word. This child believed this pervert, and really thought he was going to kill her and knew no different, so it went on for two summers and ruined her life. Now that I was twenty five years old I wanted to see this pervert and to see just what he looked like and to look at him in the face and to bring my sister Marsha along for proof of my visit and to let him know how I felt inside. I called him on the phone and let him know I was on the way with Marsha and we would be arriving soon he was not hard to find. He basically looked the same his demeanor had changed a bit being real careful around me and Marsha. He introduced me to his sixth wife. I was in shock. I said, "Sixth wife, boy you've been busy". He just looked at me with this weird look, and then changed the conversation. See, I knew this man like the back of my hand, and I knew what he had done in the past, to my Grandma, my real Grandma, my first Grandma he murdered her I witnessed it when I was 6 and a half years old when he left the bathroom door ajar while he was undressing Grandma to get ready to give her a bath in the bathroom. My memory is sharp, and like an elephant I'll never forget that night he killed my Grandmother. As he looked at me he started to remember things and was starting to shake all over. I asked him, "Grandpa, what's the matter, are you starting to remember what happened when I was a little girl"? Then all of a sudden his wife walked in with some refreshments and said; "Joe what's the matter, you're as white as a ghost"? Grandpa responds; "Nothing, I just need some air". I pulled him aside and told him that he needs to show us girls to our rooms, and to not touch me any way shape or form or I will turn him in. I am here just to see things again, and that's all. I do need some money to get back to Colorado". "He said he would see what he could come up with". Marsha and I were shown to our room. We both got ready for supper. It was a simple dinner. Not much was said. Not much to say to a person like that, anyways. His wife did most of the talking. Grandpa just stared at me with this evil look, and I looked back at him with a look like you try, and you better be ready buddy because I am younger and stronger and not afraid of you any-more! I think he got the message because he put his head down and knew he had been defeated. The next morning Marsha and I grabbed some coffee and I again asked for some money for our long trip back. Luke reached into his pocket and pulled out a $ 20.00 bill. I said; "What, this is all you have"? Grandpa exclaimed; "I'm sorry, but this is all I have today girls. I am broke. I just paid the rent and all the bills, so the well is empty." I said; "Yeah right, well the well was not empty when you molested me and all the girls in the family! The well was not empty when you killed grandma! The well was not empty when grandma and I watched her keep all the books for your trucking business and you walked away rich"! Grandpa exclaimed;" I helped all the girls in the family to make them stronger, to make them grow up to be better women". I exclaimed;" By molesting them. You Fucking pervert."! He then slipped this $20.00 bill next to my hand carefully, and tried to touch my hand, I shouted, "Don't you even try to touch me or I'll knock your teeth out"! I then told Marsha let's go, now. His wife walked in and wanted to know what all the commotion was all about, and grandpa said, "It was nothing, the girls were just saying Goodbye, that's all". With that we both left that house never to return. I hope that bastard rots in hell for the rest of his days and if there is a God, and I know there is he is in Hell right now burning at the stake not just for what he did to me but for what he did to my grandmother and the many other atrocities I'm sure of is in his past, remember he was in the Italian mafia. Marsha and I got on the bus to head home, as we handed our tickets to the bus driver to check us out, we both looked at ourselves and then took our seats opposite the seats on the way back home. Marsha wanted to be next to the window again so she could feel the cool breeze in her face while she slept. For myself, I just wanted to lay back and reflect what had just happened and to savor all the wonderful memories my sister and I had just made for life. You know, life is a funny thing, it comes in spirts, it's as if a door opens and lets you know somehow that it's time for you to go and do something like make a memory. It's a feeling you get inside you that tells you it's time to fulfill something and to do it now or never type of syndrome. It's the only way I can describe it, because that's the way it felt to me. So with that, I fulfilled my destiny and helped my mother out with her request and received her answer to her burning question at the same time. As painful as the answer will be for me to deliver, I felt confident that she needed to know how her father was doing and exactly what he said and how all her relatives were doing. I knew this news was going to upset her so I would take it slow and sit down with mom and explain slowly how her father arrived at that conclusion. I brought home pictures to share with mom and explained them all we laughed and cried together as I knew we would. I felt sorry for my mother not being able to be with her father in his last days, it was very painful for her. She said; "I was a war baby, I grew up with Daddy being in the war and gone all the time. He fought in World War I and World War II. He fought the Germans and the Japanese and he was the only one to make it back. He also got the Purple Heart for saving so many of his Platoon." Then she broke down and cried. Mom said ; "you know Emily you have your Grandpa's smile that's what I love about you". I did what I could to comfort her. She was happy I went to visit her in-laws and had that experience and most of all she was happy I was able to see her father one more time. Her sister mailed a picture of her father to mom and mom bought a special frame for Grandpa for it. This was Grandpa's last picture before he passed away.

Note: The trip to California was a long arduous trip but, a trip that needed to be made not only for my mother's sake but, for my own as well. Grandpa was one of the very few people in our family that wasn't motivated by money, he was driven by love for his family and country, unfortunately his family and country did not reciprocate this love and as a result, grandpa was a broken man who had very little to his name and stood in long lines at the VA to receive care. What a travesty.

CAN I AFFORD IT

I REALIZED THAT GETTING a good education from a quality school was going to require a lot of dedication and hard work on my part which I was willing to do. I was also sure that a quality education was going to be very expensive depending on which school that I attended. So, I would probably need some type of a student loan or else I would need to borrow money from some other source, my dad came to mind. As much as I hated to, I decided to ask him for a loan. The next day I drove up to dad's farm and I confronted him with what I was doing and what my plans were and how much I needed. He immediately froze in place. Then he responded; "Hey you see this table over here there is a whole table full of bills to pay each month on this farm, and I don't have a penny left after I finish paying them. I wish I did have some money to give to you for school but I do not, I'm barely making enough to feed me and the horse out here." I responded; "That's okay I'll find another way dad I always do." I should have known better than to go up there because I knew deep down that he would never part with any money to help me through school, but I also knew that he did have the money in a secret hiding place that only a few select family members knew about. I was disappointed but I felt sorry for him he looked miserable and his hair was much grayer and longer than it was since the last time I saw him and his face was more withered and wrinkled and he walked with a slow crocked gate and he lost quite a bit of muscle mass and his shoulders were slightly humped forward and he wore that same company regulation white jumpsuit that he wore to his job every day for twenty years and for some reason or another, he felt that he was still part of the company.

I knew I needed an education to change my life. I also knew that if you want something bad enough there is always a way to get it and I was determined to get what I needed. So I decided to apply for a student loan. I really didn't think I had a chance at getting approved. But, I did. This was one of the happiest days of my life. Now my belief system was supported with reality. I signed up for school and received my dental certificate within one year. I accomplished this goal while working a forty hour a week job. Shortly after graduation I got a job as a dental assistant. Unfortunately, the job did not work out for various reasons. I started researching the job ads in the newspapers for job openings and found an opening at the phone company for something in customer service but it was just as a temporary position. At the time, I was working for an agency and I did find a full time position up in North Western Colorado selling reverse directories for eight months or so but, the drive was too far from Colorado and too hard on me and my car. So, I found a full time position at another phone company selling pagers in Colorado and this lasted for about a year or so. Then I met my husband Tim whom I am still married to now after twenty eight years and thank God I met him just in time.

Note: I should have realized that my father was a very selfish person and only cared for his own welfare and I also knew that if he ever contributed to anyone else's welfare that it was only an illusion designed to benefit him and only him. But this episode in my life did serve to help build my self confidence and to help to define and build my own personal character of which I am grateful.

BREAKING FREE FROM THE PAIN

As our marriage progressed, my husband learned more and more about my past life and especially about the trauma that I suffered at the hands of my abusive father and my husband recommended that I seek counseling. I thought about it for a while and at first I was offended because I took it as an insult. I thought that he was trying to suggest that I was crazy, but after a while, he managed to convince me that there could be benefits if I just tried. My doctor referred me to a counselor. I was hesitant, but I kept my 1 hour appointment. The counseling session was helpful and I learned a lot about myself and how to let go of some of my anxiety and I felt at ease with the counselor and actually looked forward to our next session. With a clear head, me and my husband could plan our lives together and decide what we really wanted to do in the near future. We decided that we wanted to further our education. We both enrolled in a 4 year college degree program. We both managed to graduate as straight A students. My husband continued to earn a Master's degree in Human Resource Development and finally a Doctorate in Business Management. I Went to school for Nursing and earned an LPN and a BSN from the local University in Arizona. We purchased a home in Southern Colorado and decided to make amends with my dad and invited him down to our home.

When he came over with his truck and Airstream trailer he parked it on the side of our home. There was plenty of parking for an RV. He planned to stay for a week, but unfortunately he was only there for about two days. The first day he was there he did mow our property for us because I asked him to, he really enjoyed our riding lawn mower and he was in his element and really felt at home doing the work. Then after he was done he became bored again and started drinking beer and sitting outside alone in the sunshine in that white outfit until he became totally drunk. He then decided he wanted to have a barbecue with our outdoor barbecue pit which was a permanent fixture attached to the house and was located underneath the tile overhang of the roof. My dad started cooking the food which was steaks and brats with his special sauce and he was cussing very loud and slamming the barbecue lid down very hard then finally he came in screaming at the top of his lungs; "Here's your fuckin steaks, and your fuckin brats and started yelling and cussing at me for one reason or another then my husband got involved. Then My dad came inside the house and pushed my husband with his stomach; "Come on mother fucker". Tim then put his fists up and said; "Okay, come on you son-of-a-bitch". Then my dad ran outside and Tim instructed me to call the cops. My dad went back to his airstream to cool off for a while. The cops had a conversation with my dad and the next morning he left. I went out to speak with my dad and he said;" he would be gone in the morning and how much he dislikes my husband". I replied;" Dad my husband has nothing to do with the way you acted. You were totally drunk last night and you were the one who caused all the problems not Tim. Everything was fine, until you started drinking". Dad replies; "well I won't be back". I said; "that's fine suit yourself". I closed the door as usual, turned and walked away. I said to myself, I guess some things never change.

Note: As I sit here and try to evaluate the situation and especially what made my dad so upset I truly believe that my dad was jealous of the relationship that me and my husband had with each other and he actually envied us. Unfortunately my dad's disease process

clouded his thinking process and he was unable to logically reason internal conflicts. My dad desperately needed professional help, but first and foremost he must be willing to recognize that he had a problem.

PRICED OUT OF OUR HOUSE AND HOME

THE INSURANCE COMPANY DID a second appraisal on our house and decided to raise the insurance to cover the high value of the tile roof. Our new payments would be $400.00 more per month than we were currently paying. This was more than we could afford so we decided to move. We found a nice home that was equally as nice not too far away with payments that we could afford. The new home had a nice fenced in back yard for our dogs with quite a large lot for them to play in. It also had plenty of parking for an RV on the side of the house too. It did need a little work but it was doable and so we bought it and it was a real comfortable home for us. We ended up living in this home for ten years. During this time, I decided to call my dad and see if he would like to come over to see my new home it was about seven years since I had last seen him. He was very happy to hear my voice. He seemed a lot older now and he had forgotten about the episode back at the other home which I assumed, because he was in a different state of mind. He decided that yes he would like to come over with his Airstream trailer and ford pick-up truck to see me and maybe stay a while. He told me how bad the flooding had been in his trailer park up in Northern Colorado and how he needed to get away for a awhile because the water there was unsanitary and things were not good up there for him. So, I told him to come on down I have an RV parking area on the side of my home and he could plug in his trailer into the socket in the garage for electricity. He also offered to pay me for the electricity because it's expensive to run a line on a trailer. Everything went along fine we watched movies together, I washed his clothes, I cooked meals for him, he took a shower, we went shopping at Walmart. Everything was going just fine until one day I went to get my hair colored and the girl that colored it gave me the wrong color and I did not look like the same person he used to know so he really started to make fun of me in front of my husband. That was my husband's cue to let him have it, and his words can cut like a knife. Tim said; "You know, your daughter is suffering, she is disabled with no income, in pain all day and night, her son died, with a father that only cares about himself and his truck, now that's pretty sad". My dad replied; "You Mother Fucker, you fucken bastard, I should kill you now, and put you out of your misery as they walked into the house". Of course my husband said;" with his hand on the rolling pin behind him, go for it you son-of-a-bitch". My dad stood there for a while with his fists up then he ran out of the house. He went back to his airstream to cool off and watch T.V. for a while to think about what just happened. I just stayed in the house because I was upset at what he just did, embarrass me yet again in front of my husband and the many others in my past which I cannot fix and I am left with a broken heart and a father who has a disease of the brain which will never go away. I guess I have to face the fact that he will never be able to be around people I guess this is something I will always have to live with forever. After about five days I had purchased some presents for him earlier in the week before he came over and decided now would be a good time to give them to him. I walked over to his trailer to give them to him. I asked;" Dad can I come in"? Dad replied;" Yes, come in". As I walked in I saw him sitting there all alone in his chair I hugged him and said, "Hello, I have something for you". He smiled; "What is this, why did you do this"? I replied; "because it's getting close to Christmas and I wanted to give you some presents to make you feel better". He smiled;" well, thank you daughter dear you should not have done this". I replied;" Never mind, just try on the shirt to see if it fits, then try on the jacket, there are some warm socks so you do not have to sew your socks any more that's ridiculous and some underwear. I hope everything fits." Dad replied, Yes it's all good it all fits, you did good." Dad immediately started to hang up his shirt and coat and put away his socks and underwear and put the pretty bag it came in away. He was very happy for a moment. We stayed and talked a while. He did not like my husband, I told him Tim is what keeps me going, then he said, well I guess Tim is good for you, I just don't like him. I said that's your problem. But for me he's perfect. I love him very much because he is what keeps me going. Dad said, he would be gone tonight, he was heading back to Northern Colorado that it was dried out now and things were back to normal. He has to drive at night because his rig is long and he drives slow and needs a lot of room so he will leave at midnight. So we said our goodbyes. That afternoon, Tim and I helped dad hookup his trailer he apparently had been doing it wrong and could have gotten in a major wreck luckily, Tim showed him the right way to hook up the trailer to his pick-up truck. Dad was thankful for that. So see, I pointed out to dad that he really needs to pay attention to people and open his mind and listen to what other people say like Tim because it can save your life. He thought about that for a while. Because it was true if it was not for my husband pointing out that he was connecting the hitch to the pickup wrong he could have had a serious accident and possibly rolled the entire rig and killed himself in the process and he then realized Tim was right. He then became silent, very quiet and thankful to Tim. I noticed a big change just for a moment. Then Tim and I walked into the house for the evening and said our goodbyes and dad left at midnight. I was fast asleep but Tim was awake for the departure. Tim heard his truck startup so he looked out the window and suddenly dad turned on the lights to the truck and the trailer and it was equivalent to a thousand Christmas trees turning on at the same time. The lights were blinding and they lit up the entire neighborhood. As he drove off, it was reminiscent of a fireball rolling down the street. Tim said; "All the Neighbors lights inside their homes came on one by one to see what all the commotion was all about". Then after dad finally left the area Tim closed the curtains, turned off the, lights and came to bed.

Note: It is not our charge in life to judge people, if we do we are selling ourselves short. I truly believe that we can learn something from everyone that we meet. My dad learned this lesson from my husband, but will it make a difference?, I truly don't know, but it did for me.

MOM COMES TO SOUTHERN COLORADO

Now that dad was gone a few months had passed and things were back to normal. Had not heard from him since and did not expect to. He never calls unless it's very important or something very unusual happens. Good thing for me because at the time I was going through a lot trying to get on disability and with very little income, it was very hard times for us financially. I called my mom and asked her how she was doing and she said; "I am struggling up here in Colorado with rent and bills, it's very hard on me, I wished I had a way out of here". I told her that I was not feeling so good these days and could use a little help down here in Colorado, if she wanted to come live with me for a while she could and maybe pay just $500.00 per month which includes everything with money left over for whatever she wanted. She really liked that idea. Because right at that moment she was paying $1200.00 plus food and whatever else she had to come up with because Marsha would not work or pay a thing. I don't know why Marsha would not work, she was perfectly healthy and able to work, but she did have a serious drug and alcohol problem and I should have realized that she would give us trouble if we took mom, her meal ticket. So, mom decided to come and live with me for a while to help me out, plus get rid of her burden. But what she actually had on her mind was to destroy our lives with Marsha as her support.

From the very beginning mom was very demanding and wanted to take over the entire household. She would sit and watch T.V. with us as long as it was a program that she enjoyed, if there wasn't, she would complain and she would not allow us to enjoy a program of our choice. We would either have to change the program or she would leave in a huff. I tried to go to her room but I always found her on the telephone laughing making jokes with Marsha or making fun of us or make the conversation short when I came into the room. In the mornings when my mom woke up, she would immediately go the breakfast table and demand "what's for breakfast"? Then she would remind me how they would serve her at assisted living facilities and that's what she was expecting here that's what she told me at least. I told her; "This is not an assisted living facility, this is my home mom and I do things my way it may not be perfect, but I believe it's a happy home, and my husband has no complaints, there's no children here as you know my son is gone and I'm still grieving him so I thought you were going to help me". She said; "I will what do you want me to do"? Then I gave her a few chores to do. She helped me out for a while then after about an hour or so, I tried to give her another small chore and she said; "That's it, I'm finished I'm not going to do any more work". She simply had enough and went to her room and went to the phone to call Marsha and went to bed. My mom started to cause chaos in my home for no reason at all. She would come into the room and pick fights with me and my husband over anything she put into her mind to and then she would go to her room and call Marsha to report what she just did. It was as if Marsha was telling her what to do so she could come up with a plan to get something on us. Why I do not know, but this is what my mom did. My husband and I took my mom down to JC Penny and bought her some desperately needed clothes. I bought her some bras, underwear, and a beautiful mother's day outfit plus, a beautiful set of pearl earrings. She absolutely loved them. I wanted to go in debt and buy her a very expensive pair of earrings but she declined because I'm sure she felt guilty because of her plans that she made with Marsha on charging myself and my husband with some sort of elderly abuse and this would not look good on her case so she settled for a cheaper pair. Then afterwards we went out to lunch it went fine, until she started an argument with my husband again to make herself look good for her upcoming case. Then we all went home and all hell broke loose. Out of the blue my mom said;" I'll see if I can call Marsha to stop her". I responded; "Stop her from what"? Mom called Marsha but Marsha's phone would not pickup. So mom started to pack her car as fast as possible because she knew it was too late to change things now the ball was already in motion, her plan to hurt me and my husband was already in place. So I helped her pack her car not understanding what was going on but deciding to get into my car to show her the way to the gas station to meet Marsha and to ask Marsha what the heck is going on here.

When I arrived at the gas station I found two police cars and Marsha outside talking. Mom had pulled up to the side of the store. I immediately asked what was going on? The police officer asked me to step back and spoke to me in another area and took notes, other cop cars headed off to my home with Marsha. The officer asked if I had been holding my mom hostage in my home? I responded;" What hostage, No for heavens sakes, absolutely not! My mom has been living with me to help me out because I have been ill and she wanted to come to Colorado because it was much cheaper for her to live here and peace and quiet". Meanwhile, the cops and Marsha pull up to my home Marsha got out of the car my husband said, he was sitting in the garage Marsha got out of her car and started to run up to him the cop pulled up to the driveway and said; "Get back into your car Marsha". Then the cop came up to my husband and he had his hand on his revolver and said; "Do You know Colleen Pandora"? Tim responded; "Yes that's my mother in law." The cops responds;" I have a report that you have been holding her hostage in your home, is that true"? Tim responded;" No sir she's been staying here for a while to help my wife while she recovers from an illness. My mother in law left about ten minutes ago". Cop responds;" I have to follow up on this report I am going to have to issue a citation and you'll probably have to go to court in Allens County to get the matter cleared up there will be a Detective coming out to investigate the matter on your behalf in a few weeks." Within a few days of my mother leaving my home, Marsha started to call my home and harass me and my husband over the phone constantly. So, my husband had an idea to get the tape recorder and turn it on each and every time they would call and record their telephone conversations in order to support our case for the court hearings and to have them readily available for the detective when he came down to our home. When it came time for us to go to court, my mother and Marsha convinced the Judge that my Husband and I were terribly abusive to my mom and the Judge was so mad that she would not even allow us to present our case. As a matter of fact the Judge asked Mrs. Pandora if she wanted the restraining order to be temporary or permanent.? My mother shouted out in a fury;" I want it to be permanent your honor.". Then she started to break down in a fake cry. I could hardly believe it! I looked over at my mother in disgust and shook my head in disbelief after all I had done for her. What a liar and traitor she was I thought, but why. How could she do this to me after all these years she put a restraining order on her oldest daughter the one that stood by her side through thick and thin and always stood up for her. I took care of her and her children all those years for this? No way, I thought, No she will never get away with this one. I will never speak to her again as long as I live now. I do know that Marsha is behind this she is the expert behind putting restraining orders on people in fact, she has put one on all the family members in our family according to Lilly. Lilly told me to stay away from Marsha she is just trouble with a capitol T.

My mom was full of hate and resentment from my father because of all the beatings and ill treatment that she has received for the last forty two years of marriage and this court appearance and case against me and my husband was a perfect opportunity for her to release all of her hate and bad feelings on us. This was a way for her to lighten her load so to speak, and to free her mind and to feel free from all of her mental restraints. The only problem was that it tarnished our name and hurt me and my husband and this meant that she was not allowed to ever speak to me or my husband again ever, not until the restraining order was lifted. So I have not had any contact with her or Marsha since that day. She did it to herself, so there was nothing I could do. Mom and

Marsha filed a report in Colorado claiming that we were selling their furniture at garage sales and we refused to give it back to them.

A few weeks had passed I thought the issue was over and still had a question in my mind how my mother and my sister Marsha were going to pick up their furniture. Then I called Lilly to see she if she could call them to pick-up the furniture with Jimmy's pick- up truck and she said; "Yes that would be a good idea and Jimmy is ok with that too". Lilly called me back and said; "Marsha told her that if she attempted to come here and pick up the furniture, she would call the cops on her and have her arrested". I was devastated I had no idea what to do. So I was limited by law on what to do so I knew my next move would have to be made by my mother or my sister so I decided just to pack her things up the best I could and put everything in the garage nice and neat and try to keep them out of my way. Then I got a call from Lilly telling me that Marsha was thinking about putting a restraining order against my husband and I. I said; "What, You're kidding"? Lilly said; "Nope, I'm not kidding you, so you better prepare yourself because she has done this in the past and has put restraining orders on everyone in the family including myself in fact I have one on me right now". I could not believe what I was hearing. I thanked Lilly for the heads up and she also said that she would stand up for me when the detective Dick Sargent calls her on the phone for information on mom and Marsha. I told her I really appreciate that and will never ever forget that and told her that I was the one who raised her not my mother. She said she knew that already and said how much she loved me. I told my husband about the conversation with Lilly and he decided we needed to prepare ourselves for the court appearance and we thought about tape recording the conversations between my mother and I or Marsha and I over the phone. We did some research to see if tape recordings could be used as evidence in court and we found they were acceptable. So we purchased a high end voice activated digital tape recorder. So the harassing phone calls started coming one by one and we recorded each and every one of them and the clarity was perfect and incriminating. Then about two weeks later we received a knock on our front door so I answered it and there was a man who was standing there whom was about 6'6 he was ugly and had ruffled black hair with big hands and then quickly handed me this paper that was folded in half as he pushed the paper into my chest and shouted; "Consider yourself served". I just looked at him with total shock and my mouth was left open. Then he turned around and left my property as quick as he could and drove off. I closed the front door something told me that I had just received bad news and I hesitated to open the paperwork I wanted to call my husband but if it was bad news I didn't want to spoil his day. I forced myself to slowly open the paperwork and I immediately felt weak and sick. I found two restraining orders from the city of Allens County one for me and one for my husband each of them signed by my mother and by Marsha. I could certainly understand Marsha filing the restraining orders because she's made a habit of filing restraining orders on other members in the family but it was a complete surprise to see my mother's name on the orders. I've done so much for my mother I helped her raise her kids when she was unable to, when she was by her-self in times of need. I help protect her in times of excessive abuse from my dad. I stood up for her in court against my father. She called me her, "Right hand man". I rescued her when she could not afford to pay her rent, I would buy food I wondered what was she after? But, I do have a letter supporting the fact that the Detective Dick Sargent gave us proving that Marsha and my mother were both lying and if they continue to harass us he would take them both to jail. I am still perplexed about what my mother's reasoning was about this entire scenario and what her motivations were for creating all of this havoc in our lives. The only logical reason that I can think of is that she was jealous of what I had and she wanted to find a way to take it from me. But luckily because of my husband Tim she didn't have a chance in the world of hurting me, he stopped her dead in her tracks. First of all he drew up a bill of sale and made her sign it for the select pieces of furniture she gave me, i.e.; (clock, mirror). We taped the conversations of my mother and I and Marsha yelling and screaming at me over the phone most of the conversations were initiated by Marsha demanding their furniture back especially the clock and mirror and did not care about any of the other stuff. I said; "It's here you can come and pick it up any time you want". Marsha just kept yelling and screaming and cussing at me. We called Lilly and asked her to contact mom to arrange to see if she could pick up the furniture and drop it off for her and Marsha. But unfortunately, Marsha found out about this and said that if Lilly tried to go and pick up the furniture for mom and drop it off at their apartment that she would have Lilly and Jimmy arrested on the spot. So, I said; "To forget it, it will just have to stay in my garage I guess, until I can figure out what to do with all of this stuff". I told Lilly thank-you for all her help and thanked her for trying. I was fighting a losing battle. Marsha had mom wrapped around her little finger and mom was totally confused about everything I am sure. I am also sure that Marsha is taking advantage of my mother and not taking care of her right, I felt this in my heart. But there is nothing I can do about this Marsha is her POA now so, my mom has spoken and chosen her own path to hell.

(Incident # 15S01XXXX) Colorado County Sheriff's Office.

<u>NOTE:</u> When faced with difficult situations, the most important thing to remember is to keep a cool head. This isn't easy at times and can prove to be mentally challenging, but it is imperative that you remain cool, calm and collected for example, I knew that mom and Marsha working together would be formidable opponents, I was really surprised at my mother, but fully expected foul play from my sister. I knew that truth would be an asset on my side so I purchased a small voice activated tape recorder and got ready for the phone calls and sure enough, my mom and sister did what I expected, they called. My mom let me know that it was Marsha who actually wanted her belongings and her financial help. The tape recorded information will be helpful in removing the restraining order, but a court appearance with all the parties involved is still required to address the restraining order issue and it still may or may not be granted.

STAIRWAY TO HEAVEN

DURING THE YEAR 2014 dad was living alone and he was a religious fanatic and had plenty of time to reflect inward for some reason or another he felt that his ill deeds and his past performance as a wicked man would keep him from getting to heaven. So he wanted to find some way to make himself look right in the eyes of God and in order to do that he felt he needed to give each one 5 of 7 kids 30 thousand dollars each. Now I'm sure that this was the money given to him by his father for me because of my molestation. So I received a phone call out of the blue from him telling me that I would receive this money around February 30th. This was two months from today. February 30th came and gone and I never seen the money, but I never said a word. Then I started to get worried because he promised me, and he never broke a promise, so I called him. When I did call him, he became angry and told me that I would receive the money when he was good and ready, he just was not ready yet he had a lot of things to do so I would just have to wait, but he would keep his promise to me. Two more months passed so I called again, he became really angry at me for calling. He cussed me out and said; "You will get your Mother Fucking money when I'm good and ready, do you understand. I've had it with all you kids biting at the bit bothering me all the fucken time about the money.

I will give you kids your inheritance and after that, it's up to you to live your lives how you will. Do you understand me?" I responded;" Yes dad I was just calling to see how you were not to ask for money". Dad responded; "Ok Emily; I love you, bye". The next thing I know around June of 2014 I received a knock on the door from my mail lady and she had a package for me to sign. She greeted me saying;" Hey Emily, I think this is really important it's probably either money or a mortgage thing, I'm not really sure. Good Luck". I thanked her, signed for my package and closed the door. I looked at the return address and it was my dad's P.O. Box then I knew it was the money I had been waiting for since February. I opened the card on the outside of the large manila envelope first. It read; "Thank-you for being my daughter I will always Love you Dad". Then it had red roses all over the card. I carefully put the card back in the envelope and opened the manila envelope to find the large Cashier's check for $ 30,000. I was happy but sad at the same time. I knew deep down that all my money was being distributed to the other children which belonged to me. My grandfather left me a large sum of money because he molested me and did not want to go to jail. So he paid off my father and mother to keep quiet. I can still remember when my brother and my Dad Left for California in that brand new Cadillac to go to his father's funeral and I begged to go and they both said; "No absolutely not, besides we are only going to go to the funeral, see grandpa, stay in the hotel maybe one night and go to the reading of the will then head directly home. It will be very boring. The total trip will only take maybe three days at the most." I said" Yeah but Dad he was my grandpa and I should be at the reading of the will I was the one who spent most of my young years with his mother and maybe he left me something?" Dad responded;" No, Emily I am not taking you and that's that". Shortly after I received my check my mother called me to see if I received any money from my father. I said yes, as a matter of fact I did. I received 30,000 from dad yesterday. My mom was upset to hear this information. She was upset because Marsha received $30,000 one month ago and did not expect my dad to hand out money to any of the other children. After she heard about me I then told her that the other kids would be receiving their inheritance too. She then got pissed off and hung up on me. I wanted to express my over whelming joy with her about my money but she hung up so quickly I could not. When she hung up on me like that it also started me to thinking, why was she so upset that I received my money and the other kids were going to be receiving theirs as well. Was the truth finally coming out after all these years about how she felt deep down inside and she could not hold it any longer? Was the secret between her and my dad finally coming out? I felt like something was wrong and she wanted to tell me something but was holding it back, and I think as my dad kept talking I started to figure the whole thing out. Even though I already knew deep down what it was all about. It was about my molestation that happened to me when I was a little girl and how my grandfather made my father promise not to tell anyone about it and he would see to it that upon his death he would receive such and such amount of money to keep quiet. My father went home and told my mother and my brother the same thing and it was never spoken of ever again. Then our whole family left the state of California never to return to see our in-laws as long as we live. Which I thought was a little weird in it- self, I mean come on now, these people we grew up with and all of a sudden we were torn apart from our family that we knew and loved. My mom's in-laws, and all the relatives on both sides were really confused about our family just up and moving like that. Besides, my dad did not have a job lined up, he just sold his home in California, bought a big truck that could hold the whole family, loaded up us kids and we were off. He never wrote, or called the in-laws again only certain ones on special occasions.

Note: I really don't understand why my mother was so upset that my dad gave money to me and four of my siblings. I discussed this issue with my husband and he seems to think that my mom wanted all the money to go to Marsha. If Marsha had all the money, my mom would have easy access to all the funds. My husband was probably correct.

WHERE ARE THEY NOW

I HAVE NO IDEA where my brother **Charlie** is. I do know that my brother Charlie suffered the most intense beatings of all the kids and he was not only mentally traumatized he was also physically deformed. The last time I saw him he had a serious curvature of the spine and was unable to stand straight. This was a result of the intense beatings that he received from my father. As I mentioned earlier, he was forced out of the house at gunpoint from my father without objection from my mother. I feel so very sorry for my brother, living in a house, not a home for most of his life where both parents totally despise and hate him, where he is constantly beaten and abused, even to the point where he had to scrounge for his share of the food. I do hope that he made it and most of all that he is still alive.

Tim lives in the Colorado area, I'm not sure what part. I have not spoken to him in a while so I am not sure what his family life is like at the moment and I have not seen him in a while so I am not sure what he looks like right at the moment or sounds like. Bur if it's Tim, I'm, sure he's still the same friendly and funny guy as he always was. I do remember that Tim had a serious alcohol problem and had trouble staying sober. Tim is divorced and has 3 DUI's against him and I'm told that alcohol played a part in the dissolution of his marriage. Tim has

2 beautiful daughters, both of which drink alcohol. I believe that both daughters have children but whether or not the children have inherited my parents genes is in question and still remains to be seen and only time will tell. I can only hope for the best. I do know however, that my sister Marsha likes to party with the girls on occasion and that's a bad thing because Marsha is a bad influence.

Lilly and I speak almost every day. She is now warm and funny. I think she is the one who keeps me going most days. Lilly was always quiet and withdrawn, but this was only a facade. Lilly has been tortured by a deep dark secret that she has carried all her life and has only chosen to share with me because of my endeavor to write this book. In other words I am setting her free and releasing her from her mental prison. When Lilly was about seven years old and in the care of foster mother, her foster mother took Lilly along with her baby and put them in the back seat of the jeep outside in the driveway with the jeep running and the keys in the ignition and the mother decides she has to go to the bathroom. She then tells Lilly to ; "don't move from that spot and don't you touch my baby do you understand"? Lilly answered ; "Yes, I understand foster mom, I will be right here when you come back". So with that, the foster mom ran in to go to the bathroom with the back door left ajar, and the front door left ajar and the engine running with her 9 month old son in the back seat running around playing and going everywhere with Lilly sitting perfectly still while becoming more and more anxious. Lilly doesn't realize it yet but she will soon be diagnosed as having paranoid schizophrenia. The baby played around too close to the door until he got closer to the door Lilly started to cry with tears in her eyes she could do nothing because she remembered what she was told, "do not touch my baby, and do not move from that spot". So as the baby inched closer to the door Lilly started to pee her pants and the tears started to flow as she watched the baby fall to his death. Lilly fell apart in an emotional breakdown. The foster mother came outside and saw her baby on the ground in a blood splatter mess. She addressed Lilly by saying;" What did you do to my baby? You, killed my baby. I'm calling the cops, now. "Lilly exclaimed" I did not do anything, your baby fell out the car door that you left open when you went to the bathroom.

You left the car door open in the back seat and the front seat plus you left the car running!" So, the cops came and handcuffed Lilly thinking that she had killed the foster mom's baby. But, when taken down to the station Lilly was given a psychologist and the psychologist said that Lilly has been diagnosed with paranoid schizophrenia and cannot be held responsible for those actions. What has happened here today is the responsibility of the foster mother. So, the foster mother received first degree manslaughter and went to jail her husband divorced her and he moved away as far as I know. Lilly was removed from that foster home and was put into many foster homes after that and was put on medication to help control her paranoid schizophrenia for the rest of her life which to this day has had a negative affect on her life. Just recently, I myself helped Lilly become a Nurse and a good nurse but as things have it Lilly was a hard worker and the people at her job came down on her hard for her cussing and getting out of control. So they decided to put her on disability. She is now on permanent disability and is doing much better and under the care of a doctor and she is much happier. I asked her questions about the family but she only knows certain things, other things she cannot recall. Remember, Lilly is one of the younger children and really doesn't remember anything about interactions between my father and the older siblings. Also Lilly just recently remarried to a very nice man named Hank and they really Love each other and live in Kansas and I wish them all the best and I love her very much she was a pleasure to raise. I love you Lilly.

Marsha lives with my mom and dad in Colorado in a home my dad decided to purchase after he left Lilly's house in the summer of 2017. I am not quite sure how my mom and my sister ended up with my dad because my mom had a permanent arrangement with an assisted living home in Colorado. But according to Lilly, she just up and left her home which took Lilly a year and a half to secure for mom, and she moved in with my dad in Colorado with Marsha. Dad must have made my mom one hell of an offer to move in with him in consideration of all the years of abuse that she suffered at his hands. I really can't figure it out. He probably gave her the house along with a certain amount of money. Dad is pretty old now and he cannot walk without a walker, and needs to be taken to the Doctor's office and have his meals prepared for him and other general chores. So maybe that's what my mom does for him I do not know. They do not call here and have no contact with me what so ever. Marsha does not work and the last I heard she was an alcoholic and addicted to prescription meds. Marsha has been with my mom for years and trying to ever separate the two of them will never happen.

Regarding **Marsha**, I spoke with my sister Lily the other day and she said that Marsha never comes out of her room and won't even unpack her boxes with her clothes and personnel belongings so mom and dad decided to call jimmy in Florida to come out to help them with Marsha and other chores around the house. Jimmy said he would. I can't believe it. I would never even consider taking advantage of someone like that, especially a family member. Worst of all this is a non- emergency situation and a request from the very people who are responsible for Jimmy's inability to ever have children. Marsha Keeps in contact with Lilly and Marsha brags about all the drugs and medications that she takes and she has no medical authorization for any of these meds and Lilly says that when she calls she can barely understand her because she slurs her words and her speech is terribly distorted. She needs help, but will not face reality. Some of things that Marsha has done that has upset the family includes:

Marsha was sexually abusive toward her brother Tim when she grabbed his face and gave him a French type kiss by inserting her tongue into his mouth. Tim immediately pushed her away and exclaimed that he never wanted to see her again. Lilly found Marsha lying completely naked in bed and trying to make love to Lilly's teenage daughter. How low can you go?

Marsha tried to attract my husband with sexual advances and innuendos, but my husband just ignored her and she became very upset. Marsha visited my sister Lilly when she was married to her first husband Bob and during a conversation while Bob and Lilly were sitting on the couch, My sister Lilly left the room and Marsha who was sitting in a large easy chair across from Bob spread her legs and revealed herself and Bob was surprised to recognize that Marsha was not wearing any underwear. What a pig.

Robert Jr. my oldest brother lives in Cherry creek with his wife Vivian. They are happily married, as far as, I know but I have not spoken to my brother since my son's funeral. My Brother Robert Favors my mother's perspective on life in that he shares her love of money and his life revolves around the attainment of as much of it as he possibly can and he is quite good at it. He does not have a college degree but he has worked for the same beer brewing company for Year's and he is a millionaire and he married a millionaire. Robert walks and talks like an aristocrat and he lives like one, as well. He lives in an up-scale neighborhood. He will not associate with the rest of the family that are beneath his station in life, except for Tim. As far as morals are concerned, I can only speak from experience, Robert is the one who witnessed my grandfather molesting me when I was a child but chose to keep it quiet for money. He makes no attempt to call me. Oh what a delightful family I have, come to think of it every time I think of the family I just want to forget about it all. Remember, you can't pick your parents and you can't pick your neighbors.

WHERE'S JIMMY?

JIMMY LIVES SOMEWHERE IN Florida I'm really not too sure what part of Florida but mom and dad know how to reach him. The last time I spoke with Jimmy was in Colorado which was about two years ago. Since then Lilly has updated me on his status. Jimmy has his good days and bad days. Like the rest of the family I think all of us kids have some form of mental disability and each of us display some form of the disease in one way or another. I think some of us recognize that we have a problem and have gotten some form of help like myself and Lilly and I think well, Jimmy does contact Lilly once in a while, but has never contacted me.

MY PERSONNEL EVALUATION

As a result of the childhood molestation by my dad's father, the constant and regular beatings and mental abuse by my mother and father and watching my siblings suffer at the hands of these monsters, I have good days and bad days. I don't really feel sorry for myself, I'm sure that there are those who have it worse than me. I have a supportive husband, an understanding psychologist and hopefully, this book will help me to release some of the pain, as well as, to help others who might be living with abusive parents, spouses, etc.

Some of the negative issues that I have which are related to my childhood that bother me the most and how I deal with them include:

Fear	**Resolution**
Fear of being alone-	I purchased 2 German Shepherds
Open closet doors-Doors	I insist that my husband close all
Problem with trusting people relationships	Concentrate on building

In addition to the issues just presented, I'm always in constant pain from back problems and arthritis in my arms and hips. I have a new problem that has recently occurred and is related to a shoulder sprain that I received not too long ago while trying to walk both my German Shephard dogs with the same arm. I sprained my left arm which recently evolved into a very painful pinched nerve and as a result, I suffer from mood swings. My husband has made me aware of these since he is usually the target of my emotional outbursts. But things calm down when we both realize what the root cause is. I am currently on medication and will probably need surgery, and the medication that I take sometimes needs to be re-evaluated after it loses its effectiveness. If any of the readers are suffering from similar situations there is nothing to be ashamed of. The important thing is the realization that I do need help and having the courage to seek help but most of all, if possible, having a good support system.

Note: This is a very rough time for me and I admit that it would be very difficult to go it alone so please if you find yourself in a similar situation, please seek out someone that you can share your problems with.

THE IRONY OF IT ALL

LILLY CALLED SEVERAL DAYS ago and presented me with information that totally shocked me and I could hardly believe. It seems that my dad decided to purchase a house in Colorado in a very tight close knit neighborhood. My father finally decided to give up the trailer life and decided to buy a home in Colorado. When Marsha and my mother heard about this, they decided to help my father pick out a home. I heard through the grapevine, that this was their opportunity to get Marsha's name on the deed.

This was just the type of house and neighborhood that he has always said that he would never live in. What surprised me even more was that my mom and my sister Marsha also moved in with my dad to share his new home and according to Lilly he put Marsha's name on the deed to the property. My dad probably worked a deal with Marsha for her services to care for him and mom in their old age in exchange for the house, but I know for a fact that Marsha is not even able to care for herself and she certainly doesn't have the capability or desire to care for my mother or my father. To support what I just alluded to above, I received a follow up call from Lilly and it seems that Marsha and dad are arguing and fighting constantly and Marsha is considering on filing a restraining order on my father. Her objective is probably to get his house and have him thrown out. Marsha has a reputation for filing restraining orders on family members and other people as well. I'm surprised that the courts don't question this because most, if not all, of her filings are bogus. Marsha Even has a restraining order filed against Lilly and one of the stipulations of the order is that Marsha cannot contact Lilly, but at the time of this writing, Marsha continues to harass Lilly via constant telephone calls. Lilly is currently under the care of a psychiatrist and is very sensitive to these calls from Marsha. In fact, she can't think, eat or sleep so she is seeking additional help from the police and from her doctor. I try to feel sorry for my dad, but I simply cannot because first of all, he purchased the house in secret with the money that he probably received from his father to keep my molestation quiet and what's more, he kept this entire transaction between him and Marsha and my mom only and left all the other kids out of it. He has not changed with old age.

Note: Marsha needs to tread lightly around my father because he is a very violent and unpredictable man and just the hint of a restraining order might be enough to set him off. My sister is playing with fire.

ABOUT THE HOUSE

I DON'T HAVE TOO much information about the house itself, but I do know that they picked out a house in a nice neighborhood and Marsha and my mom moved in with my dad. My mom even gave up her assisted living apartment which took Lilly over a year to secure for her. Marsha and my mom did not stay with my dad too long, apparently they could not get along with him and he has not mellowed with age and is still a very mean man. My mom and Marsha could not tolerate his behaviors so they decided to move in with Lilly and her husband in Kansas. Now, Lilly has been diagnosed with paranoid schizophrenia and is disabled and does not work any-more because of this disease. She cannot tolerate any type of excitement in her life or she will have a nervous breakdown and is on numerous medications to help her with her everyday life and is currently under a doctor's care. Marsha and my mother are aware of this, yet they still persist on going to Lilly's house and bothering her, why I do not know. Lilly does have a vacant house which she purchased before she got married and is fully furnished, upgraded and ready to be moved into. This is where Marsha and my mom will be staying and hopefully, they will not have too much contact with my sister Lilly, but I do know that my sister Marsha has always been trouble and she will probably end up causing trouble between Lilly and her husband sometime in the near future. Unfortunately the future came too soon.

LILLY CALLED ABOUT MARSHA

As I EXPECTED, ABOUT a week later, Lilly called and told me that Marsha had another one of her episodes and came over to her house and took off her top in front of her husband. Then she wanted Lilly's dog that she got from the pound. Lilly gladly gave her the dog and her husband told Lilly to get rid of Marsha and to never let her back in their house ever again. Her actions were totally erratic and unpredictable and he never wants to see her again. My mom stayed back and was able to stay with my sister Lilly in her house. Marsha went back home to live with dad and took the dog with her. Marsha did go back to live with my father but this did not last because Lilly explained to me that my dad starved Marsha almost to death. Every time Marsha went to go and get something to eat from the refrigerator my dad would guard it and eat all the food, even all the condiments. Marsha was so thin she could hardly stand up. Between the drugs and no food, she looked like a walking skeleton. So, Marsha called Lilly to come and get her and my dad attacked Marsha who was too weak to fight back, but not Lilly and Lilly just pushed my dad aside and got Marsha and her things out of the house and took Marsha over to her house in Kansas, which Lilly would be sorry for later on but at the time had no choice but to rescue Marsha once more. While in Kansas Marsha regressed to her old self again. She told my sister Lilly that she wanted to move into the house that Lilly bought down the street and would pay for it with her settlement that she was expecting from a car accident that she had while she was in Southern Colorado. But the problem with that was that she had already received a settlement and used the money to fix her car and was not going to get any more money. In the meantime, Marsha was living off Lilly and her husband and my mom who just had a major heart attack and was also living in Lilly's house. Marsha who had no money for desperately needed drugs for her psychological disorders and was begging Lilly to help until she could see a doctor and things were starting to get out of hand. Marsha was becoming violent. She took a BRILLO pad to Lilly's refrigerator in her other home which was new, and ruined the front of it. Then she went into her husbands bedroom and broke into his cabinet and stole his collectable coins totaling $5,000 or more and took them over to her house, left part of them in the bathroom and hid the rest. Then, she went over to Lilly's house and disconnected the drain pipes in the kitchen underneath the sink. Wow, she is really destructive. So, Lilly put her in a crisis center in Kansas where they are helping her and she is receiving help and medications and will not be going back to Lilly's house any time soon. Social services will be getting involved and she will be put on disability hopefully they will help her to get her life straightened out. Meanwhile, my dad is still in Southern Colorado and does not live in the original house that I thought he lived in with Marsha's name on the title. I found out that he sold the original house that he purchased in Southern Colorado and bought a new home in the same neighborhood that I used to live in in fact, I believe it is on the same street. I'm not sure if he purchased it in his name only or if he included one of his sons in on the title and I'll probably never know because he is a very secretive and underhanded individual who plays favorites and really doesn't care too much for the girls in the family.

Note: My sister Lilly has an easy going personality but she is under the care of a psychiatrist. Lilly is prescribed medications that help to keep her in a normal frame of mind, but she is still very sensitive and can easily be provoked and as a result, I really don't agree with

her decision to have Marsha living in such close proximity by living in Lilly's small house down the street. In addition to Marsha I do not agree with my mother living with Marsha. My mother is a very greedy person and she will do what- ever she can to make my sister Lilly unhappy. My mother along with Marsha, will try to find a way to make Lilly's life as miserable and uncomfortable as possible.

THE STORY OF MY WORST MEMORIES

I COVERED MY NIGHTMARES from the time when I was a little girl and all through my life to the adult age of which I am now. All of my nightmares are created and inspired by my father and his family. These people were monsters. They were more ferocious, violent, and barbaric than any historic savage that ever existed in history including Hitler, or Vlad the Impaler or more commonly known as Dracula covered in medieval books of horror and history, my entire family was affected in a negative way by these assumed characterizations. Some more profound than others, and unfortunately, some of us, myself not included, are quite violent. Example: my sister Marsha. Out of all the kids Marsha was the most like my dad. Sometimes even worse. In fact she physically attacked my husband on several occasions for no reason at all. She was always in trouble because of her drinking and drug abuse and she could not hold a job. Even with all of her faults and short cummings, she is my dad and mom's second favorite child, of course, Robert holds the number one spot. Marsha currently lives in a crisis center in Kansas and is receiving help to get back on her feet. As far as my dad is concerned he chooses to live alone and that's probably how he'll die, alone, happy, and yet miserable. My father did have a soft heart for Marsha probably because she is a carbon copy of him and he did accept her in his life for a while, but he will probably soon grow tired of her as well, but who knows for sure. As far as the rest of the family is concerned each one of my siblings has their own problems to deal with and each lives within their own little world so to speak. Charlie I have not seen you in over thirty seven years and my memory of you is really sort or vague. Please get in touch with me there is so much I would like to talk to you about. Jimmy is somewhere in Florida with his girlfriend doing quite well and is happy as ever I over- heard from my sister Lilly. I did receive a brief phone call from Jimmy and it was very short but he is doing great and is okay. There's Robert Jr. who lives with his wife and stays to himself and surrounds himself with people and material possessions that makes him feel good about himself and what he has achieved in life. Then there's Tim my other brother who used to be an avid drinker and I am not sure if he still drinks alcohol today because I have not spoken to him in a long time. I do know he keeps in contact with Robert my oldest brother they do everything together, I am sure by looking at all the pictures. Tim is an easy going type of guy, very friendly, and likeable, and has a lot of friends and it just seems like everyone knows Tim. He's the guy who goes to Chili's restaurants on a Friday night and has all his friends with him to celebrate just because it's Friday. Yep, Tim is your man. Tim has two beautiful daughters and both of them have children of their own now, and Tim is just thrilled about being a grandpa. I do think it's a shame he became involved with alcohol and lost his marriage because of it, which I blame on my dad always drinking that beer and pushing hard liquor around the holidays and giving it to the kids. I blame my dad for that. He taught the kids to drink, then Tim introduced it to his daughters. What a shame. Sometimes I just want to scream out loud, and at other times I wished my dad could have been a father that was someone different, someone who really loved his children, I mean really loved his kids. Sat down with us, maybe read us a story, or emphasized the importance of getting a good education and how it could improve your life. In my opinion, my father really didn't want to have kids he was just following some sort of distorted religious belief when he practiced sex because he really didn't believe in contraceptives. All he believed in was making the all mighty dollar bill and what it could do for him, and what it could get for him. That's what he was always really good at working and keeping the money coming in. He used to preach how money is what you really need in this world to succeed and without it, you'll never amount to nothing. But he forgot about all the other stuff like, love and understanding, and nurturing, and bedtime stories, and just being a good father. He had no good parenting skills at all. He was totally lost when it came to being a good father. A good provider yes, a good father no. My mother tried to be both parents, but she failed because she herself became victim to his abuse and somewhere along the line I think lost her mind and with all those children to attend to, plus she breast fed each one, plus the house work, plus those horrible beatings, it all came tumbling down on her. I tried to help her as much as I could, but it was overwhelming for me, and it just became too much after a while. This book is written from my heart because I know that there are others like me who need the help and support and the knowledge of knowing that they are not alone in their world of pain and suffering. There is hope and please allow me to be that support. If you need help to find your way out of your own personal prison and the miserable life that might be causing you pain, don't wait because life is too short to allow anyone other than you to control it. I have included a list of contacts and organizations and people who care and are willing to help. Please examine the list to find the help that you need and above all remain positive and don't hesitate to call the police or 911 if the situation gets out of hand, I did. Love Always, Emily.

RESOURCES

Domestic Shelters.Org. This resource has a 24/7 hotline which provides a list of shelters and other resources. They offer programs throughout the US and Canada. Their domestic hotline is **1-800-799-7233.**

National Child Abuse Hotline. This organization provides many services and is partnered with other organizations who are dedicated to helping children who are faced with all sorts of abuse problems. Their hotline phone number is **1-800-422-4453**.

National Domestic Violence Hotline. This site offers many valuable resources including downloadable reference material and services for immediate help. They are nation wide and have a presence in all fifty states. Their phone number is **1-800-799-7233.**

Battered Women Shelters in The US. Provides a complete list of resources including, food, clothing, housing, free attorney fees, as well as shelters in all fifty states including Puerto Rico. The phone numbers are associated with shelters when you choose them at the site location on line.

Women's Shelters. Another complete list of Women's list of complete list of shelters in the US. Phone numbers are available on the state of choice that is chosen.

The National Coalition Against Domestic Violence (NCADV). Is an activist group dedicated to help and support abused women. Call **1-800-787-3224.**

Printed in the United States
By Bookmasters